THE LAWYER'S MYTH

THE LAWYER'S MYTH

Reviving Ideals in the Legal Profession

WALTER BENNETT

THE UNIVERSITY OF CHICAGO PRESS / CHICAGO & LONDON

WALTER BENNETT is a lawyer and writer living in Chapel Hill, N.C. He is a former director of the Intergenerational Legal Ethics Program at the University of North Carolina Law School and has served as a trial court judge and trial lawyer in Charlotte, N.C. He has published in the areas of legal ethics, juvenile law, human rights, and constitutional law.

The University of Chicago Press, Chicago 60637
The University of Chicago Press, Ltd., London
© 2001 by The University of Chicago
All rights reserved. Published 2001
Printed in the United States of America
10 09 08 07 06 05 04 03 02 01   1 2 3 4 5

ISBN (cloth): 0-226-04255-3

Library of Congress Cataloging-in-Publication Data

Bennett, Walter, 1943–
    The lawyer's myth : reviving ideals in the legal profession / Walter Bennett.
        p.   cm.
    Includes index.
    ISBN 0-226-04255-3 (cloth : alk. paper)
    1. Lawyers—United States.   2. Practice of law—United States.   I. Title.
    KF297 .B4   2001
    340'.023'73—dc21   2001002127

⊗The paper used in this publication meets the minimum
requirements of the American National Standard for
Information Sciences—Permanence of Paper for Printed
Library Materials, ANSI Z39.48-1992.

This book is dedicated to all lawyers who care about their profession.

CONTENTS

ACKNOWLEDGMENTS

This book is about the journey of the individual lawyer and the legal profession toward a new vision of professionalism. I could not have written it without the help of many teachers—strong, wise people who cherish the fellowship of the professional journey and who have lent me and many others a helping hand along the way. The names of some of those people—and their words—appear in the pages of this book. I will mention here but a small sampling of the people who have contributed directly to the ideas in the pages to follow.

Credit should begin with Judith Wegner, former dean of the UNC Law School, who understood that the search for professionalism is really a search for one's wholeness as a human being. She was the inspiration for much of my work in legal education, and she provided the vision, insight, and financial support—partially through a grant from the E. M. Keck Foundation—for the UNC Law School Intergenerational Legal Ethics Program. That program included both the Law School Oral History Project and the Law School Mentoring Program, which figure prominently in the ideas and solutions I attempt to develop. She also initiated two powerful vision-quest retreats for lawyers and law students, conducted in the North Carolina mountains by psychologist Pat Webster with the able help of her husband, attorney Bill Thorp. Those retreats—for the first time, to my knowledge—employed the Parcival myth as a metaphor for the lawyer's life journey, and it was Pat Webster's skillful use of that myth which inspired my own use of it as a metaphor for the lawyer's journey in this work.

I also owe deep gratitude to the attorneys and law students who participated in those retreats and in the UNC Law School Oral History Project and the Mentoring Program. They renewed my faith in the profession, in its capacity to seek community and maintain ideals, and in the capacity of its members to grow in wisdom and to impart that wisdom to each other. There are great and good lawyers practicing today who are also great and good people. They confirmed Dean Wegner's faith that our society can revive its great institutions.

Other individuals lent specific expertise: Jaquelyn Hall and Kathy Walbert of the University of North Carolina Oral History Program, and Kathy Nasstrom, formerly of that program, advised me and my students on oral history techniques and boosted our efforts with moral support. Ruel Tyson, director of the UNC Institute for the Arts and Humanities, and the participants in his 1996 summer workshop on education and the professions, assisted my thinking on professionalism and helped provide the encouragement to pursue ideas for this book. Grady Balentine, Patricia Bryan, Bari Burke, Leary Davis, James Elkins, John Frey, John Hagan, Joe Harbaugh, Tom Kelley, David Luban, Soyini Madison, Hon. Harry Martin, Pender McElroy, B. B. Olive, Wade Smith, Mark Weisberg, and Lucie White served as advisors to the Intergenerational Legal Ethics Program and provided valuable support and insight on professionalism and the role of lawyers. Patricia Bryan and Mark Weisberg read and critiqued drafts of this book and became close friends and advisors to my work as a teacher and writer as the ideas for this book took shape. Tom Faison and Ken Broun also read and critiqued drafts of the manuscript.

Tom Shaffer of Notre Dame Law School read the manuscript and graciously led me on a rewarding journey into deeper and broader thinking on questions of professionalism, community, and the common good. Without his help and insights, this entire enterprise would have been much less complete. Richard Allen, editor for the University of Chicago Press, helped prepare the manuscript for printing and provided valuable insights and suggestions as to content. Geoff Huck of the University of Chicago Press first recognized the value in this work, and it was primarily through his efforts and encouragement that I was able to bring the manuscript to publication. I am grateful also to Syd Nathans and Kermit Hall for assistance in finding a publisher.

Finally, I appreciate the patience and assistance of my wife, Betsy Bennett, who offered encouragement and critical suggestions throughout my work on this book. And I owe a special word of thanks to the late Judge James B. McMillan of Charlotte, a true giant of the law and an exceptional human being, who, in that confined and often frightening space between the bar and bench in his court, taught me how to be a lawyer and a professional.

If a man has the soul of Sancho Panza, the world to him will be Sancho Panza's world; but if he has the soul of an idealist, he will make—I do not say find—his world ideal. Of course the law is not the place for the artist or poet. The law is the calling of thinkers. But to those who believe with me that not the least godlike of man's activities is the large survey of causes, that to know is not less than to feel, I say—and I say no longer with any doubt—that a man may live greatly in the law as well as elsewhere; that there as well as elsewhere his thought may find its unity in an infinite perspective; that there as well as elsewhere he may wreak himself upon life, may drink the bitter cup of heroism, may wear his heart out after the unattainable.

Oliver Wendell Holmes[1]

From the conception the increase,
From the increase the thought,
From the thought the remembrance,
From the remembrance the consciousness,
From the consciousness the desire.

From one of the Four Maori Cosmologies[2]

INTRODUCTION

This book is the culmination of a personal quest that began sixteen years ago when I left law practice and began to cast about for other ways to make a living through my self-bred compulsion to live and think like a lawyer. It has been a meandering journey.

I was a trial lawyer. My case load consisted of everything from complex federal litigation to domestic and criminal cases in state courts. I was working long hours, but, as most trial lawyers know, even when I was not working, I was "working." My focus on my cases never ceased, and so intense was I in that preoccupation that it was a struggle for me to imagine any other way to live. Finally, the only plan I could devise to pry myself out of my self-made rut was to go back to school. I applied to my law school alma mater to obtain a graduate degree in law with the idea that it would eventually lead me into a more theoretical area of legal work where I would spend less time working on weekends and fewer hours on the telephone, aspects of trial practice that "they" don't tell you about in law school.

Graduate school in law was an enlivening experience and very different from the heartless grind of the J.D. years. It was intellectual in a way the earlier law school experience was not. One could ruminate on theory and spend hours in unhurried research. My LL.M. classmates were mostly from foreign countries and had not been exposed to or consumed by the intensely competitive atmosphere of the J.D. track. Student gatherings were relaxed and joyful occasions imbued with genuine feelings of comradeship, trust, and mutual admiration. Unlike my J.D. experience, which I found fraught with jealousy and anxiety, the graduate law experience was both intellectually animating and soothing. Compared to my life as a trial lawyer, it seemed as though I had returned to a more real world

1

where human feelings, self-reflection, and intellectual curiosity had room to prosper.

So, it was in the LL.M. year that I began to perceive where the intensity of the J.D. experience and thirteen years of practice as a trial lawyer (including five years as a trial court judge) had taken me. I saw that there were people who were accomplished persons of the law who lived lives much more balanced and holistic than my own. I perceived this, but I had no clue as to how they got there or how I might emulate them.

After graduate school in law, I took a job as clinical professor of law at the University of North Carolina Law School, where I spent one-on-one time with students who were struggling to prove themselves in the skills of their chosen profession and to come to terms with their law school experience. I saw aspects of myself as a law student and young lawyer in many of the students I supervised in the UNC Clinic. They had in various measures both respect for lawyers' work and fear of it, and some of them developed a passion for it. Many of their egos had been maimed in law school, and they yearned for a chance to regain self-respect in the "real world" of practice where, they hoped, their other life-skills—those not measured in the narrow and closed laboratory of law school examinations—could be put to good use. Frequently that happened. And after their year of clinical experience, I would suffer through their graduation on some humid Sunday in mid-May in the un-air-conditioned auditorium on the main campus at UNC, wish them good luck on the bar exam, and say goodbye as they moved into the life I had left behind.

While I ended each of those years with the feeling that I had done a good job of teaching my students the basic skills of lawyering, I also had the feeling that there was something I had not told them. They never asked me why I had left law practice to teach, and I never volunteered an explanation. My job was to teach the skills of lawyering. But I knew by that point in my life that there was much more to living a lawyer's life than graduating from law school and being minimally competent at practical skills. I knew, or at least suspected, that in order to do it well and to avoid the descent that so many lawyers take into the narrow tunnel of one-mindedness—of thinking like a lawyer and doing or being very little else—a reorientation of the soul was required, a reopening of the intellectual and emotional gates that so many people begin to shut in law school. But I also knew that I was incompetent to teach them that because I did not understand it myself, and I had never practiced it.

At some point around my fourth year at Carolina, I was offered a chance to teach a section in legal ethics (called "professional responsibility" in most law schools). Professional responsibility courses were largely third-year courses and were oriented almost entirely toward teaching the ethics codes. Many students viewed them as merely a hurdle one must jump and of minimal importance. P.R. teachers were frustrated with the lack of student interest and the lack of peer recognition for teaching a course considered to be peripheral.

So my first job in teaching professional responsibility was to convince students the course was important, and my first step in that process was to find out why they thought it wasn't. A primary suspect was close at hand. It soon became clear to me that the attitudes fostered by the law school culture itself discouraged law students from thinking seriously about ethics. This didn't surprise me when I sat back and thought about it. Law students are taught to view laws critically and skeptically and to parse codes and cases for their limits and exceptions. They are also taught that aggressive advocacy is an essential tool for success as a lawyer. One effect of these hard-taught lessons is to foster in students an attitude of moral minimalism: moral predilections should be repressed lest they complicate legal analysis and inhibit decisive, winning action. This is not an attitude likely to promote a heavy application of the rules of ethics, which are often more aspirational than normative.

But there was something else about law students' approach to ethics that disturbed me even more. It usually surfaced toward the end of a semester when we had finished discussing some ethical case that presented hard moral choices. I would glance around the classroom at the looks of consternation, and sometimes something close to anger, on the faces of many of the students. And then I would ask a question to try to get at what the problem was, and someone would come out with it: "Why are you teaching us these lofty notions about ethics and lawyers' behavior? When we pass the bar, we're going to be scrambling to find and hold jobs, pay off student loans, win cases, and make partner. We're going to have to play by the rules that are out there, not the nice moral rules we dream about in law school."

My first reaction to this type of statement was to sympathize with their plight and then to try to soften it—to make it seem that the choices were really not that hard. But these efforts rang hollow, and I finally had to face the students' anguish for what it was: an expression of moral impotency, of a lack of control over one's moral life. It was not the feeling I recalled having when I exited law school in the early 1970s, when, harboring my own illusions, I assumed that my classmates and I were acquiring the legal power and moral will to change the world. But the economic picture and consequently the moral picture had changed since I was in law school. I soon learned that the *average* educational debt for students graduating from UNC Law School, one of the least expensive state law schools in the country, exceeded $30,000.00. I also began to perceive that law students knew very little about the human side of practicing law. They assumed that when they left law school, they would be alone, and that the loneliness which had gripped them during their first year of law school, when the reality of grade competition set in, would be the defining aspect of their practice.

The recognition of my students' feelings of moral impotency was depressing to me because I knew that in some respects their premonition was true. Many lawyers do feel trapped and morally impotent. They become trapped economically by adopting lifestyles which they think are expected of lawyers and to which they think they are entitled. They become trapped in the hierarchy of success and failure: winning cases, making partner, gaining and keeping clients. They become trapped in the methodology of the law, the linear, oppositional, hyper-rational style of the law, which they adopt and pursue with such intensity that they become incompetent to think any other way. And they become trapped in the pure intensity of it, the constant pressure of the lawyer's life to work harder and harder and concentrate more and more to gain the advantage it takes to win, an intensity so pronounced and consuming that in many cases the other parts of one's life are left to wither and sometimes to vanish completely.

I also knew that many lawyers feel alone. About the time I was hearing students express their powerlessness, the North Carolina Bar Association conducted a survey on the quality of lawyers lives.[1] The results painted a picture of loneliness and lack of control. Twenty-three percent of the lawyers responding said that they would not become attorneys again, and only 53.9 percent desired to remain attorneys for the remainder of their careers. Eight to twelve percent had symptoms of serious psychological or physical ill health. Twenty-four percent reported significant symptoms of depression, including appetite loss, trouble sleeping, suicidal thoughts, and extreme lethargy. Twenty-five percent had anxiety symptoms (hands trembling, heart racing, hands clammy, faintness). More than 22 percent had been diagnosed with anxiety related conditions, including ulcers, hypertension, and coronary artery disease. Almost 17 percent consumed at least three to five alcoholic drinks per day, and approximately the same percentage took one week or less vacation per year. Eighteen and one-half percent said they had no one with whom to share their feelings, and 43 percent felt they did not have enough time for a satisfying life outside their work. I looked back at my own life in the law. I had made friends, but it had taken me a long time to learn that making close friendships with other lawyers was possible. I knew that as a young lawyer, when the chips were down, I had felt time and time again that I was basically on my own. The adversary system tends to foster that type of feeling, and young lawyers, in particular, are susceptible to it.

So in my new life as an ethics teacher, it became clear to me that it was virtually useless to talk about rules of ethics and ethical case law without first dealing with these two, fundamental attitudinal problems: the compulsion to moral minimalism, and the feelings of impotency and loneliness. I decided that the solution to the first problem was to tackle it head-on. I did this by assigning readings and writing exercises that addressed the effect of the law school experience on students' moral character. This was a reflective process intended to draw students into thinking of themselves as people first and lawyers second. I hoped they would begin to perceive that while legal analysis might be essential to good lawyering, it alone was not enough for good ethics or a good life. I think in the main students welcomed this chance to "rediscover" a lost part of themselves.

The solution to the second problem was more difficult. How could I, a law teacher who had fled law practice for the softer and less pressured life of a professor, convince students that their premonitions of powerlessness and loneliness, premonitions that I shared to some degree, could be overcome? In the few occasions when I tried to convince them from the classroom lectern, I could feel the waters of my own hypocrisy rise about me. This spectacle was not lost on the students. If they were to be thrown a lifeline, it had to come from someone other than me.

Then one day during summer break I trekked down to the dean's office for my annual half-hour conference to discuss my progress as a law professor. The problem of student morale was fresh on my mind, and I had just left a meeting with members of the medical and business school faculties where we had discussed conducting a cross-disciplinary study of some large case that held medical, legal, and economic lessons. Our idea had been to use students to gather oral histories about the case and then to use those oral histories to teach a cross-disciplinary course. I mentioned both the student morale problem and the idea of using oral histories to the dean, and as we spoke we began to see that some version of the latter idea might be a solution to the former problem. By the time

I left her office, I had agreed to teach a seminar on the oral histories of lawyers and judges, in which students would go into the field to take the life stories of noted members of the profession. Perhaps by listening to these stories from professional elders, I thought, students could learn not only wisdom and acumen as a lawyer, but see firsthand a life dedicated to moral purpose and know that even in the legal profession, there is help for the lonely.

When the seminar got underway the next fall and the recorded, oral histories began to come alive in the classroom through the oral presentations of the students, I experienced something close to euphoria. Yes, there were lawyers and judges out there who were living lives dedicated to a higher purpose, who loved what they were doing, and who found intellectual richness and creativity in lawyers' work. There were lawyers and judges who had faced loneliness and feelings of powerlessness and had overcome them, sometimes after great struggle and heartache. There were lawyers and judges—very successful, dedicated lawyers and judges—who had learned how to balance their lives at work with their lives as citizens and family members. And, most important, there were lawyers and judges who were proud of being members of the profession, who felt that being a lawyer involved a deep moral commitment, that it was a position not only of prestige but of honor.

These life stories had a profound effect on me, and they had a profound effect on the students who heard them and retold them to their fellow students. The stories taught me that the profession had a heritage that was still alive and cried out to be passed on and that there were members of the profession who were ready to do that by sharing a part of their humanity with law students and other lawyers. This was getting very close to what Oliver Wendell Holmes called a life of "passion" in the law—a term at which I had marveled when I first read it and wondered if I would ever experience what he was talking about. My students and I studied intently the stories of the lawyers we interviewed for the secrets their lives would yield. Perhaps the most important of those secrets is that passion in one's life's work does not come from a perfection of lawyer's skills or monetary success. It comes from connection with parts of oneself that are rarely recognized in law school or in much of the current lore about being a good lawyer. I found that a passionate life called on something much deeper and greater than anything yielded by the traditional notions of professional success. It had to do with finding within oneself those hungry, persistent, and inspired remnants of selfhood where passion resides. It had to do with placing one's work as a lawyer, with all the attendant skills and devotion it requires, in the larger context of one's life and one's place in the world. And most of all, it had to do with balance, with finding a balance within oneself between the demands of a lawyer's work and the humanity within one's own life and that of other people.

There are many quotations from the oral histories which illustrate this type of balance, but I will present three that speak directly of lawyers' work and that portray the balance I am talking about implicitly. The speakers are three of North Carolina's most skilled, successful, and renowned trial lawyers.[2]

> It's not like it's some magic. It's certainly not that I'm unique or something. I have my share of fatal flaws. But I also think I have my share of those few little gifts, and one of them would be the ability to talk to people, to listen to them, to understand what they are saying, to get inside where they are, to empathize, to help them think through what they ought to do, to help them solve their problems. [It's] just part of my life. It's always been amazing to me. There are some folk who enjoy working in the fire department putting out fires. Thank God for them. And people who enjoy being police officers, teachers, and so on. And there are people who can communicate, who can be lawyers. And I think it just happened that when I was being made, they put me over in that group.[3]

> As lawyers we are taught that we're to look at cases and find the legal issues and address those issues, that we use facts to address issues. I think what moves people is not issues, but human events, the story of what happened to someone who was wronged in some way will move the jury far better, far quicker, than the greatest exposition in the world of a legal issue [or] what the law says. So I think if you can take every case and relate it to the human story that's there—[and] there's a human story in every case, I don't care what kind of case it is . . . —and you find that story, develop that story and effectively present that story, then ninety-five percent of your work is done.[4]

> The other thing that [Harvard Law School] Professor [Charles] Ogletree talked about in his article was empathy, and that is seeing yourself . . . in human beings who made terrible choices and who do terrible things and get themselves in terrible trouble. I think that I can do that, although most of the people I see don't have an upbringing anything like my upbringing. I can see some of me in them and some of them in me, and so I think that's been very important in making [death penalty] work worthwhile and rewarding. . . . I mean, I enjoy coming to work every day, and I took forward to it . . . , and although there's lots of tragedy and sadness in it . . . , I feel very lucky.[5]

These comments reveal what I would call a softer, more human (some would say more "feminine") side to the practice of law, which was my first clue to what it might mean to develop a balanced life as a lawyer. Developing such a life and, in so doing, finding a moral purpose for being a professional are what this book is about. In the discussion that follows, I treat this process of development as I experienced it (and continue to experience it), as a journey of the profession and of the individual lawyer. I see this journey as a quest, though I know that this linear version, which traditionally seeks some form of psychic grail, may not suit for everyone. Some may see the process as more circular and holistic. But regardless of the form it takes—linear quest, holistic discovery—it is a process that all of us must undertake over and over, daily, weekly, yearly and for a lifetime, in order to reap its rewards. It is the process itself, I suggest, and the knowledge that one is engaged in it, which are most important.

For those readers who prefer their material in careful, syllogistic order, a warning: this book is more on the order of a narrative. It was written as a narrative and roams about some, as narratives often do, exploring the landscape of the legal profession. But I hope in the end it takes you to where you want to go.

1

The Professional Wound

To begin our process of self-discovery, let us peer into the dim and timeless pasts of our ancestors as they grope for the answers to the eternal questions: Where do we come from? Where are we going? How do we find meaning in our lives? We see our forebears in the dark forests of Wales, the misty moors of Scotland and Ireland, the smoky plains and mountains of America, Europe, and Asia, the rocky hills of the Middle East and the deserts and jungles of Africa. If we go back far enough, we will discover a common thread—the thread of narrative—that may lead us to the truth about ourselves and our profession. The details of this ancient story vary from place to place, but the essence of it is the same. It tells us of a land far away and a time long ago where a great chieftain reigned over a bountiful and beautiful kingdom. The people who lived in this kingdom prospered. It was a place of peace, harmony, and well-lived lives. But eventually all of this began to change. Conditions in the kingdom began to deteriorate, and the kingdom soon became a wasteland. Crops would not grow; calves, lambs, and colts were stillborn; livestock died. The people suffered greatly, both in body and spirit.

In most versions of the story, the deterioration of the kingdom is preceded by a physical weakening of the king. In the Celtic version, the people of the kingdom trace the beginning of their decline to the wounding of their king in the groin in a duel with a powerful warrior. The wound, which will not heal, is ghastly to behold and constantly runs poison. The king suffers terribly, and as the poison from his wound seeps into the soil of his kingdom, the kingdom is poisoned as well. Only one pastime distracts the king from his endless suffering, and so when we first see him he is fishing in the lakes and rivers about his kingdom, trying to find relief from the constant pain. But the suffering never stops, and, as the story goes, it will not stop until a questing knight comes seeking a talisman—in the Christian version, the holy grail. The savior will be the knight who has developed consciously and spiritually enough to ask the essential question that will begin the healing process: Whom does the grail serve?

Like the kingdom in this myth of the Fisher King, the legal profession in America is wounded and suffering, and many of the lawyers in it are wounded and suffering as well.[1] This has been catalogued in numerous books, studies, and personal anecdotes.[2] It has gone on for some time and, at least until recently, has been growing worse. Attempts to address this malaise in the profession and in law schools by a renewed emphasis on ethics training and through workshops on the quality of lawyers' lives are commendable and are of some help. But as anyone knows who has sat down and seriously tried to deal with the problems gripping the legal profession, those problems, like the wound to the Fisher King, are wide and deep and will not heal easily. They share other characteristics similar to the wound of the Fisher King as well.

First, like the wound to the Fisher King, who, in fighting the warrior who wounded him was metaphorically fighting his own ego and self-pride, they are largely self-inflicted. There is a tendency in addressing the wound of the legal profession to want to cast blame outward on other forces—e.g., changes in the economics of practice, Supreme Court rulings on professional advertising, bad press, or poor public understanding of the justice system. These are no doubt contributing factors, but they are generally not factors over which we, as a profession, exercise much control, and they are not the causes of what really ails the legal profession. It is perhaps more accurate to see them as spears that we use to wound ourselves in our internal struggle to develop as lawyers and professionals. Our wound is too deep and complex to have been caused only by such external factors. It is upon the wound itself, and not the visible "causes," that we should first focus in our efforts to find solutions. What is the wound? What really ails the legal profession? When we understand that, we may be more able to find the healing salve.

One clue is found in another similarity between the wound to the profession and the mythical wound of the Fisher King. The king's wound is a sexual wound, and—though this at first may sound startling—metaphorically speaking the wound to the profession is a sexual wound as well. It is significant that the Fisher King's wound is to the area of his groin (some versions of the myth say the wound is in his thigh; others identify it as the wound of a spear or arrow through his testicles), for it is a symbolic wounding of his creative and procreative powers. As the spiritual leader of his kingdom, if he is so wounded, his kingdom suffers accordingly: it loses its procreative power; crops do not grow; animals are unable to reproduce; fetuses are stillborn. In the metaphorical context of mythology, as the physical world goes, so goes the world of the spirit. Or, perhaps it is more accurate to say that physical infirmities are outward manifestations of the ailing soul. The Fisher King's kingdom is spiritually dead. It has lost its way and has therefore, like its king, lost the power to grow and heal itself.

The malaise affecting the legal profession is also a wounding of its creative and procreative powers, and that malaise also grows primarily out of the fight with, and wounding by, our own warrior selves. In essence, the warrior-like, super-masculine part of our professional psyche has at least temporarily prevailed in the internal struggle for the soul of the profession. The dominant professional archetype is the "no-holds-barred," "go-for-the-jugular" trial lawyer or the overbearing, relentless, and humorless office lawyer, who measures success only by winning or otherwise demonstrating superiority and is often driven by ego and greed. The dominance of this type, this negative ideal, which I suggest is present to some degree in all of us (including women attorneys), has deeply affected the professional psyche. It has elevated winning (and attendant financial rewards) as the only true measures of success. It has encouraged an adversarial atmosphere where moral doubt and civility toward others are impediments to achieving that success and where endless hours or work and increased competition at all levels are assumed to be essential ingredients of the professional life. It has devalued the things human beings do to give their lives greater purpose and a spiritual meaning. Basically it has destroyed our professional mythology and, more importantly, our capacity to create professional myths that allow us to grow and to understand ourselves and the social and moral significance of our profession. This is the true nature of our self-inflicted wound—a wound that will not heal until we begin to ask ourselves the essential mythmaking questions about who we are and whom we serve.

The myth of the Fisher King is sometimes a prelude to other stories, and in later derivations it figures most importantly in the Arthurian myth of Parcival's search for the Holy Grail. In the Parcival myth,[3] an untutored and largely inept youth watches knights from King Arthur's Round Table as they pass his woodland home. He is dazzled at the sight of them and naively sets out to follow them, hoping to join them. He succeeds in this because, we eventually learn, he is a chosen one, chosen because of his simplicity to become a knight and to successfully complete the grail quest by asking the essential question, "Whom does the grail serve?," thereby healing the Fisher King and restoring the kingdom. But first he must undergo a long and difficult quest in which he will endure many hardships, commit many errors, and suffer mightily in the process of becoming spiritually whole enough and conscious enough to ask the necessary question. The myth of Parcival is a "hero" myth in the traditional sense, but on its most profound level, it is much deeper than that and speaks to us universally, regardless of gender. And it speaks particularly to lawyers, for the primary task in Parcival's long and arduous quest for consciousness is to bring his warrior self into balance with the rest of him, to honor the feminine in his nature and to learn to use his feminine power in harmony with his masculine power to save the kingdom. He must first learn that his soul is out of balance, that he has an exaggerated view of his own importance and a deficient understanding of his duty toward other people. Only then can he begin to grow socially and spiritually so that he eventually gains sufficient consciousness to ask the question that will heal the king and save the community. Parcival's story is about the quest each of us makes, or should make, for psychic wholeness and a realization of self and, ultimately, the reconstitution of community—for our purposes, the legal profession. On a spiritual level, if we wish to take the myth that far, it portrays the maturing of the individual soul and the movement of mankind toward God.

The legal profession sometimes behaves as if it is waiting for a knight in shining armor to rescue it from the evils of professional advertising, the forces of the marketplace, and the other afflictions we identify as the sources of our problems. But the practice of law is not a fairytale, and there is no knight in shining armor coming to the rescue. There are only we, its members. If the legal profession is going to save itself, we are the people who must do it. We are the wounded king, and our profession is the wounded kingdom. But we are also Parcival. Parcival *c'est moi!* It is we who must take up the long and difficult quest that will lead us to ask the essential question. And a good way to begin our part of that quest is to understand where we have come so far and where the dragons are. Like the Fisher King, whose fishing is a metaphor for his soul-searching in the realm of his own unconscious, we will need to do some fishing as well into our professional past and the landscape of our own unconscious. I will begin this journey with a personal story which probes the darkness of this landscape in the hope of shedding some light on how we got to where we are.

2

The Dark Landscape of the Profession: The Legal Academy and the Loss of Ideals

The Murder of Moral Purpose

This story begins in torts class when I was a first-year student at the University of Virginia Law School in the fall of 1969. The class met in a first floor lecture hall with high, bare walls and heavily sashed windows that reached almost to the ceiling. The floors were stepped wooden platforms covered with dull, brown linoleum, and the well-worn desks were wood and metal and bolted to the floor. Our teacher was a short man who moved back and forth in front of the class like a leopard stalking a herd of zebras. His voice was high pitched and challenging, and in the cavernous old classroom he used it effectively, lowering it to a purr as he contemplated a student's answer to a question he had just posed, or raising it to a roar as he pounced upon an idea that had emerged from the thicket of our Socratic dialogue. I had never seen a teacher perform this way, and I was scared to death by it.

Early in the semester our reading assignment included *Beatty v. Central Iowa Railway*,[1] a relatively short nineteenth-century case presenting the elements of negligence and reasonable care, and we had discussed the case exhaustively under my professor's tutelage for the better part of two class meetings. I recall my intellectual and emotional disorientation in those first law school classes and the eagerness with which most of us sought direction in the jungle of questions that our teacher planted around us. I recall the cacophony of ideas, viewpoints, and voices our professor used to lead us about in that jungle and my feelings of being lost and bewildered when one attempt at closure after another was exposed as a false trail. And I remember the growing panic in my gut at discovering the realization of my deepest fear: I was not very smart after all, and I was incompetent at the one subject I had chosen as my life's work.

Finally, at a point well into the third class period when I was bound limb-for-limb in the dialectical tangle and feeling the hot breath of the leopard, one of my more vocal classmates (he actually volunteered answers—or, attempted answers) lunged for daylight. His attempted breakout came in his response to the last in a series of increasingly pointed questions from our professor about how reasoned analysis of the case could have led to the result my classmate had just proposed. At last cornered and growing desperate, my classmate blurted out: "Because it seems to be the best way to achieve justice." The professor, who was pacing by this time, whirled in his tracks, thrust both hands in the air and shouted in a voice louder than any I had ever heard indoors, "Don't speak to me of justice! I do not wish to hear about justice. I wish to hear about the rule of law."*

This was the early 1970s. Many of us had come to law school to pursue various social agendas, some well defined, some quite indefinite. But all of those agendas contained at their heart some notion of justice. There was dead silence in the classroom after the professor shouted those words. For me, and I suspect for many of my classmates, an internal shift began to occur. I imagine it was like the shifts that begin in Marine recruits on the bus to Paris Island when the drill sergeant first begins to scream at them. The ideas and values I had accumulated in no particular order during my first twenty-four years seemed to be under attack. I had assumed, as had the student who uttered the fatal words on justice, that justice was the whole point of law and the reason I was in law school. But no—not only was it not the point, it was not even in the equation.† I had entered a system where such concepts were apparently viewed as worthless or worse, a hindrance to my success in the system.

Now I will admit that at this point in my life, I probably had more stars in my eyes than the average law student and may have been, for that reason, less prepared than many law students to resist the pressures to conform. I had twenty-four months previously returned from a tour of duty

---

*This story is true and was written before I read about similar episodes in Benjamin Sells's *The Soul of the Law* (Rockport, Maine: Element, 1994), 36.

†I understand that for some, this will appear an overly narrow, hyperbolic, and condemnatory view of the philosophy of legal education that prevailed in the early 1970s, and to some degree that criticism is accurate. If asked, most law professors of that era would have probably said that justice (and other such ideals) were the ultimate purpose of the law. But the method in law schools—at least from my experience and that of many of my classmates with whom I spoke—did not reflect that belief. And the effect of the method upon the unsophisticated mind—which I concede describes my own intellectual state at the time (as well as that of many of my classmates)—is what I am describing here.

with the United States Army in Vietnam, entered graduate school at the University of North Carolina, and become involved in a fairly emotional way in the student protest movement against the war. I decided to attend law school as a direct result of the helplessness I felt while watching on television the events surrounding the 1968 Democratic National Convention. I was particularly disturbed by the dissonance between the messages of the protesters in the Chicago streets and the ceremonies occurring inside the convention hall and the ineffectiveness of the Democratic nominee, Hubert Humphrey, who was a hero of my parents and a national leader in whom I had at one time placed great trust, to respond meaningfully to the protesters. In addition, as was true of a lot of other white, middle-class Americans of my generation, I was beginning to understand for the first time some of the truth about American racism, and particularly, the Southern version, of which I and most of my relatives and ancestors were a part. And there was even a glimmer at this point of emerging issues of gender inequality, though I was only beginning to stumble down that path, still largely in the dark. So, not only was I newly infused with ideals of justice, I was just beginning in many ways to imagine what justice meant. And I assumed that law school would be a good place to find that out.

THE ILLUSION OF A MORAL VOID

The first year of law school is notoriously stressful, and my first year was no exception. In the introductory address to our assembled class by the aging ex-dean, we were warned that we were entering a new discipline of study that would demand from us things we had never been tested on before. We would be asked to stretch our minds in ways they had never been stretched. We would feel disoriented from our traditional ways of studying and problem solving. And for many of us the disorientation set in very quickly. The admonition of my torts teacher against the confusing effects of idealistic thinking, and the messages from other law school classes that supported that admonition, intensified my intellectual and emotional disorientation and added an ethical disorientation as well. I began to feel myself severed from my roots—adrift in a moral vacuum where the ranking hierarchy, immersed completely in the process of the law, not only gave no moral direction but seemed indifferent to whether you had one. Moral commitment, or the lack thereof, was superfluous. What counted was one's ability to "think like a lawyer," to suspect and discredit easy answers and to find comfort in the briar patch of seemingly endless questions—and within the briar patch to find the ever narrowing passageways that led to the illusive, and sometimes illusory, final, ultimate "Issue of the Case."

I have discussed the torts class vignette with my colleagues at UNC Law School and at other law schools. Some of them defend my torts professor by saying that he was simply implementing a necessary pedagogical step in teaching neophyte students to think like lawyers. He was admonishing them to forget (at least temporarily) the fuzzier notions of justice and morality in order to learn the rigorous process of legal analysis—to learn, as Oliver Wendell Holmes put it, "to predict the incidence of public force through the instruments of the courts."[2] I think this analysis of my tort's professor's purpose is probably correct. But the problem is that no one told me and my classmates that the separation of law from morality was temporary. Indeed, the entire attitude of the law school hierarchy, both in the law school I attended and in many others then and now, is that man's highest achievement is rigorous legal analysis and that serious students of the law must pay primary, if not exclusive, fealty to that purpose. Notions of justice and a higher morality are treated as distractions.

It was the narrowing aspect of the law school process that I did not fully appreciate at the time.* Instead of accumulating knowledge and information in a process of continual augmentation with fairly cursory evaluation as I had done as an undergraduate, the primary objective now became to evaluate and discriminate, to rate information in terms of relevancy and irrelevancy, and to weed out the irrelevant and discount the marginal. Justice was irrelevant. So were many other fuzzy concepts and principles we had brought with us from our experiences of growing up. We had to discard these unfinished assumptions before we could even begin to accurately weigh the ingredients in the cases we studied on the systematic scales of rationality.

---

*The method itself, as well as the creed of the system, works mightily to narrow the focus of the student and the practitioner. Numerous commentators have noted this facet of legal education, one of the more famous being Erwin Griswold, former dean at Harvard: "It has often been said, for a smile, that legal education sharpens the mind by narrowing it. To my mind, there is more truth to this than we have been willing to admit. The methods of legal education fostered at this school and widely adopted elsewhere do have a tendency to exalt dialectical skill, to focus the mind on narrow issues, and to obscure the fact that no reasoning, however logical, can rise above the premises on which it is based. The making of nice distinctions is an important part of the lawyer's craft, and I have already indicated my agreement with Karl Llewellyn's statement that a lawyer must be a sound craftsman. But it is not enough." Erwin N. Griswold, "Intellect and Spirit," *Harvard Law Review* 81 (1967): 292, 299. See Roger C. Cramton, "The Ordinary Religion of the Law School Class Room," *Journal of Legal Education* 29 (1978): 247, 260–61, quoting Griswold and suggesting further aspects of the narrowing effect of legal education.

For some people this step was relatively easy (perhaps for some, no step at all), and others of us began to be awed by the apparent quickness in our classmates to fathom the hidden mysteries. We began to feel left behind. Though we would not admit it even to ourselves, we began to feel intellectually clumsy and stupid: "Some have it; some don't." Were we to remain among the unwashed, the outcasts? The internal pressure to learn the techniques that still eluded us became intense. The energy with which we devoted ourselves to the task increased. Our efforts to unburden ourselves from the notions we now believed the system deemed irrelevant grew more and more rigorous.

I recall a conversation in the crowded coffee shop in the basement of the law school about halfway through the first semester. A number of us began to meet there, at first to discuss politics or whatever subject came up, but more and more as the semester progressed, to discuss only "The Law." I'm not even sure what the conversation was about, but it was fairly intense—they were almost all intense by that point—and I can hear the tone of my own voice in that conversation through the slurps of coffee and nervous sucking in and exhaling of cigarette smoke. And the voice I hear is that of a person trying very hard to sound like he thinks he is supposed to sound, searching for the dialectical attitude that unites him with the fraternity of which he wishes to be a part. There is even a certain smarminess to it and a condescension to other people present—my fellow students—who either out of self-confidence or principle or ignorance were still not playing by the new rules.

The aphrodisiac in this process was a growing feeling of power. When my fellow students and I began law school, our professors seemed all powerful. In their classrooms and offices, in the halls and stacks of the library, they seemed to move about as knights in a list, thriving on the perils and glories of the endless tournament and supremely confident in their own skills. We wanted to join the joust, to learn and test our own skills, to feel the exhilaration of power and confidence that they felt. And as we began to master the process and to try our skills out on each other and then on other friends and family members, the feeling of power began to grow. The system worked. We were learning to think like lawyers. And we were learning to act like lawyers, too.

Though I believe the harshness of law school teaching methods and the attitudes of law school teachers have softened considerably since I left law school in 1972, my conversations with today's students convince me that much of what I describe here continues to occur. Every year I asked students in my professional responsibility classes to write short papers on "The Moral Reasons (if any) Why I Came to Law School" and "The Effects of Law School upon My Personal Value System." These papers testify that many students still experience the moral alienation and attitude changes I describe.

Sixteen years after that memorable torts class, I returned to the University of Virginia to obtain an LL.M. and again took traditional law school courses with another group of law students whose average LSAT scores were even higher than those against whom I had competed for the J.D. I was astonished at how well I did and how naturally the work came to me. This was testament to the thoroughness with which the legal method consumes one's intelligence and not to the power of the intelligence itself. I had been a lawyer and judge for almost thirteen years by then, and I simply had more years of training and experience in thinking like a lawyer than did my fellow law students. In fact, I could hardly do it any other way: it was a reflex, or, perhaps more than that, it was a compulsion.

I did not realize it when I was in law school in the 1970s or later when I was a lawyer and judge, but another of the byproducts of my learning to think like a lawyer (in addition to a narrowed intellectual focus), and one of the frequent symptoms of that mind-set, was an abiding cynicism.[3] I had never thought of myself as a cynical person. In fact, I had always considered myself to be dangerously idealistic. I sought out civil rights and public service work long after many of my classmates, who promoted themselves as idealists, had veered into more lucrative fields. But I now know that in terms of the work itself—in the way we went about it—almost all of us were cynical, and I was as cynical as any of them.

I have an image of myself behind my desk in my law office in about 1985, during the two years I practiced law between leaving my judgeship and returning to law school for my LL.M. I am wrestling with a legal problem in one of my cases, and, with my issue-spotting antennae working at warp speed, I detect an ethical problem in one of the tactical options I am considering. I whirl in my leather-upholstered swivel chair to my credenza, pull out the statute book containing the North Carolina Rules of Professional Conduct, find the appropriate sections, parse them to see if any apply, ascertain that there are at least plausible arguments that they don't, and then return to the original problem, satisfied—nay, delighted— that I have slid deftly around the potential ethical roadblock.

When I first recalled this image of myself some years ago, I found it astounding that at that point in my life I saw an ethical problem as confined and rule-specific. Now I realize that I was simply doing with it what I had been trained to do and had been practicing for a considerable period of time. I treated it as another legal problem, subject to the same type of analysis I had learned so well in law school. There were no moral questions beyond the plausible bounds of the Rules of Professional Conduct. There were no higher principles to consult or personal standards to bring into play. There was no conscience.

I know that all lawyers are not as cynical as I became, and I suspect that I was not always that cynical either. But during my time as a judge, when I saw lawyer behavior from a more objective standpoint, it was clear to me that many lawyers were that cynical, and that within some fairly wide bounds, if pushed hard enough in the adversary process, most lawyers could become as cynical as they needed to be to win. That cynicism is frequently turned against them in standard lawyer jokes. ("What is brown and black and looks good on a lawyer?" Answer: "A Rottweiler.") Such brutal cynicism in lawyer jokes is, I suspect, no accident. It reflects the way a lot of people feel about lawyers. And those feelings spring, at least in part, from the cynical way many lawyers behave and the cynicism with which they view themselves and their work.

Of course, in my observations of lawyer behavior as a judge, I did not recognize what I was seeing as cynicism. At that time I would have simply felt that a lawyer was pushing the skills we learned in law school and in practice a little too far or was shaving the ethical rules a little too closely. It was a matter, for example, of a lawyer arguing in a bench trial a point of law that any objective observer would recognize as absurd, or of demanding a jury trial in a simple divorce merely to frustrate the other side, or of subtly insinuating irrelevant issues of race or gender to influence a jury. It was always something that made me uneasy and made my role as an impartial decision-maker more difficult to sustain.

And the effect was cumulative. By the time I returned to private practice after five years as a trial court judge, the attorney behavior that had merely irritated me when I was on the bench was grating and sometimes infuriating to me as an advocate. So how did I respond? I was rarely able to simply ignore it. In my more skilled moments as an advocate, I found ways to use the attorney's behavior against him. In my worse moments, I responded in kind. And I'm not sure what it was, but during this time around as an attorney—as opposed to the five years I had spent in practice before becoming a judge—I began to realize that I didn't much like my role in either response. I didn't like the cynicism. I had been able to stay aloof from the rough and tumble as a judge. I felt degraded being back in it.

There are many people in the legal profession who have resisted better than I the pressures to push the limits of advocacy. And I feel that I resisted it better than a lot of others. But the feeling of degradation caused by my participation in it was powerful. Why had I not felt it to be degrading before? Why had I never really questioned the adversary ethic? Why in the torts class described above did I not speak up and say that I thought the principle of justice had some place in the study of law? I cannot speak for others, but I think for me it was a mixture of fear and testosterone. I was afraid of rebuke and ridicule. I wanted to prove I could be a tough guy in a system where toughness was a very important currency. And I think that the forces that drove me drive many other lawyers as well. I have discussed these feelings with women attorneys and women law students who tell me that for women the fear is not only of being viewed as not "tough" enough but also of being viewed as emotional or irrational.

Though I did not know it at the time, my recognition of this feeling of degradation was a life-changing awakening—a beginning of awareness about who I was and what I had become as a lawyer and a human being. It was the prick to my consciousness about how I related to the world around me much as, in the myth of the grail quest, the innocent fool, Parcival, is awakened from his torporous life in the woods by his vision of the wandering knights of the Round Table. Parcival abandons his old, unconscious life to take up the quest that will lead him to consciousness sufficient to ask the question necessary to heal the wounded king. In a sense, at the point of my first understanding of what I had become as a lawyer, I attempted in my own clumsy fashion to stumble toward a more conscious life. For someone in a profession, this quest is (and will continue to be) an excruciatingly slow process. It involves the truthful telling of two very difficult stories: the story of one's profession and the story of one's own life. Both of these stories contain parts which, like the degradation I felt as a lawyer, we are either afraid to know or reluctant to admit, and both of them are constantly expanding.

The Arrogance of the Legal Method

While there is a legitimate pedagogical purpose in the educational method exemplified in the story I have just told about my first-year torts class, there is a great fallacy in that method as well. That fallacy is the notion that one can dismiss ideals from an educational process without them being replaced by other goals and motivations. It is the notion that by dismissing those higher, often confusing ideals such as justice, one can simply learn to think like a lawyer in some sort of antiseptic space uncontaminated by moral considerations. And it is the notion that, having encouraged students to set aside ideals such as justice in order to learn to think like lawyers, law schools have no obligation to (and no time for) reintroducing those ideals in the educational process.

This persistence in decontextualizing the study (and practice) of law from other, less definite aspects of behavior and character can be traced at least in part to Oliver Wendell Holmes's famous lecture at the dedication of the new hall of the Boston University School of Law in 1897. The lecture was entitled "The Path of the Law,"[4] and in it Holmes advocated, for the limited purpose of learning the law, a separation of law from the confusion of moral terminology and the concerns of conscience. Because of the importance of this speech in the culture of the modern law school, it is worthwhile now to take a closer look at it. The legal academy has applied Holmes's limited-purpose formula quite broadly and given it an interpretation that appeals to those who advocate a very limited moral role for lawyers: i.e., the lawyer's job is simply to advise, counsel, and assist his client in, as Holmes puts it, "the prediction of the incidence of public force through the instrumentalities of the courts"[5]—that and nothing more. The result is not only a misreading of Holmes but a perversion of his purpose, for Holmes states his limited goals very early in his speech: "When I emphasize the difference between law and morals I do so with reference to a single end, that of learning and understanding the law. For that purpose you must definitely master its specific marks, and it is for that I ask you *for the moment* to imagine yourselves indifferent to *other and greater things*" (emphasis added).[6]

Later in the speech Holmes uses the metaphor of the "bad man" as a reference point to understand the force of law ("If you want to know the law and nothing else, you must look at it as a bad man, who cares only for the material consequences which such knowledge enables him to predict"). But it is compiling error to view this metaphor, as the legal academy has tended to do, as a complete formula for educating lawyers. Holmes added to his proposal that we view the law temporarily from the perspective of a "bad man" the following: " . . . not as a good one, who finds his reasons for conduct, *whether inside the law or outside of it,* in the vaguer notions of conscience" (emphasis added).[7] I think it is safe to assume that Holmes viewed lawyers, at least in the ideal, as "good" men and not "bad" ones and saw a life in the law (including both the study and practice of it) in the much larger context of "good" and "bad" human emotions and motivations.[8] It is quite clear that Holmes was himself well grounded in an intricate moral code as part of his heritage as a well-educated and well-bred New England gentleman. In his comprehensive biography of Holmes, G. Edward White says:

The heritage of Calvinist religion thus primarily manifested itself for Holmes in the Puritan concept of a "calling," which by Holmes' time had evolved from its initial theological context to the secularized world of educated elite professionals. Among Holmes' beliefs throughout his adult life were the need for moderation and self-control, the obligation of continued and persistent education, and a consciousness of the qualities and duties of the "elect," which for him meant not a class of predestined souls but his Brahmin contemporaries. The last set of "class" values included a distaste for "vulgarity," whether in conspicuous consumption or elsewhere, and contributed to Holmes' belief in what he called "jobbism," the idea that someone with Holmes' heritage did his best in his profession not only for self-gratification but also out of an obligation to hold up the standards of the elect.[9]

This does not describe a man who circumscribes his professional morality to the standards of a "bad" man. Rather, it is the image of a man who saw his professional life in a much broader moral context. It is the recognition of the need for this context and the role of law schools in developing it that has been missing from law school curricula.

My purpose in this critique of the singularity of focus of the legal academy is not to proclaim that traditional legal reasoning is useless or to advocate its abandonment. The type of analysis which Holmes was describing and which has comprised the central focus of law school education is, and I believe will continue to be, the most fundamental skill practiced by the profession. I will have more to say in chapter 8 about the importance of reasoned analysis both in the work lawyers do and in the service they may render to society. So in the tradition of Holmes (and, I hope, with better results), I want to make it quite clear that when I criticize the legal method as it is taught in law schools, I do so for the limited purpose of suggesting that legal method does not comprise or even imply a moral universe. It is a basic skill, perhaps *the* basic skill, lawyers must learn, but it is morally accountable only if it is understood in the broader context of one's life and place in society.

The attempt in the academy to separate legal education from moral considerations, without an attendant effort to in some fashion reunite them, is an arrogant act and has lead to much of the ethical malaise present in the profession today. It is arrogant in at least several respects. First, to the typical, fledgling law student, it appears to judge the relevance of the moral ideals and concepts that students bring with them to law school in terms of their utility in legal analysis. This is not so much a conscious intent of the legal method as an unconscious result. If "moral" language and moral reflection are banned from legal analysis, as much law school teaching appears to do, the only standards left for judging ideas and concepts are those supplied by the method itself. It may be, as Holmes tells us, that it is necessary to rid ourselves of the unnecessary "confusion" of moral language to see the law clearly and predict its force.[10] Hence words like "malice," "intent," and "negligence," which have moral roots and reference, lend confusion to an understanding of their operation in legal context.[11] But it is quite another step to presume to banish moral reflection and ideals from the practice and application of the law and from one's professional life. And this banishment is what legal education appears to do for many law students.

The attempt to cleanse legal analysis of idealistic thinking in law school is also arrogant because it appears to discount the value of the moral character of individual students. Again, if this separation of moral ideals from legal thinking was simply a step in an educational exercise to teach legal analysis and recognized as such, it might not have the effect it does. But for many students and practitioners, unsure of other ideals and goals, it has become a pedagogical and professional end in itself. That end manifests in the image of the penultimate law school product: the perfect abstractionist, the predictor "of the incidence of public force through the instrumentalities of the courts," unhampered by the confusing moral issues and emotions that distract lay people. Adopting this image as a pedagogical goal—as the model law school product—is a moral judgment about how lawyers should think and about the kind of people they should be as members of the profession. This is a great leap beyond simply teaching the law, which has been our simplistic and morally myopic myth about what legal educators are doing. It is creating professional (and individual) character, and that is a very presumptuous undertaking unless it is faced honestly and humbly with an understanding of the implications of the task.

But the primary arrogance in the assumption that one can teach legal analysis devoid of moral reference lies in its discounting of the nature and power of narrative. That is, it discounts the innate human compulsion to fashion our experiences and perceptions into morally meaningful forms. By "narrative" I mean more than simply relating a sequence of disconnected events. Morally meaningful narrative involves the "refashioning" of events, experiences, and thoughts into a story with meaning and a meaning which affects consciousness. Therein lies the moral dimension.[12]

It is the presumption that we can simply wipe out one moral story about who we are without it being replaced by another (or, perhaps, many others) which is arrogant. That presumption ignores what novelist Reynolds Price has called "the narrative hunger so basic to man."[13] It ignores the primacy of narrative in the human psyche—that it is there, active and productive just as surely as we are breathing. It is not something we can simply turn on and turn off.[14] The arrogance that discounts the power of narrative also contains a simplistic notion of how people think and live. As legal scholars who are feminists or from racial minorities argue forcefully in the debate now raging over the use of narrative in legal scholarship, and as anyone who will look inward at his own life will see, narrative gives voice to many things largely excluded from traditional, scientific legal analysis. Emotions, desires, hopes, values, ideals, the hidden and ever present voices from the unconscious, all are expressed through narrative. And while they may be revealed in other ways as well (as when one shouts in anger or cries in sadness), they become meaningful to us as they relate to our life story, which is our contextual understanding (sometimes real and sometimes illusory) of who we are. Each of us has a continuously evolving story of who she is that gives meaning to (or sometimes shows the absurdity of) our lives. And this instinct for our own narrative, this function that is as real as consciousness or breathing, cannot be discontinued for law students by educational fiat or rigorous training. The process will continue, inevitably, but the story will almost certainly be changed.

At some point well into my first semester of law school, the same torts teacher who banished justice from the classroom told us of the crowning moment in his short experience in private practice when his mentor, an elderly trial attorney for whom he worked, told him, "The thing I like about you is that you go for the jugular." That was the first time I had heard that phrase, which has perhaps become the most clichéd description of the vaunted instincts of the skilled American trial lawyer.[15] While I do not wish to imply that my torts teacher's reference to "going for the jugular" determined my moral destiny as a lawyer, the image it conveyed fairly well depicts the revised story I was beginning to tell about myself to myself and others by the time I left law school and entered practice. I conceived myself to be in the process of becoming a very different person from the person I was when I entered law school, with a new and clearer view of the realities of life and the skills to control and manipulate them. I had that power because I had learned what it meant to "go for the jugular."

This is not an absence of moral reference. It is simply a new story of who I was and a new set of moral values within which to operate. Instead of conceiving my story as primarily that of a professional using his newfound skills to achieve ends of social justice, my story was becoming that of a man known for his instinct for the jugular and his ability to fight hard and win. Thus in my instinctual "hunger for narrative," I simply replaced one dominant story with another, and it made all the difference in my self-image and in how I conducted myself as a professional.

Though I cannot look into the souls of my law school classmates, I can identify several other stories that seemed to emerge among us (in various shadings and configurations) from our law school experience—stories which replaced the ones we told to each other when we first arrived about our reasons for going to law school:

The Ends-Justify-the-Means Story: "I'm really a good person who will dedicate his life to the ends of truth and justice, as I hoped when I came to law school, but sometimes—perhaps a lot of the time—I will have to be an s.o.b. to do it." This is a version of the "nice guys finish last" maxim, and it is built on the illusion that most people have the ability to comfortably lead dual and morally conflicted lives.[16] My story of myself, as one who goes for the jugular, adopted part of this story, because I assured myself that my newfound ability was being put to good use and therefore was not morally deprecatory to my character.

The Nihilist Story: "In the 'real world' there are no altruistic goals (or altruistic goals are for suckers) (or altruistic goals are O.K. for some people but not for me)." For absolutists in the first year of law school, this story may seem like the only alternative when they are told that the ideals with which they entered law school are hindrances in the "real world" of law practice. This response is, in my experiences as both law student and law teacher, partly a function of the feeling of powerlessness that students experience in law school, particularly in their first year. They are told that the world is not as they imagined it, and that, if they want a job after law school, they had better learn the new version. They begin to feel that they really have no choice but to "get on board" and with as much enthusiasm as they can muster. Students who adopt this story, in which the profession (as they understand it) sets the "real world" parameters of what is morally relevant, also adopt new goals which are compatible with the story and which can be delivered by the profession itself. Frequently those goals are in the categories of money and power. And for some, the ultimate goal becomes the means themselves—that is, to become as skilled as possible at using their newfound mental acuity, the measure of which is to win and only to win.

The Super-Competence Story: "My goal is to be the best lawyer I can be and render the best possible service for my clients (and it is not my concern what the client's goals are). In doing this I will be a good lawyer and a good person." This is another version of what for many lawyers becomes the "adversary system excuse,"[17] in which the issue of the morality of one's work is not faced in any personal sense but is loaded onto the legal system itself. If the system is morally supportable, the work one does within it, if it is high-quality work, is also morally supportable regardless of the social consequences in any individual case.[18] This story represents an effort by law students (and lawyers) to reconcile using one's skills to obtain objectives for clients which are or might be morally repugnant to the lawyer, if the lawyer really thought about those objectives. Like the other stories, this one is not true for many of the people who use it, but it suffices to prevent the internal reflection which leads to real stories—those that tell us the truth about ourselves—coming out.

One of my first cases as a young lawyer illustrates my use of this story. As an aspiring civil rights lawyer in a small firm, I was assigned to obtain a parade permit for the Ku Klux Klan to march down the main street in Charlotte, North Carolina. There are "good" reasons to help the Klan obtain a parade permit, mostly based on the First Amendment, and the moral debate is a tough one between one's belief in constitutional rights for *everyone* and one's abhorrence of racism. But I never really entered that debate, even with myself. I simply placed all of my moral predilections about the Klan into the closet of my law-school-learned reverence for the First Amendment. I convinced myself that in doing the best job I could for my client, I was simply defending the Bill of Rights. I did not look at the costs on the other side. I did not address the moral quandary. But that quandary became more and more apparent as, during the application process for the permit, I got closer and closer to defending the real reason for the march.

These are rough sketches of some of the stories that began to surface to replace the moral stories which my classmates and I brought to law school. There are some who will argue that as morally limited as these stories are, they may be better for society in the long run than the moral outlooks which some people bring to law school. While I do not share that pessimistic view of the moral values of prospective law students, I will admit that in some cases one's moral outlook may be broadened, and thereby improved, in law school. But the real danger is not so much in the change in one's moral story about oneself, but in the damage to one's capacity for moral growth. The incapacitation for moral growth, about which I will have more to say in chapter 6, begins in law school. It is replicated in the profession and is the primary reason many lawyers are ailing in their personal and professional lives.

3

The Profession and the Loss
of Professional Mythology

Something roughly parallel to the displacement of the personal stories of law students has happened on a larger scale in the legal profession itself. As the legal profession developed in America, narratives evolved which helped define lawyers in terms of their own character and identity and of their relation to the greater society.[1] These were orienting stories— stories which told lawyers who they were, which gave lawyers their identity, both to themselves and to the society they served. Some of these narratives were favorable to the profession, with the lawyer in the role of hero, champion, and community-builder. Others, at least on first impression, were decidedly derogatory. The favorable stories about lawyers crystallized into ideals of professionalism and the good lawyer. The unfavorable ones crystallized into archetypal stories of the bully, shyster, and trickster.

In a profession given to testing stories against factual proof, one is tempted to ask whether any of these ideals and archetypes (and, indeed, the stories which underlay them) were factually correct. This is akin to asking whether there was really a Welsh king named Arthur and a Round Table. Probably most of the underlying narratives about early American lawyers were based on actual events in the courts and the lives of real lawyers and then were reformed, enhanced, and merged with other stories in repeated tellings.[2] How true to life the emerging ideals were is open to question.

But, of course, that is not the point. The power of narratives and the ideals they foster is not dependent upon legal proof. It is a power inherent in the narratives themselves. Narratives are powerful insofar as the story they tell has the power to engage our minds, spirit, and emotions and to

28

open us to the possibility of growth in the form of deeper understanding, broader perception, and greater consciousness.[3] Whether the stories are actually true or not may affect their ability to sway us in this way, but not necessarily. Factual truth or accuracy is only one of many factors that may contribute to the power of a narrative.

The important point is that powerful stories and ideals of who lawyers are and of the roles they play have circulated in this country both in the profession and in the larger society. We know they have existed because most of us have heard them in one form or another, and we know they are powerful because they have persisted. They (at one time at least) helped us understand what it could mean to be a lawyer and what a "good lawyer" or "bad lawyer" was. In his book *The Lost Lawyer*, Dean Anthony Kronman chronicles (and laments) the historical demise of one version of the stories of the good lawyer—the ideal of the lawyer-statesman—and doubts the efficacy of filling the resulting void with the intellectual ideals of what Kronman calls "policy science":[4]

> The lawyer-statesman ideal is an ideal of character. It calls upon the lawyer who adopts it not just to acquire a set of intellectual skills, but to develop certain character traits as well. It engages his affects along with his intellect and forces him to feel as well as think in certain ways. The lawyer-statesman ideal poses a challenge to the whole person, and this helps to explain why it is capable of offering such deep personal meaning to those who view their professional responsibilities in its light.
>
> The ideal set up by the proponents of policy science is by contrast narrowly intellectual. It is an ideal directed at the thinking part of the soul only.[5]

It is, of course, impossible to ascertain precisely how true to life the ideal Kronman speaks of was in the lives of lawyers prior to, say, 1960.[6] But it is clear from what Kronman and others before him have said that the ideal of the lawyer-statesman was a powerful image in the minds of Americans and, perhaps more importantly, in the minds of members of the profession. It was one of the stories—one of the positive stories—that informed us about who we were, how we should behave, and why. What happened to the ideal of the lawyer-statesman, and what were the other positive stories that informed us about lawyers and the nature of the profession?

The ideal of the lawyer-statesman was a logical extrapolation of the role of the lawyer-professional in the republican society conceived by the founding fathers after the American Revolution.[7] Republicanism embraced the notion of public virtue—which was the capacity of people in a representative government to strike a balance between private interest and public duty that protected the common good.[8] Lawyers, because of the nature of their work and skills, were eminently placed to function as a highly trained and principled elite whose primary role was to serve as protectors of public virtue. But in order to maintain this place—which as professionals they were obligated to do—they must view themselves as allied to the greater good of society at large and preserve a degree of independence from both political forces and the forces of the marketplace. This role for lawyers was doubly important to the republicans because they believed that the forces of greed and self-interest in a market-driven society would naturally undermine any higher tendency toward civic virtue and the common good.[9] As a principled elite, lawyers were thought to be best able to resist these temptations.

Translated into terms of lawyer's work, this meant that a lawyer was himself a virtuous person who set limits upon how far he would push a client's interest when he deemed that interest harmful to public welfare. Translated into terms of lawyers' training, it meant that lawyers were trained to be public servants first, advocates for clients' interests second, and money-getters last. Thomas Jefferson, perhaps the leading American republican theorist, in promoting professorships in law at William and Mary and the University of Virginia, conceived a curriculum to train lawyers to assume this crucial public role.[10] Central to the ideal was the paradox of maintaining individual liberty through devotion to the common good. And central to the resolution of that paradox was a classical notion of balance between the two potentially opposing goals. The key to maintaining that balance was the belief in and practice among citizens—and lawyers as the elite of society—of both personal and public virtue.

Dean Kronman details a number of reasons why the lawyer-statesman ideal is no longer viable in modern practice. One is the legal academy's hostility to "the notions of character and prudence that lie at the ideal's heart"[11] (a hostility rooted in scientific realism, which has been a dominant theme in legal education and which Kronman finds particularly present in both the Law and Economics Movement and the Critical Legal Studies Movement now present in law schools). Second, there are the new realities of the economically driven, client-oriented, technologically invested, specialized, multi-officed law firm. Third, Kronman cites the bureaucratic focus in courts—particularly appellate courts—upon economic management of dockets and caseloads and maximizing distribution of justice rather than upon the historical role of the judge as statesman and purveyor and protector of political wisdom.

Oral histories of lawyers and judges taken by students in a seminar I taught on the lives of judges and lawyers in North Carolina support Kronman's conclusions. A retired judge says in response to a question about the decline in lawyer professionalism:

> I think the public is worse off, and I think that maybe lawyers are worse off [now than in the 1940s, 50s, and 60s]. The profession has lost a whole lot of its dignity and a whole lot of public confidence. [In] my opinion, the profession in general, not being specific, in general overcharges—does not really have any sense of public service. They've become a mere money-getting trade, on the order of a brick mason or an automotive mechanic. Not that those are not good folks, but they're not professionals. From the time I started practicing law, 1946 in January, . . . the profession has steadily deteriorated. I like the law. I'm proud of being a lawyer, but a lot of lawyers do things that I'm not proud of.[12]

A highly respected North Carolina corporate lawyer adds:

> I think the law has become a business rather than a profession. I think there was more professional feeling back then [prior to the early 1980s] than there is now. Now people are looking for the bucks, and the law firms are looking to do all kinds of marketing programs and all that. . . . For the first . . . fifteen years I practiced law, lawyers could not advertise. . . . No professionals could advertise. So it really was more of a profession, and you did what came to you. But you couldn't advertise. Once that changed, then law firms started hiring marketing experts and all kinds of stuff, and the whole thing changed. And law firms got to be so big [and] they got such big overhead that dollars became more important than doing a good job. . . . It's really something that most of us older lawyers lament. It's really too bad.[13]

While all of these debilitating factors may be real, and while the ideal of the lawyer-statesman is without question on the decline in the areas where Dean Kronman looks for it, there are at least two qualifications that need to be made to Kronman's model.

First, the ideal was never universal—it was merely one version of who lawyers were in our society.[14] It is perhaps the version most familiar to Dean Kronman and the one historically fostered by America's elite law schools and larger, corporate firms. But, to put it simply, Kronman betrays a myopia that inhibits the view of many commentators on the legal profession in this country. Not everyone practicing law went to an elite law school and practiced in a corporate firm or as house counsel in a major corporation. Throughout the history of the country, there have been thousands of lawyers in small firms in medium-sized cities and relatively small towns, and recent studies indicate that approximately 70 percent of lawyers in private practice in the United States work in firms of ten people or less and over 60 percent in firms of five or less.[15]

Second, the ideal of the lawyer-statesman is not the only ideal that informs us what, as Kronman says, "a life in the law should be"[16] or what virtues a lawyer should possess. It is one version—in its many variations, perhaps a central version—but, as we shall see below, it was accompanied by other versions as well. Significantly, however, some of the same forces which Kronman identifies as eroding the lawyer-statesman ideal have also undermined and replaced the other stories and ideals.

So what is left of the story of the lawyer-statesman and the ideal it embodies? And if it is vanishing, at least on a national level, what is replacing it? A glance at some relatively recent histories of fallen lawyer-statesmen tells us more about the answers to these questions than we want to know. We see the modern, shabbier version of the lawyer-statesman in the 1970s testifying before the Senate Judiciary Committee, standing at the dock of Judge Sirica's court, and boarding a plane for San Clemente in the denouement of the Watergate investigation. More recently he is pleading guilty to defrauding clients in Federal Court in Little Rock as part of the "Whitewater" investigation or facing impeachment by Congress for lying to cover up sex acts in the Oval Office. This is the reductio ad absurdum of the republican ideal once personified by Jefferson, Holmes, and John W. Davis. It is true that the public lives of Jefferson, Holmes, and Davis were not subjected to the scrutiny directed at Presidents Nixon and Clinton, though Jefferson certainly received his share of personal and political attack. Perhaps if they had been, the ideal of the lawyer statesman would have been tarnished earlier. It is also true that there are people in high places in public life today who personify the old ideal.[*] But in the old world of the lawyer statesman, the ideal was the lodestar for the well-lived life of the public man. Today that ideal has been overshadowed by the rising specters of high-priced lobbyists, political operatives, and good-lawyers-gone-bad. Kromnan's explanation of the demise of the true ideal gives us some of the academic and institutional reasons for this cataclysmic fall. And to be sure, there is at the heart of that demise a basic loss of—or misdirection of—moral purpose. But there is something much more basic missing in the characters of the current, dominant version of the lawyer-

---

[*]There were lawyers both in the Watergate scandal and during the more recent Clinton investigations who upheld the old ideal of the lawyer-statesman. Examples are Archibald Cox, Elliot Richardson, and Samuel Dash.

statesman. It's as if any instincts for personal and civic virtue, which they may at one time have possessed, were displaced by another, much more cynical code, a code which was disconnected from internal reflection and which allows them to be pulled into whatever escapade excites their egos, lines their pockets, and draws upon their lawyering skills and instincts. It is a disconnection from self and a disconnection from any realistic concept of community welfare, both of which figured strongly in the republican ideal. A look at some of the other positive stories about who lawyers are and the ideals those stories embody may explain this further.

THE PILLAR OF THE COMMUNITY

The Pillar of the Community ideal is in some ways a localized and less formal version of the lawyer-statesman. The pillar of the community was well known in his town and handled the legal matters that allowed the affairs of the local people, businesses, and town government to operate. He was usually a prominent member of a prominent church or synagogue. He served on various civic boards and committees and functioned informally as counselor to people on innumerable problems that were frequently not, at their heart, legal issues. In this capacity he was an arbiter of fairness, morality, and common sense and served, as did the lawyer-statesman, as a pivot to keep the various forces of society in balance. His calling was thus far beyond that of legal technician and courtroom operator, though not on as grand a scale as the lawyer-statesman. The work of the pillar of the community was ultimately tied to interpersonal relationships among people, between people and businesses, and between people and their government. On the local level, he was the glue that held all of that together and the grease that made it work.

As the ideal of the elite lawyer-statesman was forming in the mind of Jefferson and other intellectuals and aristocrats in the power centers emerging on the east coast, the ideal of the pillar of the community was developing in the settlements along the expanding frontier.[17] While the ideal of the lawyer-statesman began as an intellectual conception of the role of lawyers in the new republic and was based on republican theory and grounded in the teachings of Locke, Hume, Montesquieu, and Adam Smith, the pillar of the community was a natural response of one trained in the law to a social necessity. The frontier needed leadership and order. The lawyer provided both.

Perhaps one of the earliest and most famous examples of the pillar of the community was Abraham Lincoln of Illinois, whose practice in Springfield and the surrounding circuit made him a leading member of his community, both civically and morally. During the first part of his life, he essentially lived out the small town American dream, rising from inconsequence and poverty to economic and political prosperity. His ambition in the early stage of his legal career seems almost Babbitt-like. His marriage to Mary Todd was a social step upward, and he devoted himself to acquiring the status and the accouterments of the solid middle class.[18] At some point in Lincoln's career—and there is no clear demarcation—his increasing political involvement took him beyond the ideal of pillar of the community and into the ranks of lawyer-statesman—a not infrequent transformation for early American lawyers who began as leaders in their local communities. In Lincoln's case, there is reason to believe that this career change stemmed from a vestige of what we would now call a "mid-life crisis."[19] In any event, he developed from a local, frontier community leader and politician into a statesman of national stature. Probably by the time of his election to Congress in 1847, and certainly by the time he stood across the platform from Stephen Douglas in their debates over slavery in Lincoln's unsuccessful senatorial campaign of 1858, Lincoln was the frontier epitome of the republican lawyer-statesman, negotiating and articulating the force and structure of the overriding legal issues of the day in the lives of his fellow countrymen.

But it is the nature of Lincoln's law practice in Springfield that best portrays his status as pillar of the community. We see Lincoln riding the circuit with Judge David Davis and other lawyer friends who would appear in court with him the next day as judge and adversaries. Sometimes he would share a bed with one or more of them in the crowded boarding houses along the way. We see him enjoying their fellowship among the locals in the taverns at night; joining in discussions of the law, politics, and community gossip; regaling a circle of listeners with jokes and stories and eventually trying, very imperfectly, to join them in song.[20] He was highly respected by his fellow professionals and viewed by people in Springfield and the other towns along the circuit as one of them and often as a wise, charming, and trusted friend.[21]

In addition to being a lawyer, Lincoln was the first choice among his fellows as substitute judge when one was needed and a first choice among quarreling acquaintances as informal arbiter.[22] Frequently he assumed this latter role when one of the disputants came to him with a case that Lincoln felt could best be settled informally, as between friends. Lincoln would forego both the role and fee of advocate to assume the more healing role of arbitrator.[23] And it is this image that most informs the ideal of the community pillar: that of the lawyer at the center of his community, protecting and advancing the cause of justice and the rule of law, performing as skilled and fair advocate, but preserving above all the welfare of the community and the good relations of his fellow citizens.

This ideal still exists in smaller towns and communities throughout the United States. It has figured in relatively recent literature,[24] and my students and I have found numerous local Lincolns in the oral histories we have conducted of lawyers in small towns in North Carolina. But like the lawyer-statesman, and for many of the same reasons, the pillar of the community is becoming a depleted ideal. Lawyers who are focused upon the number of hours they bill are obviously not as likely to find time to engage in the affairs of their communities and are not as likely as Abe Lincoln to turn away a fee. There is, in addition, the growing complexity of practice, including specialization and increased use of technology and impersonal communication, plus, simply, the increasing size of local bars.

Two of North Carolina's more famous members of the profession testify to the tradition of the pillar of the community in North Carolina and to its demise. Wade Smith of the Raleigh, North Carolina bar states:

> To be a lawyer in the 1960s [when I graduated from law school] was a great honor. . . . The lawyers returned to the small towns in North Carolina. They were president of the PTA; they formed the corporations; they defended people accused of crimes; they headed the United Way campaigns. They really became leaders in their communities. They were very, very much respected in their communities. . . . The lawyers ran for the legislature. The lawyers went to the legislature and passed the laws. The lawyers became judges. The lawyers were the governors. Lawyers were an honorable, honest, distinguished group of people. They wanted to make the world better. They were idealists. They struggled to make the world better. . . . They went to law school because it was a way to make the world better.[25]

Judge Sam J. Ervin III, who served on the Fourth Circuit Court of Appeals and as a revered member of the Morganton, North Carolina bar, also remembered a more community-oriented bar and sees that that is not the case today:

> Lawyers had a much higher standing in the average town or city in North Carolina than they have now. I think they were looked up to as the leaders of the community, the people that you would respect to take on civic responsibilities, people who were primarily interested in seeing that justice was being done and who were not primarily interested in seeing how much money they could make. And I think the lawyer has lost a great deal of prestige and respect. Not all lawyers,

but the profession as a group, I think, is not nearly as highly regarded today as it was when I started practicing law. And I think we've done it largely to ourselves.[26]

THE CHAMPION OF PEOPLE AND CAUSES

In 1853, twenty-eight years after hearing Daniel Webster's four-hour argument before the Supreme Court in *Dartmouth College v. Woodard*,[27] Chauncey A. Goodrich, then professor of oratory at Yale, told the story of Webster's performance to Rufus Choate, who was to deliver a memorial oration on Webster's life.* The story, through Choate's telling, became an archetypal legend of the lawyer as champion of a cause—there the defense of the autonomy of a privately chartered college from virtual appropriation and control by the State of New Hampshire.[28] The argument proceeded before the aging Chief Justice John Marshall and a full bench in a relatively small, temporary hearing room in the North Wing of the Capitol.[29] Through most of the argument, Webster stuck to the facts and law of his case, presenting an argument which was, by contemporary standards, a "model of lucidity."[30] When he had come to the end of his argument, he stood silently for a few moments as if contemplating whether to proceed or sit down, and then suddenly turned toward the Chief Justice and said:

> This, sir, is my case. It is the case, not merely of that humble institution, it is the case of every college in our land. It is more. It is the case of every eleemosynary institution throughout out country, of all those great charities founded by the piety of our ancestors to alleviate human misery, and scatter blessings along the pathway of human life. It is more. It is, in some sense, the case of every man who has property of which he may be stripped,—for the question is simply this: Shall our state legislature be allowed to take that which is not their own, to turn it from its original use, and apply it to such

---

*The story of Rufus Choate provides perhaps another real-life example of the demise of the lawyer-statesman ideal, for he was one of the leading lawyer-statesmen of his day— at least of the New England/Whig variety—and yet is largely unrecognized in today's profession. He was a leading attorney in Boston in the mid-nineteenth century, frequent courtroom opponent of (and great admirer and political ally of) Daniel Webster and himself holder of various political offices, including a seat in the United States Senate. Like Webster, he was a great orator and jury arguer, and much of his influence as a leading Whig came from his public speeches on national issues, particularly slavery. An excellent account of his career appears in an appropriately named biography for a lawyer-statesman: Jean V. Matthews, *Rufus Choate: The Law and Civic Virtue* (Philadelphia: Temple University Press, 1980).

ends or purposes as they, in their discretion, shall see fit? Sir, you may destroy this little institution, it is weak; it is in your hands! You may put it out; but if you do, you must carry on your work! You must extinguish, one after another, all those great lights of science, which, for more than a century, have thrown their radiance over the land! It is, sir, as I have said, a small college, and yet there are those who love it.[31]

At this point, Webster's hands were shaking, his voice began to break, his lips trembled, and his eyes filled with tears. As he struggled to regain his composure, Justice Marshall was visibly moved, and in the temporary silence of Webster's great voice could be heard the sounds of others present in the room weeping. Webster, recovered, glanced briefly at his opponents and then continued:

> Sir, I know not how others may feel, but, for myself, when I see my alma mater surrounded, like Caesar in the senate house, by those who are reiterating stab upon stab, I would not, for this right hand, have her turn to me and say,—"*et tu quoque, mi fili!*,"—"and thou too, my son."[32]

Webster sat down. Justice Story, sitting at the end of the bench as one of the two most recent appointments to the Court, later described the overall and final effect:

> There was an earnestness of manner, and a depth of research, and a potency of phrase, which at once convinced you that his whole soul was in the cause; and that he had meditated over it in the deep silence of the night and studied it in the broad sunshine of the day.... And when he came to his peroration, there was in his whole air and manner, in the fiery flashings of his eye, the darkness of his contracted brow, the sudden and flying flushes of his cheeks, the quivering and scarcely manageable movements of his lips, in the deep guttural tones of his voice, in the struggle to suppress his emotions, in the almost convulsive clenchings of his hands without a seeming consciousness of the act, there was in these things what gave to his oratory an almost superhuman influence.... There was a painful anxiety towards the close. The whole audience had been wrought up to the highest excitement; many were sinking under exhausting efforts to conceal their own emotion. When Mr. Webster ceased to speak, it was some minutes before anyone seemed inclined to break the silence. The whole seemed but an agonizing dream, from which the audience was slowly and almost unconsciously awakening.[33]

This image of Webster, passed down to us through multiple retellings, is certainly romanticized. We know also that there was a darker, more cynical side to Webster that is considerably less admirable.[34] But it is the ideal here which is important, romanticized though it may be, of the lawyer as champion of a cause for the less powerful.[35] The lawyer is the great equalizer who brings the power of his brain, his voice, and his character to the bar for his client and fights the good fight against what would be, without his help, overwhelming odds. He fights with rational argument, drawing upon his great skill as a lawyer and thinker, and with emotion through the power of his voice, personality, and compelling presence. The response of those who see him, even in a lost cause, is often admiration, gratitude, and a kind of reverence. We see a fictional version of this response in the novel *To Kill a Mockingbird*, when Atticus Finch, having lost his case to free Tom Robinson, walks out of the courtroom under the racially segregated gallery where his young daughter Jean Louise, the narrator of the story, is seated with her brother, Jem; the black preacher, Reverend Sykes; and the black residents of Maycomb, Alabama. As Atticus Finch passes beneath them, the people in the gallery rise to show their gratitude and respect. Jean Louise describes the scene:

> Someone was punching me, but I was reluctant to take my eyes from the people below us, and from the image of Atticus's lonely walk down the aisle.
> "Miss Jean Louise?"
> I looked around. They were standing. All around us and in the balcony on the opposite wall, the Negroes were getting to their feet. Reverend Sykes's voice was as distant as Judge Taylor's:
> "Miss Jean Louise, stand up. Your father's passin'."[36]

The champion of people and of causes appears not only in the crucible of famous trials but in the context of a life's work. There are many examples of this "long distance" champion, including Clarence Darrow, Louis Nizer, and Jack Greenberg. But perhaps the most prominent recent example is that of Thurgood Marshall, who, from the time he graduated from Howard Law School until his appointment to the Supreme Court, devoted his legal career to the cause of civil rights for black Americans.[37] Here, it is not so much the skill and emotional power of the attorney that we admire, but the dedication, perseverance, and courage. For Marshall, his championship season culminated in the arguments before the Supreme Court in *Brown v. Board of Education*,[38] where he and his team of NAACP lawyers took on history, the prevailing law of the land, and the era's most skilled appellate advocate, John W. Davis. The story of Marshall's victory in Brown is a story of the victory of will, spirit, and a just cause over skill, resources, and encased tradition. It is a classic story of the lawyer as champion for the underdog.

The ideal of the lawyer as champion of people and causes has become tarnished since the heyday of the civil rights movement. Now, when we think of lawyers championing people in court, rather than Thurgood Marshall and Atticus Finch, we are more likely to envision Johnnie Cochrane or F. Lee Bailey. This is in part due to the replacement of simpler, clearer issues of good and evil in the legal arena with highly complex cases concerning highly complex social issues. No longer is the person to be championed a poor, oppressed, but honest man like Tom Robinson, who is innocent, but a wealthy and powerful sports hero who is, perhaps, guilty of murder and certainly guilty of spouse abuse. No longer is the jury racist and all white, but predominantly black and carrying the distrust of white men and white police officers earned through generations of oppression. It is hard to find the champion in this complex, latter-day version. It is harder to identify the virtuous causes and virtuous people for a champion to represent.

THE PARAGON OF VIRTUE AND RECTITUDE AND CONSCIENCE OF THE COMMUNITY

To be the paragon of virtue and rectitude and the conscience of the community is to be the solid moral center of society—the righteous prism against which moral confusion and ambiguities are refracted in perfect and redeeming clarity. Sometimes the moral solidity is coterminous with the hard letter of the law, but not necessarily. And frequently the models for this ideal are judges. Two examples of the judicial version of this ideal appear in two famous western novels: Judge Henry, in Owen Wister's *The Virginian*,[39] and "the judge" in Cormac McCarthy's much more recent *All the Pretty Horses*.[40] Toward the end of *The Virginian*, Judge Henry, who has until then remained a secondary figure, is brought to center stage to set straight a central, moral quandary—a quandary both for the reader and for the hero and heroine. Judge Henry is a patriarchal figure, a rancher, a good citizen, and the employer of the hero, the Virginian. The Virginian is an archetype of the rugged individualist and a "good American." He is honest and respects justice.[41] At the bequest of the judge, he has captured and hanged, without benefit of trial, two cattle rustlers who had for some time managed to evade the long arm of the law. Molly Wood, a cultured school teacher from Vermont, who is in love with the Virginian, and who, like the presumed reader, sees him as a model of justice and integrity, learns of the deed and is distraught. The judge, described by Wister as an "upright judge" and "a stanch servant of the law," is dispatched by Molly's guardian to enlighten her on the law of the West. He is faced with the tough moral task of defending what, "at first sight, nay, even at second and third sight, must always seem a defiance of the law more injurious than the crime itself." But he is equal to it.

It is clear that the judge's mission to morally educate Molly is directed at the reader as well. By this stage of the novel, if the "tenderfoot reader"[42] of Wister's era has followed the formula Wister intends, he has identified the Virginian as the hero and Molly as the heroine and has invested emotionally in the morality of their characters and the justice of their imminent union. To reach the happy ending, which seems so "right" and reaffirming of all we know to be good and just, this apparently serious moral failing, this lynching by the Virginian, our hero, must be morally explained. Only one character in the novel possesses the moral authority to set us and Molly straight: Judge Henry.

The judge devotes to his task his considerable dexterity in the Socratic method aided by a fair degree of what may appear to the modern reader as cynicism. He opens softly, admitting that "some dark things have happened," and then proceeds under her attack to try to distinguish the difference in principle between lynching African-Americans in the South and lynching cattle thieves in Wyoming. "What is the difference?" she demands. The judge replies that in the South the act is secretive, "semi-barbarous," and disgraceful, but that the hanging of cattle thieves is an effort to "become civilized." Molly concedes that the "way" of execution may be different, but holds fast on the principle. The judge then leads her through a Socratic sleight-of-hand in which he traps her into admitting that while both instances involve ordinary citizens taking law into their own hands, in Wyoming legitimate authority has failed while in the South that is not so. The Wyoming cattlemen are therefore justified because as "ordinary citizens" in a democracy, they are the ultimate source of the law. The judge is defining what is moral from a position above the law and above the predilections of Molly and the reader:

> "Call them the ordinary citizens," said the Judge. "I like your term. They are where the law comes from, you see. For they chose the delegates who made the Constitution that provided for the courts. There's your machinery. These are the hands into which ordinary citizens have put the law. So you see, at best, when they lynch they only take back what they once gave. Now we'll take your two cases

that you say are the same principle. I think that they are not. For in the South they take a Negro from jail where he was waiting to be duly hung. The South has never claimed that the law would let him go. But in Wyoming the law has been letting our cattle-thieves go for two years. We are in a very bad way, and we are trying to make that way a little better until civilization can reach us. At present we lie beyond its pale. The courts, or rather the juries, into whose hands we have put the law, are imitation hands made for the show, with no life in them, no grip. They cannot hold a cattle thief. And so when your ordinary citizen sees this, and sees that he has placed justice in a dead hand, he must take justice back into his own hands where it was once at the beginning of all things. Call this primitive, if you will. But so far from being a *defiance* of the law, it is an *assertion* of it—the fundamental assertion of self-governing men, upon whom our whole social fabric is based. There is your principle, Miss Wood, as I see it. Now can you help me to see anything different?"

She could not.[43]

While there is much to quarrel with in this passage—including not only the judge's erroneous assumptions about the legal status of the African-Americans lynched in the South, as well as his condescension toward Molly and toward the reader—the moral image Wister intends for us is clear. The judge is presented as a man of such moral rectitude that when he tells us that that which breaks the law and our own moral code is nevertheless morally right, we (the readers) are presumed to accept it, as does Molly Wood. He basically gives us a new moral view of the universe, and we are supposed to trust him to do it because of his moral authority.* And the moral authority comes primarily from his position as judge in a thoroughly patriarchal society.

Cormac McCarthy's judge in *All the Pretty Horses* plays much the same role, though in a much less preachy and high-handed way. McCarthy's judge appears only briefly in the novel, but, as in Wister's work, toward the end when some sort of final moral measure is needed. McCarthy's novel is set in the 1940s. The protagonist, John Grady Cole, a teenager, has returned to west Texas from an extended venture in Mexico in which he has suffered much in body and spirit, fallen in love and lost, gone to

---

*Implicit in Wister's character of the Judge is an over-arching patriarchal correctness which appears in the younger hero, the Virginian, as manly virtue and strength of character. It is a fair reading of *The Virginian* to say that Wister's message to the reader in the presentation of these characters and their moral code is that if one does not understand and approve this code, one is not truly a man.

prison and barely escaped with his life, killed one man, come close to killing others, and in the process has essentially grown—or been forced—into manhood. He brings with him the horse of a now dead companion who accompanied him on part of the journey. He is hoping to find its original owner. The horse is soon impounded on the testimony of three local citizens, and John Grady is required to appear before the local judge to try to establish ownership. He tells the judge the saga of his trip, and the judge, who is portrayed as a sort of backwoods Solomon, asks him three questions to test his veracity, the last one being a request to take down his pants and reveal scars from rifle shots which John Grady had testified passed through his thigh during his escape from Mexican authorities. The judge observes the scars, is satisfied, and awards ownership of the horse to John Grady.

That evening John Grady goes uninvited to the judge's house, and the judge, seeing that he is troubled, invites him in. In spite of the judge's acceptance of his story in court earlier that day, John Grady is still unsettled about having killed a fellow prisoner in Mexico in self-defense, and he seeks further justification. He and the judge talk for some time, with John Grady going back over the things he told the judge in court and adding details which he had not mentioned. The conversation reads like a sacramental confession, which is essentially what it is. When John Grady tells the judge about the killing, the judge can see how much it weighs on him. He listens, probes gently to be sure he is getting the truth, and begins to ask questions which lead to consolation and ultimately a form of absolution. He makes the excuses and articulates the rationale for what John Grady has done, and because the justification comes from the judge and because the judge appears so fundamentally good and kind, John Grady accepts it, and we do too. The scene ends with the judge returning to the subject of the horse:

> The judge leaned from his chair and took the poker standing on the hearth and jostled the coals and stood the poker back and folded his hands and looked at the boy.
> What would you have done if I'd found against you today?
> I don't know.
> Well, that's a fair answer, I guess.
> It wasn't their horse. It would have bothered me.
> Yes, said the judge. I expect it would.
> I need to find out who the horse belongs to. It's gotten to be like a millstone around my neck.
> There's nothin wrong with you son. I think you'll get it sorted out.

Yessir. I guess I will. If I live.

He stood.

I thank you for your time. And for invitin me into your home and all.

The judge stood up. You come back and visit any time, he said.

Yessir. I appreciate it.

It was cold out but the judge stood on the porch in his robe and slippers while he untied the horse and got the other two horses sorted out and then mounted up. He turned the horse and looked at him standing in the door light and he raised his hand and the judge raised a hand back and he rode out down the street from pool to pool of lamplight until he had vanished in the dark.[44]

This is close to being a religious scene, with the judge, framed in the light from the open door, lifting his hand in benediction as John Grady slips back into the world of darkness. The judge has, like Wister's Judge Henry, assumed a moral role on a level far above interpreting and applying the law, although he has done it in a much more humble and compassionate way. He seems possessed of infinite wisdom and goodness and an almost spiritual aspect. He is equal to or perhaps above the role of priest. He is for that moment the moral judge of John Grady's universe.

In both of Wister's and McCarthy's judges, we are presented with quite different versions of a character of the law who commands and sanctifies moral authority. In the case of both, they are the ultimate moral measure in the narratives in which they appear—representing a sure morality that transcends even the law they are sworn to uphold. They personify virtue and rectitude and community conscience. By virtue of their character, training as judges, and position in the community, they are the only people we can ultimately trust to justify what we have done.

When we see this ideal in the lives of lawyers (as opposed to judges), it appears in three different guises. Perhaps the most obvious and currently viable of these is the image of the incorruptible prosecuting attorney, who, in the face of political corruption and social malaise, cleans up an ailing city. Novels and movies frequently rely on this basic story, and politicians continue to rise from the ranks of honest prosecutors who have wielded their office like the sword of the people's justice. Thomas Dewey and the young Rudolph Giuliani are but two examples. In this version of the archetype, we see more the hand of vengeance than that of mercy, but this is only because the times call for it. We assume that once the job of cleaning up is done and order is restored, the kinder judge can resume his rightful place.

The paragon of virtue ideal also appears among lawyers as a righteous refusal to do something which, though perhaps legal, is deemed by the lawyer to be immoral. And frequently, though it is the lawyer's personal morals which are being asserted, there is an underlying assumption, not without a trace of arrogance, that the lawyer's morals are aligned with the bedrock morals of society—morals of which the lawyer presumes to be both savant and at least part-time enforcer. Professor Thomas L. Shaffer gives us a clear example of this presumption in his story, borrowed from Harrop Freeman, of the "horsewhip lawyer."[45] In the story, as Shaffer relates it, the horsewhip lawyer refuses to help a young woman who wants to leave her admittedly good husband and three children to marry her lover, who is also married with children of his own. One of the lawyer's possible responses (and Shaffer posits several)[46] is that he will not help the woman in a divorce action that will result in two people leaving their families.* Here is the lawyer as moral stop, enforcing, at least in his own domain, what he conceives to be the basic morality of society. Another example is provided by the lore on Abraham Lincoln, who would not— and apparently felt he could not—take or continue to pursue a cause which he felt was false or unjust. He was notorious for this and on occasion was known to abandon his client in court when he decided his client was lying and the other side was telling the truth.[47]

A third version of the virtuous, rectitudinous lawyer is that of the lawyer who takes on an unpopular case and, in pursuing it, acts as the conscience of the community, somewhat in the mode of Judge Henry and the judge from *All the Pretty Horses*. These are lawyers who act against the will of their communities on the basis of moral principle, which we come to recognize—and which history eventually proves—they under-stand more deeply and thoroughly than their fellow citizens. Frequently this involves advocacy for a client who, for whatever reason (often racial prejudice or political views), is a social outcast. Of course, in such cases, the lawyer is acting as an agent of both law and ultimate morality, and it is his community which is out of sync with both. Atticus Finch's defense of Tom Robinson is a good example of this brand of rectitude. Clifford

---

*This type of rectitude has been criticized by some legal ethicists as a morally limited approach to the attorney's role in the attorney-client relationship. Thomas L. Shaffer refers to it as the "ethics of isolation." Thomas L. Shaffer, *On Being a Christian and a Lawyer* (Provo, Utah: Brigham Young University Press, 1981), 13–20. Other critics have objected to the lawyer assuming the role of moral filter in relation to the needs and desires of their clients and, ultimately thereby, to the moral actions of society. See Stephen Pepper, "The Lawyer's Amoral Ethical Role: A Defense, A Problem, and Some Possibilities," *American Bar Foundation Research Journal* (1986): 613, 617.

Durr's representation of black civil rights demonstrators in Montgomery, Alabama, in the 1950s and Julius Chambers's representation of blacks seeking integration and equal treatment in Charlotte, North Carolina, in the 1960s and 1970s are further examples.[48] In such cases, the lawyer presumes that his understanding of morality and justice is more correct than that of the society around him, but he does so more out of conviction than arrogance. And, unlike the lawyer who acts as the moral stop for his client, he does so at great social, and sometimes physical, risk. We admire what he does because it is an act of both physical and moral courage. Judges have also served as models for this version of the ideal of virtue. Notable examples are Judge Frank Johnson in Montgomery, Alabama; Waties Waring in Charleston, South Carolina; and James B. McMillan in Charlotte, North Carolina—all of whom suffered the opprobrium of their communities for courageous decisions in the area of civil rights.[49]

Of the ideal stories of lawyers, the one that has probably suffered most from the passage of time is that of the paragon of virtue or rectitude. This erosion is less evident where the ideal appears in the "community conscience" vein—a judge assuming moral authority or a lawyer taking an unpopular case—rather than a lawyer who, through his own certainty about morality and the lack thereof in his client, refuses to take or further pursue a case. But many people either do not recognize or do not credit the virtuous lawyer now in any form. There are probably many reasons for this. One intrinsic reason is that this ideal of virtue and rectitude, or at least the image of the virtuous and rectitudinous lawyer, runs superficially counter to much of the work lawyers do. A central part of lawyers' work *is* to represent people and advocate causes that are unaligned with the moral mainstream and are frequently viewed as blatantly immoral. That part of lawyers' work is fundamental to their role in society. And since the civil rights era, in which lawyers championed not only righteous, unpopular causes but also protected the rights of unrighteous criminal defendants and groups like the American Nazi Party and the Ku Klux Klan, that aspect of lawyers' work has become relatively expected. Thus a lawyer's taking of an unpopular case is generally not perceived as a morally courageous act or an exercise of moral virtue. In other cases where the lawyer acts as a moral stop to the "immoral" aims of his client, it is generally done in the privacy of the attorney-client relation and, therefore, is unknown to the public. And if it does come to light, it is often viewed as overreaching by the lawyer.[50] The ideal of the paragon of rectitude, then, is often not particularly visible, and if it exists, is frequently couched in subtleties that most people—including apparently a large number of lawyers—do not understand.

Another reason why this ideal is less visible today is evident in the posture and attitude of Judge Henry in the excerpt quoted above from Wister's novel. It is an attitude that is probably more familiar to lawyers than the more deferential and gentle approach of McCarthy's judge. Judge Henry's posture toward Molly Wood is one of patriarchal condescension and even cynical manipulation. And through the character of the judge, one suspects a similar attitude in Owen Wister toward the reader. If we look more carefully, we can see even more which makes Judge Henry an unappealing model. The morality of which Judge Henry is the center and which Wister promotes is at its core a patriarchal morality, coming to us in the form of unwritten codes forged by a self-appointed, elite group of men—codes which are understood by them, guarded by them, and interpreted for the rest of us by them, and codes which reaffirm that those men are the natural, moral custodians of society. This image exudes arrogance and is not one likely to attract followers in a professional society that is increasingly diversified by race and gender.

The Lawyer and Gentleman

By the early part of this century, the concept of what it meant to be a great lawyer was sufficiently developed in America that the ideal was realizable: one knew what greatness meant in the context of the legal profession, and, if one was of the right race and gender, one could aspire to become such a lawyer.* To achieve it required not only proportional shares of all the attributes and archetypal qualities we have examined so far, but in addition keen intelligence, well-practiced skills, and a willingness to work very hard. If one possessed those qualities, acquired those habits, and developed the right connections, one could achieve greatness not only in terms of professional stature and public power but in wealth as well. The accumulation of private wealth was finally reaching such proportions in the United States that those lawyers who served the rich and powerful were themselves becoming wealthy.

---

*The ideal of the gentleman-lawyer is described by Thomas and Mary Shaffer as a person of civility towards others, self-possession in terms of personal morality, discrimination in his dealings with others, and diffidence in regard to those things which he does not or cannot know. Thomas L. Shaffer with Mary M. Shaffer, *American Lawyers and Their Communities* (Notre Dame: University of Notre Dame Press, 1991), 43–47. The Shaffers recognize, however, that the gentleman's ethic as historically practiced was patriarchal, elitist, and oppressive to women and racial minorities, and much of their book is devoted to the question of what good can be salvaged from the ideal to apply in today's professional context.

There are, however, contradictions in the lawyer's role and in the ideal of the great lawyer that often made achieving the ideal difficult. Chief among them is that while greatness required being accepted and admired by one's fellow man for one's skills as a lawyer and virtues as a public person, lawyers were engaged in work that was almost certain to offend people. They contended with others; they tried to thwart and defeat the interests of others; they spoke publicly against their opponents; they represented people and interests who were often anathemas to other people and sometimes to the population as a whole. In addition, there was (and is) the underlying hypocrisy in lawyer's work: They advocate positions in which they do not believe and sometimes even positions they know to be wrong.[51] Doing this work and doing it well and at the same time maintaining a patina of gentility and public virtue requires an extraordinary degree of mental dexterity and social aplomb. These skills were the crowning attributes of the gentleman lawyer.

In 1895 a young lawyer entered the West Virginia bar who had not only the potential for greatness but the social skills necessary to achieve and maintain it to an advanced degree. John W. Davis had read law for a year in his father's law office in Clarksville and studied law for a year at Washington and Lee.[52] Davis was very bright and ambitious, and he developed early the traits that would lead him to the top of his profession. One such attribute was a tremendous capacity for hard work. From the outset, he worked late at night and never felt he was as prepared as he wanted to be in his court appearances. Another trait was a sharpened intelligence and a phenomenal ability to speak both precisely and movingly so that, as one observer put it, "he would create a bias in his favor by the brevity of his statement."[53] Davis became the greatest appellate advocate of his day, arguing 140 cases before the United States Supreme Court and winning most of them.[54] Oliver Wendell Holmes said of Davis's performance as United States Solicitor General between 1913 and 1918, during which Davis argued sixty-seven cases before the Court, "Of all the persons who appeared before the Court in my time, there was never anybody more elegant, more clear, more concise, or more logical than John W. Davis."[55] Other members of the Court and the bar shared this opinion.[56]

But Davis's success did not result from hard work and forensic skill alone. He also possessed that nebulous quality which, in describing lawyers and public figures, people sometimes refer to as "presence."[57] He brought an aura into the courtroom and wherever he went. People expected to hear eminent reason from him. They wanted him to persuade them. Learned Hand said, "I do not like to have John W. Davis come into my courtroom. . . . I am so fascinated by his eloquence and charm that I always fear that I am going to decide in his favor irrespective of the merits of the case."[58] He had a way, Hand said, "of stating differences that left no record of ill feeling. . . . He had no sign of passion."[59]

A large part of this "presence" was what people perceived as graciousness, charm, and character. From his childhood through law school, Davis was the "fair haired boy" of his parents, four elder sisters, and a successive group of cherished mentors. Under their attention, he cultivated his extraordinary charm and adopted the gentlemanly principles of honesty, propriety, courtesy, and fair dealing. These came largely from the example of his mother, a high-minded woman of considerable poise and erudition; the training of his father, a lawyer of high but rigidly conservative principles;[*] and his mentors at Washington & Lee University and the Washington & Lee Law School, where he received his undergraduate and legal training.[†] This culminated in a remarkable combination of charisma, eloquence, and social grace. Lloyd Paul Stryker, renowned trial lawyer of that era, described Davis thus: "In my heart what makes him live was his gentle kindliness and unfailing sympathy, his gift of humor and his flashing wit, the ability to laugh with and not at his fellow men, his invariable simplicity, his human understanding, his patience to listen to those less gifted and less wise, his readiness to help those who had no justifiable claim upon his time, his unaffected modesty."[60]

Admiration of Davis for his gentlemanly status and manner extended to those who would have otherwise opposed him philosophically and politically. Lloyd K. Garrison, a director of the ACLU, the National Urban League, and chairman of the National Labor Relations Board, who brought Davis in as his co-counsel to defend Robert J. Oppenheimer against charges of communist sympathizing before the Personnel Security

---

[*]Davis said of his father, John J. Davis, himself a state legislator and minor statesman, "I have never known any man who was more insistent on making up his own mind and really less inclined to yield to the opinions of others." William H. Harbaugh, *Lawyer's Lawyer: The Life of John W. Davis* (New York: Oxford University Press, 1973), 7. These were traits that would appear in his son as well, but there under the gloss of a mannered Virginia gentleman.

[†]Harbaugh, *Lawyer's Lawyer*, 22–24. It is no accident that Davis was a product of a college and law school steeped in the Southern courtly tradition. Indeed, it is likely that the ideal of the gentleman lawyer was largely a creation and outgrowth of the Southern ideal. Justice Lewis Powell, another graduate of Washington and Lee Law School (and college) is often thought of as an example of this archetype. See John Calvin Jeffries, *Lewis F. Powell, Jr.* (New York: C. Scribner's Sons, 1994), 54–56, 507–508. Behind this courtly ideal lies the long shadow of the ultimate Southern gentleman and former president of Washington and Lee, Robert E. Lee.

Board of the Atomic Energy Commission, considered Davis "a man of courage and honor."[61] And, even during the most conflicted stage of the Supreme Court arguments in *Brown v. Board of Education*,[62] which was Davis's last case, his opponent, Thurgood Marshall,* expressed his admiration for Davis as a great lawyer and man of honor, saying that Davis's animus in defending public school segregation was not racism but state's rights and calling him the "greatest Solicitor General we ever had" and "a great advocate, the greatest."[63]

As one reads about Davis's life, it becomes clear that his courtliness and status as a gentleman were not only a carefully adopted and maintained way of life, but weapons in his professional arsenal. Above all, he was a consummately devoted lawyer, and when he was thus engaged, which was most of his life, it is difficult to see his remarkable attributes at work in any role other than winning cases. And he did not hesitate to use them for that purpose. Indeed, because they were so pronounced and because respect for him was so profound and widespread, he was able to effectively put his own character in play in behalf of clients who were themselves subjects of public opprobrium. He did this successfully in representing a number of prominent lawyers and judges who were charged with forms of malfeasance or criminal activity. He also used it to the advantage of one of his most notorious clients, J. P. Morgan Jr., while defending Morgan in an investigation by the Senate Banking Committee.

In a real sense, John W. Davis represents the culmination of the professional ideals which were building and solidifying through the late eighteenth and the nineteenth centuries in America. He was a pillar of his community during his early years of practice in West Virginia, and was deeply involved in public life and community organizations. He was a lawyer-statesman of the first rank throughout his career, serving as congressman from West Virginia, United States Solicitor General, ambassador to Great Britain and unsuccessful, Democratic candidate for president against Calvin Coolidge in 1924. He was a champion of people and causes, and, while these tended to be politically conservative causes for clients who could afford his substantial fees, Davis also worked for individual rights when the issue, for whatever reason, struck a chord with him. One

---

*"The worst [Marshall] would say was that his adversary as 'all wrong' on civil rights." Harbaugh, *Lawyer's Lawyer*, 503. As a law student at Howard University, Marshall would skip classes to watch Davis perform before the Supreme Court and adopted Davis as his ideal advocate. Marshall recalled, "Every time John Davis argued, I'd ask myself, 'Will I ever, ever . . . ?' and every time I had to answer, 'No, never.'" Ibid. (quoting from "The Segregation Issue," *Time*, December 22, 1952, 12–13).

example is his enthusiastic, pro bono representation of two pacifists, Dr. Douglas C. MacIntosh and Marie Averill Bland, who had been denied citizenship under a section of the United States Naturalization Act. The ACLU had represented both parties until Davis and his partner, Allen Wardell, took the case.[64]

And finally, Davis presented himself as a man of great rectitude. This attribute was most apparent when it was used as a weapon in Davis's adversary arsenal, where it appears, forged from his sterling reputation, as righteous indignation. When used carefully and sparingly and at appropriate targets, this weapon can have devastating effect. Davis used his own indignation masterfully in his defense of attorney Isador J. Kresel on charges of bank fraud. Kresel was convicted at trial under fairly flimsy charges after a particularly scathing and inflammatory, ten-hour harangue of the jury by the prosecutor, James G. Wallace. On appeal before the New York Appellate Division, Davis argued for five hours during which time,

> he defended his client and castigated Wallace in words such as he had rarely, if ever, used in an appellate court. Gone was the gracious deference to opposing counsel, the poetic allusions and swift flashes of humor, the generous concessions on minor points—gone were most of the other traits that had made him the most polished appellate lawyer in the nation. Kresel . . . had been convicted of an offense which involved no moral turpitude and which was based on a transaction which caused no injury to anyone and by which neither the defendant nor anyone else profited in the slightest. . . . Furthermore, the case had been seriously prejudiced by a summation "unparalleled in the history of jurisprudence" and "transcending all limits of professional propriety."[65]

Davis accomplished all of these feats while building one of America's leading law firms,[66] accumulating impressive personal wealth, and maintaining his reputation as a perfect gentleman. He was Lancelot, the personification of the ideal. The mold he cast became the mold which law schools tried to reproduce in their deans, professors, and graduates and which the leading firms tried to hire: hard-working men, rigorous in reasoning power and intricate of thought, articulate, well-mannered, poised, and self-confident. And the persona for this model was the appellate advocate. Of all the varied types of work that lawyers did, appellate argument is the one skill that law schools chose to teach. It is the skill exemplified more than any other by John W. Davis.

4

The Mythological
Function of the Lost Ideals

What is the value of these old the stories of Abe Lincoln, Daniel Webster, John W. Davis, and others legends of the bar? How have we used them? What social and moral purposes have they served? The answer to these questions is more profound than at first appears and is central to problems currently faced by the legal profession. We have used these ideals, I suggest, as our professional mythology.

Myths are narratives, but they are narratives of a special and powerful kind. They are narratives which have evolved through numerous retellings until they are distilled to a purer and deeper form which connects to the timeless forces in our own natures—forces in the individual and collective subconscious which teach us eternal lessons. They reassure us on an emotional level about who we are, how we connect to the world around us, and how we relate to the great truths about our lives. For lawyers and other professionals, they give transcendent meaning to professional lives, and they do this on basically two levels. The first of these levels is easy to comprehend. On that level the mythological functions are practical and widely recognized by experts in mythology. Myths help us define ourselves in relation to our communities and to our greater society and help explain our and our society's eternal significance. They help us interpret the unknowable so that we can begin to comprehend it and to envision our role in the universe. Rollo May, who has written extensively on myths and the uses of mythology, has this to say about how we use myths:

> A myth is a way of making sense in a senseless world. Myths are narrative patterns that give significance to our existence. Whether the meaning of existence is only what we put into life by our own individual fortitude, as Sartre would hold, or whether there is a meaning we need to discover, as Kierkegaard would state, the result is

the same: myths are our way of finding this meaning and significance. Myths are like the beams of a house: not exposed to outside view, they are the structure which holds the house together so people can live in it.[1]

He then adds: "The myth, or story, carries the values of society: by myth the individual finds his sense of identity. . . . By their myths, we would say, we shall know them."[2]

The noted mythologist Joseph Campbell cites four essentially orienting functions for myth: (1) the mystical function—"realizing what a wonder the universe is, and what a wonder you are, and experiencing awe before this mystery"; (2) the cosmological function—"the dimension with which science is concerned—showing you what the shape of the universe is, but showing it in such a way that the mystery again comes through"; (3) the sociological function—"supporting and validating a certain social order"; and (4) the pedagogical function—"how to live a human life under any circumstances."[3]

Myths about the lawyer's life and what it means to be a professional serve all of these orienting functions. Through stories of the lives and works of mythological heros, lawyer myths reveal to us the "great mysteries" of the law and the transcendent power of the profession when we have the skill and industry to pursue it to its lofty heights. They show us the science of the law and how it works and how the mystery of the law is embedded in what Rollo May calls its structure. They inform us about the society of lawyers itself—again as May says, "the values it carries"—the practices, traditions, beliefs, expectations, and mores of the profession. They give us a purpose for lawyers' work that is community based and spiritually transcendent. They teach us how to live a life in the law and—this is important—how to live a life in the law that is a complete life, grounded in something greater than the profession itself, rather than a life which is consumed by the mysteries, science, and society of the law.

In addition to the orienting functions, myths serve us on a primal level. The primal function is, in a sense, a deeper part of the orienting function, but it occurs on a much less conscious and visible level—a level so deep, opaque, and timeless that intellect not only does not control or manipulate it but is at that level essentially nonexistent. This is the level which C. G. Jung called the dark realm of the collective unconscious, the unknown but instinctual heritage which we all possess as descendants of the human race. It is not a product of our individual consciousness, repressed or otherwise. It is more universal than that and is revealed to us in the form of universal archetypes that appear as images in dreams and mythology and that emerge through the creative process. The mother and father archetypes are but two of the more common examples. When we dream about an older man who helps us out of trouble, or when we read about Zeus in Greek mythology or Judge Henry in Owen Wister's novel *The Virginian,* we are seeing examples of the father archetype.

These archetypal images are the keys to the transcendent, precognitive truths of our existence. And while we do not consciously create or extract them, and though they speak to us on a psycho-emotional level, we may look upon them and reflect upon them consciously. When we do that carefully, they can help us understand both our inner and outer worlds. Myths are one method by which we can raise archetypal lessons from our unconscious (and from the universal unconscious which informs it) to consciousness. They portray the unknowable archetypes of the collective unconscious in forms that speak to our consciousness and upon which we can then reflect, learn, and grow.

Because they portray universal archetypes, myths are infinitely renewable and recyclable. Jung said of myths and the unconscious:

> The primitive mentality does not *invent* myths, it *experiences* them. Myths are original revelations of the preconscious psyche, involuntary statements about unconscious psychic processes. . . . A tribe's mythology is its living religion, whose loss is always and everywhere, even among the civilized, a moral catastrophe. But religion is a vital link with psychic processes independent of and beyond consciousness, in the dark hinterland of the psyche. Many of these unconscious processes may be indirectly occasioned by consciousness, but never by conscious choice. Others appear to arise spontaneously, that is to say, from no discernible or demonstrable conscious cause.[4]

This primal connection, which is present for all humans but to which some people are more attuned than others, is essential for a healthy, vibrant, and unstagnated society. It connects us to an eternal dimension, to the timeless, the incomprehensible, and, for some, to the great mystery of creation— for some, to God. At the very least, whether it is interpreted religiously or not, it provides us with the perception of an Other which is greater than ourselves and with an experience of our disconnectedness from that Other—with the result that we yearn to unite (or reunite) with it. This is the greatest source of creative energy. And while this kind of energy may not be essential to scoring high on a law school exam or winning a case (though, I would suggest, even that is debatable), it is essential to living a purposeful life, to the thriving of a community, and to the building and maintenance of a profession. At the very least a professional life should be a purposeful life, and, at its heart, a profession should be a community dedicated to something greater than itself.

Understanding these transcendental links is crucial to our hopes for revitalization of the legal profession. In terms of the myth of Parcival and the Fisher King, with which we began this discussion, that understanding is the answer to the question which Parcival must ask to heal the ailing king and restore the kingdom: "Whom does the grail serve?" The grail serves, and we as seekers of the grail serve, that which is greater than ourselves. But what is that for lawyers? This is not a question for which there is a simple answer. Rather it involves a coming to consciousness about ourselves and our work and learning that, to have eternal meaning, work must serve something greater than ourselves. And here is where myth can help us, because that coming to consciousness is the life-long quest in the myth of Parcival and the Fisher King. In a way typical of myths, the story of the grail quest doubles back on us. The message to lawyers (and to all who engage in the quest for the meaning of life) is that the answer to the question with which we began the quest is found in the quest itself. The consciousness we gain in our quest is a growing perception that we are not the center of the universe but merely a part of it, that there are causes and purposes much greater than ourselves: other people, the common good, public welfare, principles of justice and righteousness, universal love, God, and many others, which we can serve, which are worthy of service, and which will give our lives moral meaning. This must be more than an intellectual understanding. It must be an emotional acceptance and a psychic (and, we may hope, a spiritual) commitment. The mythological quest, then, becomes all important. It teaches us the meaning of our lives if we attend its mysteries; it provides us the means of fulfilling that meaning by giving us a venue for service. It helps us understand the essential question and live out the answer to it.

The ideal stories of lawyers which we examined in chapter 3 provided this crucial psychic structure for the professionals who went before us in the American legal profession. They were myths which helped lawyers bridge the gap between their everyday work and their human need for a life-purpose. They provided a vision of who lawyers were and who they might become. Dean Kronman describes this visionary function for the myth of the lawyer-statesman:

> The ideal of the lawyer-statesman offered an answer to the question
> of what a life in the law should be. It provided a foundation on which

a sense of professional identity might be built. And because the foundation it provided was rich in human values, this ideal was appealing at a personal level too. The decline of the lawyer-statesman ideal has undermined that foundation, throwing the professional identity of lawyers into doubt. It has ceased to be clear what that identity is and why its attainment should be a reason for personal pride. This is the great inward change that has overtaken the legal profession in my generation, and its outward manifestations, which are visible in every branch of professional life, all point to a collective identity crisis of immense—if largely unacknowledged—proportions.[5]

I believe Kronman's statement applies to all of the lost ideals I have outlined above. Each of them, in its own way, provided members of the legal profession with "a foundation on which a sense of professional identity might be built." And as a composite—and, indeed, that is how mythological images of this nature work—they answered the numerous questions of "what a life in the law should be," including moral and ethical questions of how to behave in professional contexts. In essence they helped us understand that we served something greater than ourselves and gave us an image of what that was and what the nature of our service could be.

The ideal of the lawyer-statesman told of the proper relation of the lawyer to his country and the greater community. It was an ideal of service in the great enterprise of nation-building and management, of commitment to the delicate and essential tasks of balancing the forces of democracy and making them work. The ideal told us how our profession fit into the great national undertaking and identified the important roles lawyers were expected to play in the public sphere. It connected us to the public welfare and identified us as patriots—indeed, in the most essential patriotic role as protectors of the intellectual heritage of democracy. These are exalted images. They interpret for lawyers the "mystical," "cosmological," and "sociological" functions, which Campbell identifies, of our professional mythology.[6]

The lawyer's role as pillar of the community served much the same purpose on a different level because it presented a more personal image of lawyers relating directly with other people in localized and contiguous settings. But the function was much the same, with more emphasis, perhaps, on Campbell's third and fourth functions of myth: the "sociological" function ("supporting and validating a certain social order")[7] and the "pedagogical" function ("how to live a human life under any circumstances").

We see in the pillar of the community images of how the lawyer should relate to his fellow man, again in the sense of service—and of the lawyer's responsibility for the well-being of the local community and the people in it. This ideal also includes a localized version of the lawyer-statesman's role—making democracy work on the local level—but there is something more personal here as well. Implicit in this image is the notion that a life so lived is a life well lived, and that it will bring, not only local fame and status, but also the love and appreciation of one's neighbors and personal satisfaction.

The champion of the people presents a different image but one no less important to the workings of democracy. Here is the lawyer-hero who takes the unpopular cases, champions the weaker voice and, through sheer courage and skill, rights power imbalances. In this sense, like both the lawyer-statesman and pillar of the community, he too is making democracy work and participating in the great national enterprise. But he does this not as facilitator and interpreter but as warrior. He will not be elected to the local school board or appointed secretary of state, but he may sue them both. He will frequently be outside the power structure and antagonistic to it. This role can be lonely, as it is clear much of lawyers' work is. And the image of the lawyer as champion helps to give those lawyers who undertake that difficult work the courage and the will to persevere through the disparagement of others. It is the role and image of hero—a primarily masculine image.[*] As such, it speaks to a primarily masculine profession.[8] It is more closely related to Campbell's fourth function of myth: it teaches us how to live under any circumstances.

The paragon of rectitude is the lawyer in the seat of judgment—the lawyer as an ultimate arbiter of and enforcer of core standards of

---

[*]On one level, the myth of Parcival and the grail quest is such a masculine myth. It is the tale of a lone knight, a hero, engaged in a long quest in which he faces and overcomes great trials at great odds to arrive at victory—for himself and the kingdom he serves. In Jungian terms, this hero is a masculine archetype. See R. W. Connell, *Masculinities* (Berkeley and Los Angeles: University of California Press, 1995), 213–14; Edward C. Whitmont, *The Symbolic Quest* (Princeton: Princeton University Press, 1991), 182. Atticus Finch's defense of Tom Robinson in *To Kill a Mockingbird,* including his heroic walk down the isle of the courtroom at the end of the trial, is a modern example of the hero's journey. As occurs in the Arthurian myths, the questing hero often is part of a community of noble knights or warriors who represent the highest masculine ideal. See Emma Jung and Marie-Louise von Franz, *The Grail Legend* (Boston: Sigo Press, 1986), 61. The progress of the Parcival myth, however, is the story of psychic change from the masculine ideal to a more complete ideal, balanced equally by the masculine and the feminine. In that sense, it is a true "hero's" journey and a metaphor for the life story of every man and woman.

morality that are essential to the maintenance both of his own character and, because of his position, of civil society as a whole. This role is also a lonely one, and the existence of the ideal version of that role helps lawyers find the courage to say to a client, "I won't do that," or, "I won't help you do that," and even more emphatically, "That is wrong!" The ideal helps lawyers assert their power as sturdy soldiers, defending the moral center. The unspoken attitude of the lawyer is, "There are some things I, as a lawyer and person, will not do because they are deleterious to the fabric of society, and, by virtue of my intelligence, training, and professional character, I have the insight to know what those are and the will to refuse to do them."[9] This image of straight-backed rectitude has historically been essential to the respectability of a profession that has assumed the privilege and power to charge fees and to manipulate levers of power on behalf of others. With such privilege and power at one's disposal, it is easy to drift from the frame of propriety into one where privilege and power are devoted to more selfish ends. The ideal of rectitude is an anchor against this drift. The conscience of the community and paragon of rectitude illustrates Campbell's third and fourth functions for myth: the sociological function—supporting and validating a certain social order; and the pedagogical function—how to live a human life under any circumstances.

For all its shortcomings, and there are many,[10] the ideal of the gentleman-lawyer perhaps served the most important function of all the images we have discussed, because it linked all of the other myths with an additional concept that was essential to the survival of the profession. The ideal of the gentleman-lawyer told lawyers how to behave toward other people—including clients and other lawyers. No matter how emotional the case, there were certain lines of behavior that were not crossed, because to do so reflected badly on one's character and destroyed the possibility of friendship on the other side. James Dorset, a lawyer from Raleigh, North Carolina, explains the code of behavior in this way:

> *Interviewer:* Do you think that the closeness of the relationships in the bar back then [in the years immediately following World War II] affected the quality of legal representation for clients?
>
> *Dorset:* . . . I truly do not, because I think there was still the strong sense of being a good adversary to your fellow lawyer. That is, you were going to represent your client to the best of your ability. You were going to prepare your case carefully and well. Yet you could go in the courtroom and contest a case strongly, but without rancor or dislike and without spoiling a friendship.

Interviewer: Were there any particular instances where you felt your
relationship with another lawyer was tested by the adversary
[system]?

Dorset: Well, I think just inevitably in the course of the intensity
of an important case and one that was strongly contested and
strongly tried, that there were certainly emotions felt. But so long
as the lawyers were not being uncivil, that made a great deal of
difference. I do believe . . . that [in those days] lawyers treated
their fellow lawyers, the judges, and even witnesses with more
consideration and courtesy than they now do.[11]

Mutual respect and civility fulfill an essential function in a profession
that is inherently adversarial and antagonistic and that rewards aggressive
behavior. Without it, we begin to develop the type of work environments
that legal practice seems to create today,[12] together with the growing
feelings in the profession of alienation and loneliness.[13]

The gentleman-lawyer represents the zenith of the old profession. In
terms of the Parcival myth, he is the knight of the Holy Grail. The ideal
law firms, consisting of gatherings of gentleman-lawyers, were Arthurian
courts where the knights sallied forth to fight good fights for what they
perceived as noble causes and where chivalry reigned. Such a court is
imbued with its own ideals of status and achievement. And for those
who were admitted to it (in the pre-1950s American legal profession as
in the legendary court of Arthur, almost all of whom were men), it was
a noble place where, as Holmes suggested, "a man may live greatly in
the law."[14] It had its limits, as we will see, but for its time, it was the
epitome of the ideal. Of Campbell's four enumerated functions, the myth
of the gentleman-lawyer served all four but concentrated on the latter
two: the sociological function (with emphasis on the society of lawyers
itself), and the pedagogical function (how to live a good life under any
circumstances).

These are the legacies of the old myths of the profession—legacies
which have now been largely lost. It might seem that the logical next
step in profession-building is to imagine ways to restore those myths or
to replace them with new ones. But before we undertake that, there is a
bit more work to be done in understanding how myths work and how
they might inform the professional life. First, while we have examined
the "good" myths of the profession, there are other old stories about
lawyers which are not so ideal. Those stories figure in the mythology
of the profession as well, and it is important to understand that myths
teach us by both "positive" and "negative" images of "positive" and

"negative" archetypes. (I do not use these terms as a moral judgment on the images or archetypes but rather in terms of their emotional impact.) Myths teach both by inspiring us toward the path of truth and enlightenment (the ideal "Other" in ourselves) and by showing us another, darker side of our personal or professional psyche which is frequently, but not always, fraught with warnings and danger. Jung saw this darker side as one aspect of what he called the "shadow,"[15] and both the shadow and its archetypal, polar opposite, the ideal "Other," are important to deeper self-understanding and growth. For lawyers, the darker side of the legal profession is frequently depicted as the shyster, trickster, or bullying lawyer. As this discussion of the mythology of the legal profession continues, it will be important to take a close look at this "shadow" side of the professional psyche to understand where it comes from, what it teaches us, and why it persists in the public perception of lawyers.

Second, while myths are not consciously constructed (in that they derive from a priori, unconscious archetypes), their emergence as teaching lessons on the conscious level may well depend upon our conscious and, to some degree, our unconscious receptivity to them. And our unconscious receptivity may depend upon our conscious receptivity. As the quotation from Jung near the beginning of this chapter suggests, the raw material for myth formation is present already in our collective unconscious. But the shape of the myths which evolve and manifest themselves, and how we use those myths and what they teach us, depend upon real-world experience and the conscious act of valuing myths and their teaching power. For myths to teach people, their culture must practice an openness to *mythos*—to the holistic narrative of life—and provide time and space for myths to grow and evolve. In the culture of the legal profession, that time and space is in short supply. Where this type of communal reflection is missing, the darker myths—the "shadow" myths, which tend to reflect our deepest fears and insecurities and which depend less on the light of conscious telling to survive, tend to move to the front of and dominate our individual and collective perceptions of ourselves. As I have said, these dark myths teach us also if we will listen. But their venue is frequently fear, self-hatred, and pain. We will do well to ask two questions: What are we as members of the legal culture learning from the dark myths that now dominate our professional story? What do we need to do about our lives, our work, and our culture to allow for the resurrection and renewal of our old, positive mythology and the creation of new, positive myths? But before we address those questions, we need to take a close look at our shadow mythology and begin to understand how we can learn from it.

The Negative Archetype in Professional Mythology

THE SHYSTER/TRICKSTER LAWYER

A darker, unheroic image of lawyers is also present in common consciousness. This is the image of the "shyster" lawyer—devious, underhanded, and unscrupulous, willing to manipulate the system and everyone in it, including his clients, for his own advantage. The methods of the shyster often extend beyond devious trickiness into bullying, abuse of power, and even sycophancy when it suits his purposes. And in doing whatever it takes to win, the shyster is utterly without shame. He takes society's opprobrium, which is heaped upon him constantly, into his identity. He expects nothing but scorn from society, and, rather than let it inhibit him, he uses such scorn to sink to the level he needs in order to survive. He survives by a combination of his wiles and a total lack of principle.

Where does this depraved character exist? Or, does he exist in fact? It is difficult to find this extreme brand of villainy in literary portrayals of lawyers,[1] and, I suggest, it is difficult to identify people as utterly cynical and ruthless as this in real life. But we all know that the image is present in our consciousness. This should tell us that it is rooted much deeper in our collective unconscious as well. It is, then, a mythological archetype, which, regardless of its literal accuracy, informs our idea of lawyers and of their socio-cultural role.* But if it does not exist or rarely exists in fact, where did it come from, and, more to the point, what function does it

---

*Variations of the shyster/trickster archetype have historically been applied to ethnic and cultural groups as well, with perhaps the most vicious and persistent application in recent history having been against Jews. It has also appeared in the culture of Western Europe and America in regard to Gypsies, and, in the American South, to African-Americans and even to poor whites. (See, for example, William Faulkner's portrayal of Flem Snopes in his novel, *The Mansion,* and in the short story, "Spotted Horses"). From my observation, however, the archetypal image of the trickster in the legal profession is not ethnically or culturally

serve? The answers to these questions are both interesting and complex and tell us a great deal about the function of myth in the formation and maintenance of our profession.

It is helpful to begin this inquiry by searching for a defining archetype in universal mythology. A number of scholars in folklore and psychology, including Carl Jung, have studied the phenomenon of the trickster.[2] The trickster is a complex and multifaceted mythological figure who appears in numerous cultures and societies.[3] He is a central figure in Native American myth and spirituality, where he has been much studied, but the aspects of the archetype appear in other cultures as well.[4] Jung says:

> In picaresque tales, in carnivals and revels, in magic rites of healing, in man's religious fears and exaltations, this phantom of the trickster haunts the mythology of all ages, sometimes in quite unmistakable form, sometimes in strangely modulated guise. He is obviously a "psycholgem," an archetypal psychic structure of extreme antiquity. In his clearest manifestations he is a faithful reflection of an absolutely undifferentiated human consciousness, corresponding to a psyche that has hardly left the animal level.[5]

In one sense, the trickster is basic and one-dimensional. He is frequently a moral simpleton who knows nothing of and cares nothing for the consequences of his acts, which are motivated primarily by his need for personal gratification. He survives by his wiles and a sort of moral recklessness and even malice, which frequently manifests in tricks he plays on people—sometimes to manipulate them into doing things they would not otherwise do and which are frequently harmful to them. In this characterization, he is an uncaring foil to human existence, particularly to the unwary and sometimes in an almost mocking way,[6] and he often appears in the form of an animal or other creature we associate with craftiness and trickery: the coyote, the fox, the raven, the rabbit (or hare), and the spider,[7] and in other contexts as devils or poltergeists. As part of his deception, the trickster can often change guises, appearing to people in different forms for different purposes, and the changes in guises may also denote a transformation, and even a progression, of character.

---

focused but applies across the board to lawyers of every type and of every financial and social strata. This is in part because the trickster archetype among lawyers derives as much from their privileged access to and manipulation of the levers of power as it does from their perceived use of trickery and wiles. At the "higher" ends of the profession, the image may be refined and gentrified, but it is still there.

The psychic role of the trickster in mythology and cultural orientation is very close to the pejorative image of the lawyer in modern consciousness. Central to this similarity, I believe, are two perceptions about lawyers which identify them with the trickster archetype. First, like the wily coyote and the poltergeist, lawyers are perceived to possess powers that ordinary people do not have (and, perhaps more accurately, to be privy to the use of powers to which others are not privy). This perception is due in part, of course, to lawyers' training, but the context in which lawyers operate is important as well. Lawyers are perceived by some to matriculate in a realm, if not of their own making, then at least of their own maintenance, in which the secrets of power over the political and legal machinery are reserved, protected, and ultimately manipulated for their own advantage and to the detriment and divestment of others. Their power is exercised largely through sophistry and verbal skills that are frequently perceived as trickery.* Those skills give them power in the social context that many see as unfair and dangerous, both to society and to individuals, and that many people resent.

The resentment of the power of lawyers is not new but is deeply embedded in our social history. American colonists brought with them from England a dislike of lawyers who, in the "old world," were part of the political and financial elite.[8] In the colonies this dislike intensified as resentment toward the power of the Crown grew and lawyers became more entrenched as purveyors of and complicitors with that power. Lawyers were seen as part of an evil and unnatural apparatus that worked to repress and disenfranchise the common man and to undermine the ideal of a utopian republic. Many colonies outlawed "advocating for hire," and there were numerous instances of both legal and extra-legal attacks on

---

*Two examples of public perception of the lawyer as trickster appear in the modern film, *To Kill a Mockingbird* (Robert Mulligan, dir. 1962), and Robert Bolt's play (and later, screenplay), *A Man for All Seasons.* In *To Kill a Mockingbird,* Bob Ewell, the father of the alleged rape victim, confronts Atticus Finch, the attorney for the defendant, Tom Robinson, after the trial and says, "You got to watch out for tricky lawyers like Atticus Finch." Ewell then spits in Atticus' face. The spitting scene occurs also in Harper Lee's novel but there without the reference to "tricky lawyers." In Bolt's play, Sir Thomas More is warned by his daughter, Meg, and son-in-law, Roper, not to appear before Secretary Thomas Cromwell to answer charges because Cromwell will try to trap him. Roper says, "While we are witty, the Devil may enter us unawares." More responds, "He's not the Devil, son Roper, he's a lawyer. And my case is watertight." More, who is not only a lawyer himself but a brilliant one, is more than a match for the legal tricks of the secretary. At the end of the inquiry, he dismisses Cromwell's charges with a "contemptuous sweep of his arm": "They are terrors for children, Master Secretary—an empty cupboard! To frighten children in the dark, not me." Bolt, *A Man for All Seasons,* act 2.

lawyers. Legal historian Lawrence W. Friedman describes the atmosphere in colonial America:

> In 18th-century New Jersey, the "table of the Assembly groaned beneath the weight of petitions . . . invoking vengeance on the heads of attorneys." The "Regulators" in late colonial North Carolina—a kind of vigilante group—rose up to squash corrupt and incompetent government. Lawyers were in the camp of the enemy. They perverted justice; they were "cursed hungry Caterpillars." In Monmouth and Essex counties [New Jersey], in 1769 and 1770, mobs rioted against the lawyers.[9]

The dislike of lawyers survived the revolution in spite of the fact that many of the founding fathers were lawyers. And, ironically, it was the special, political capacities attributed to Kronman's lawyer-statesman that supported the public dislike. The common man held a deep-seated distrust of political power in any form, and a particular distrust where power was held and exercised by persons who, by training, birth, or social standing, constituted some form of elite.[10] Lawyers, as Alexis De Tocqueville and others testified in adulation,[11] fit that category perhaps more than any other group. But the common man interpreted this power differently from De Tocqueville and Kronman. Because lawyers were trained in the language and reason of the law, people believed they could manipulate it at will and, therefore, rather than serving democracy by tempering and balancing its exercise to make it work, were among its chief subverters.[12] An anonymous author of the period expressed the sentiments of the common man toward the influence of lawyers in the formation of the new government:

> When sires, whom patriot virtues warm,
> Assembled government to form,
> Then note, the *Foxes* too were there,
> With learned and important air;
> The fabricators in debate,
> Of ev'ry mystic turn of state;
> So intricate to grovel thro'
> That none but they can find the clue.
> They rack'd their oratorial might
> That spreads a mist, or holds up light;
> Can fright by terror-feign'd extremes,
> Or fasenate by golden dreams;
> Can make the just corruption's tools,

And sages oft the dupes of fools:
For still the wise and good we find
Of noble unsuspecting kind.[13]

This same brand of distrust was expressed recently by the Chief Justice of the North Carolina Supreme Court in describing his view of lawyers when he was growing up in the small town of Ellerbe, North Carolina: "Growing up in Ellerbe . . . with a lot of the things I saw, I had a very negative idea with regard to lawyers. I just got the wrong impression. I suppose that most of them were very terrible people whose job it was, as a lot of folks said around there, . . . to lie people out of trouble. So I did not have a very high opinion of lawyers."[14]

A second factor that tends to align lawyers in the public mind with the trickster archetype is the perception by many people that lawyers are moral eunuchs, unencumbered by qualms that limit the behavior of other people. This view posits that lawyers lack ordinary moral development, that they possess a character defect which prevents them from gaining the moral consciousness that other people develop naturally as part of growing up in society. The image that emerges is but another version of the stunted moral consciousness of the trickster, and predictably the response of society is much the same: moral opprobrium, scorn, and ridicule (and, perhaps, a little envy). A nineteenth-century American essayist expressed it thus:

> [There is] a certain class of men, in short, we know by the name of lawyers, whom we find swarming in every hole and corner of society. . . .
>
> Their business is with statutes, dictates, decisions, and authority. They go on emptying volume after volume, of all their heterogeneous contents, till they become so laden with other men's thoughts, as scarce to have any of their own. Seldom do their sad eyes look beyond the musty walls of authority, in which their souls are all perpetually immured. And now, as soon as their minds have come to be duly instructed, first, in the antique sophistries, substantial fictions, wise absurdities, and profound dogmas of buried sages, and then fairly liberalized by all the light of modern innovation, and of precious salutary change, do we see them step forward into the world full blown with the most triumphal pretensions, to deal out blessings to mankind. Now, indeed, they are ready to execute a prescription of either justice or injustice—to lend themselves to any side—to advocate any doctrine, for they are well provided with the means in venerable print. Eager for employment, they pry

into the business of men, with snakish smoothness slip into the secrets of their affairs, discern the ingredients of litigation, and blow
them up into strife. This is, indeed, but laboring in their vocation.
For an honest lawyer, if, in strictness, there be such a phenomenon
on earth, is an appearance entirely out of the common course of
nature—a violent exception, and must therefore be esteemed a sort
of prodigy.

Abject slaves of authority themselves, these counterfeits of men
are now to be the proud dictators of human destiny, and withal the
glittering favorites of fortune![15]

It is disturbing how close the sentiments in this more than a century-and-
a-half-old essay come to present complaints about the use of adversarial
ethics and partisanship as excuses for lawyer behavior. And it is important
to note that in neither case are the complainers attacking behavior that is
professionally unethical. They are attacking an attitude and consequent
behavior that is presumed (at least by many) to be an inherent part of the
creed and practice of the profession.

This is why efforts to address public perception of lawyers as the
tricksters of society by attempting to eradicate the image of the shyster
are likely to fail. In an effort to improve the image of lawyers (and to
genuinely improve ethical standards), law schools enhance their ethics
offerings and bars institute continuing education requirements in ethics,
promulgate ethical rules and procedures to insure lawyer honesty, and
fund publicity efforts to improve lawyers' public image. While these
efforts may be worthy for any number of reasons, they are unlikely to
significantly change the public image of lawyers. That is true because
the archetype of the trickster is a part of the collective unconscious of
society and because the characteristics of that archetype are inherent in
the work lawyers do.* Lawyers *do* possess special knowledge that gives
them special legal, political, and economic power. They *do* manipulate
language to protect but also to trick and entrap people. They *do* speak
for and advocate positions they do not believe in and that appear immoral
to laypersons.† And they *do* profit immensely from their work. As long as

---

*"It is human nature to abhor those who remind us of our gravest flaws. . . . Lawyers
serve as constant reminders of some of our most grievous shortcomings as individuals and
as a nation." Walt Bachman, *Law v. Life: What Lawyers Are Afraid to Say About the Legal
Profession* (Rhinebeck, N.Y.: Four Directions Press, 1995), 91.

†When I taught professional responsibility at UNC Law School, each year I played for my
classes a portion of the film *Ethics on Trial* (WETA-TV, 1986), in which the infamous Belge
Case (sometimes called "the hidden bodies case") from Syracuse, New York is examined.

these practices continue, the trickster archetype will stir in the collective unconscious and attach itself to the public perception of lawyers.

There is a sort of perversion at work here as well. While the public frequently appears to hate lawyers, it is also fascinated with them. Though it would be impossible to prove empirically, I strongly suspect that the public's fascination with the legal profession is induced through the same archetype which engenders the hatred and disgust. In effect it is one side of what we hear referred to as the public's "love/hate" relationship to lawyers. It is the same impulse that attracts us to the dark characters in literature, so that the villains become more attractive than the heroes and heroines. Thus we find that in Milton's *Paradise Lost,* Satan is more fascinating than Gabriel, and in Shakespeare's *Othello,* deceptive, manipulative Iago is more so than Othello. And, of course, in Shakespeare's *Richard III,* we find the most fascinating villain of all—Richard of York, who engages us more than all of the "good" people in the play. There is a part of us that not only likes what he does but almost wants him to get away with it.

And that is the key to the attraction of the trickster. In a sense he is a part, not only of the collective unconscious, but, as an archetype of the collective unconscious, of each of us. In Jungian terms, this phenomenon is labeled the "shadow" part of our individual and collective subconscious. One Jungian scholar explains:

> Besides the persona there is another, darker side to our personality which we do not consciously display in public: the *shadow*. It is what is inferior in our personality, that part of us which we will not allow ourselves to express. . . . The shadow finds its own means of expression, though, particularly in projections. What we cannot admit in ourselves we often find in others. If, when an individual speaks of another person whom he hates with a vehemence that

---

The attorney who is the focus of that inquiry, Frank Armani, refused to divulge his client's confidences about where he had buried the bodies of two young women he had murdered. This is, of course, perfectly ethical under applicable professional rules on confidentiality. (In fact, it is almost certainly mandated. See Rule 1.6 of the ABA *Model Rules of Professional Conduct.*) Yet, as the film demonstrates, once the truth was finally known to members of Armani's community, they were uncomprehending, angry, and disgusted with his refusal to divulge. He was shunned and received death threats. Armani also attempted to use the information his client divulged to him to plea bargain for his client on another murder charge. While it is arguable whether this action was mandated by professional rules, it is certainly not prohibited. This, too, greatly offended the moral sensibilities of Armani's community. The district attorney called it "reprehensible."

seems nearly irrational, he can be brought to describe that person's characteristics which he most dislikes, you will frequently have a picture of his own repressed aspects, which are unrecognized by him though obvious to others. The shadow is a dominant of the personal unconscious and consists of all those uncivilized desires and emotions that are incompatible with social standards and with the persona; it is all that we are ashamed of. It also has its collective aspects which are expressed mythologically, for example, as the devil or a witch. But the shadow also has a positive value, at least in its potential. There is no shadow without consciousness, no darkness without light. The shadow is a necessary aspect of man; he would be incomplete, utterly shallow without it.[16]

Thus the image of the trickster lawyer is not something we can simply "overcome" through better behavior and better efforts at public relations. It is a part of our social and cultural psyche. The best way to deal with this reality is to recognize it and understand it and, in particular, to understand how it informs our professional mythology. As we will see, the trickster's role in our mythological process is not entirely negative.

Before moving on to a discussion of how trickster works with the positive myths of the profession, one further point should be addressed about the negative effect of the trickster image upon the development of the profession. In my efforts to discuss the ideals of the lawyer-statesman and gentleman-lawyer with colleagues and students in my professional responsibility classes, I have become keenly aware of an underlying distrust of these ideals by women and racial minorities. It seems arguable that that distrust is exacerbated, not only by the historical elitism and exclusiveness embodied in these two ideals, but also by the subliminal, shadow image of the trickster that accompanies them. Lawyers—perceived by some as gentlemen and statesmen who devoted their lives to civility toward their fellow man and who labored to make democracy work for the common good—are now perceived by many women and African-Americans as the manipulators of power who preserved the status quo of an oppressive regime. Not only was the profession exclusive, it was clandestine and secretive in its use of and preservation of power in the hands of wealthy and influential white males. If this image is in some manner connected to and rooted in the collective unconscious of women and racial minorities, it is not likely to be eradicated by any amount of argument for the abstract virtues of the gentleman-lawyer. We must look for a new and better approach.

How the Positive and Negative Myths of
the Profession Work Together to
Complete a Professional Mythology

The negative mythology about lawyers, based on the trickster archetype, informs us about the profession by its interaction with the loftier images and ideals we discussed in chapter 3. At first blush, there seems to be little that is positive about the trickster image of lawyers, and parallels between the low public image of lawyers and the darker shades of the trickster archetype are disturbing and disheartening. But the mythological pattern of the trickster is more complex than its darker implications, and the archetype carries positive psycho-social implications that are central to its mythological purpose. Jung explains a basic dichotomy as it appears in the trickster myths of Native Americans: On the one hand, the trickster represents the undeveloped consciousness—"a very much earlier stage of consciousness which existed before the birth of the myth, when the Indian was still groping in . . . mental darkness."[17] This is a state of moral unconsciousness which is necessary for the trickster to live his immoral life. In this primordial, undeveloped state, the trickster resembles the youthful Parcival, who, when his story begins, lives deep in the woods with his mother, oblivious to moral issues in the world around him and unable to grow in consciousness. (Of course Parcival, whose consciousness is awakened by the glamour of the Roundtable knights passing his woodland home, rises out of his moral topor. Tricksters, who are unable to see such visions, do not.) Like the youthful Parcival, the trickster in this stage of undeveloped consciousness is himself the object of ridicule and the subject of jokes.

On the other hand, as it appears in Native American mythology, the story of the trickster also serves to reveal to us a higher consciousness. Though the story of the trickster, we are able to perceive simultaneously our own baseness and our own ideal. And to truly understand ourselves and our relation to others and the world around us—to thus become "conscious" of who we are and the meaning of our lives—this dual perception is necessary. It is also necessary that the perceptions of both our baseness and our ideal self occur simultaneously because the perception of one depends upon the perception of the other. The dualities define each other.

This simultaneous perception seems an impossible task. How does one perceive one aspect of himself which depends upon the perception of another aspect of himself without having the latter perception in place?

The solution to this quandary is found in narrative. Narratives provide the images of the dual natures—the shadowy trickster and the positive ideals—to help us find the way to perceive both of these aspects of ourselves simultaneously. And now we see the true value in a myth like that of Parcival and the Fisher King. The journey of Parcival replicates the life journey of everyman—of ourselves. We see in Parcival's story both our baseness (our morally unconscious trickster side) as Parcival lives in the torpor of his woodland home, and our ideal, as he follows the grail, advancing in knighthood and eventually rescuing the ailing kingdom. And most important, we see the importance of the quest. For it is only through the quest that we can move from one pole of the duality to the other.

But until we learn to identify our own journey as a version of the archetypal journey, until we understand that our journey is the journey of everyman, the ideals we hope to internalize will be merely "out there." So the lawyer's journey in quest of lawyer's ideals, like the journey of Parcival in search of the grail, must begin largely as a journey of faith. And that faith must be based upon the stories we believe about the profession—the articulation of the meaning of the journey through narrative—either the stories we tell ourselves about our profession and our own journey in it or, on the more cosmic level, the old myths of the quest, such as the myth of Parcival and the Fisher King.

The journey—or, at least, the possibility of a life's journey toward greater consciousness—is, then, the ultimate gift of the trickster archetype. Without the trickster, there is no journey and no perception of the ideal. Where there are no opposites, there is no movement, no growth toward consciousness.* Thus, the *complete* story of the trickster includes not only stories that portray and define his character in a negative way, but also the act (and fact) of telling those stories, which signify a progression of human consciousness toward higher ideals that permit us to see the trickster image for what it is. That is the complete myth of the trickster: the stories, the process of developing and telling those stories, *and* the self-awareness and understanding which emerge from that process. Through this "oppositional" process,[18] we learn from the character of the trickster (from an image of the shadow) and progress. In this context

---

*As one commentator on the trickster has said: "Trickster accounts for the twinness in humans. He is both a giver and a taker, one who tricks and is tricked. He seems not to know good from evil; at the same time, his actions bring about both. He often acts as if there are no moral, ethical, or social values; he is driven by his desires and passions. And yet, because of the Trickster most values come into existence." Suzanne E. Lundquist, *The Trickster: A Transformative Archetype* (San Francisco: Mellen Research University Press, 1991), 25.

the trickster is a creative force and a life force, both for the individual and for society.

This process (moving from total unconsciousness—from ignorance and stupidity—to the ideal of total consciousness) is in Jungian terms the process of the movement (and progression) of history and the process of deification (movement of man toward God).[19] It occurs on both the cosmic and individual levels. As Parcival leaves his woodland home and begins his journey toward individual consciousness, the hopes of the Fisher King and the ailing kingdom move with him. At Arthur's court, he meets his teacher, Gournamond, who trains him in the ways of knighthood and tells him that he must undertake the life-long quest and that the goal of that quest is to ask the question that will heal the Fisher King. This question, which provides the mystery that propels the story of Parcival's quest, is simple enough: Whom does the grail serve? So why is it so hard for Parcival to ask it? Why does it take him so long?

The answer is that it is more than a simple question. It is *the* question. It cannot be asked until the purpose of the question and its answer are fully understood, and Parcival cannot reach that understanding without the hard work of the quest itself. For it is only in the long and difficult life quest that we gain individual consciousness and realize the higher ideals of service to others. And it is only though individuals gaining consciousness that the greater goals—healing a kingdom (healing a profession), building a society (building a profession), moving a society closer to God—can occur. The individual and cosmic levels are co-dependent and must also proceed simultaneously.

Thus the trickster, despite his reputation for moral ignorance, malice, underhandedness, and stealth, is also essential to the civil and spiritual development of humanity and especially essential to the mythology of the legal profession. He is both an object of hatred, disgust, and ridicule and the basis against which we discover the ideals and inspiration that allow for growth and moral development. He is, in short, the embodiment of contradiction and ambivalence and the object of ambivalence as well.

We have seen this ambivalence manifested in what we have already learned about the myths of the legal profession. The high ideal of the lawyer-statesman, elite mechanic and preserver of the machinery of democracy, is shadowed by the underhanded, manipulating treachery of the shyster. We can aspire to the higher ideal because it exists in stark contrast to what lies in the other direction. But frequently the difference between the two is very difficult to see. When we try to win a case for a client who is pursuing it for purely selfish ends, are we serving our justice system and the ends of democracy or our own private interests at the expense of society and, perhaps, at the expense of a more honest party on the other side?

Frequently, I would suggest, we are doing both. And this is where the importance of ideals comes in for lawyers—especially for lawyers. The lawyer's role as advocate is fraught with moral ambivalence, and the lawyer's morality exists in a constant tension between the actuality of what he is doing and a vision of higher ideals which must be implicit in his work. Added to the burden of moral ambivalence is the public's limited understanding of lawyers' work, which breeds a cynical view of lawyers and what they do. The public often sees only the shadowy, trickster side, which is that part of themselves that they most readily identify in lawyers. Thus there are powerful messages both from the public's limited perception of lawyers' work and from the reality of the work itself that push us toward the caricature of the trickster. A powerful vision of higher ideals is an essential counterweight to these messages in order for lawyers to maintain a life of moral purpose. Without that vision, the crucial dichotomy is lost, the crucial balance between the two opposites is lost, and movement toward the ideal ceases. We feel ourselves sliding back into the trickster caricature, and soon we begin to identify ourselves with that negative archetype. We are re-inforced in this identity by the public's view of us in that mode as well. Because we have no other vision of who we are, society's label sticks. In short, we desperately need the ideal stories. We need a positive mythology.

The goal of the profession, therefore, should not be to eradicate the trickster image of the lawyer, which is ultimately impossible given the history of the profession in this country and the basic role lawyers maintain in American society, but to rediscover the positive opposites to the trickster that give the trickster archetype its meaning, reactivate its mythological power, and restore its teaching potential. We need to reestablish the dynamic of the oppositional process in order to rise above the characteristics of the trickster and achieve a greater professional consciousness. This dynamic is not a one-time event, but for individuals a life-long process that repeats itself over and over, and for a community (or profession) an ongoing process that passes from generation to generation. It is hard, constant, long-term work to rebuild a professional mythology, and it cannot be created out of thin air. It must arise out of the context of a community. And thus we arrive at the true, comprehensive problem facing the legal profession: we no longer exist as and do not perceive ourselves as a community. It is difficult to know which occurred first in regard to the legal profession: the loss of community or the loss of professional mythology. But there is no doubt that the two are closely intertwined.

6

Professional Mythology
and the Loss of Community

The Loss of Mythological Power in the Old Stories

What happens to a community that loses its mythological power? Of the
four orienting functions of myth that Joseph Campbell identifies (outlined
in chapter 4), it is the third function that is particularly important to our
analysis here—the sociological function—because the legal profession is,
in truth, a society—or, at least it has historically tried to see itself that
way. And it is in this crucial connection between mythology and society
that the problem lies. Joseph Campbell, speaking of the breakdown in
mythology and Western society in general, explains:

> We have seen what has happened, for example, to primitive commu-
> nities unsettled by the white man's civilization. With their old taboos
> discredited, they immediately go to pieces, disintegrate, and become
> resorts of vice and disease.
>
> Today the same thing is happening to us. With our old mytholog-
> ically founded taboos unsettled by our own modern sciences, there
> is everywhere in the civilized world a rapidly rising incidence of vice
> and crime, mental disorders, suicides and dope addictions, shattered
> homes, impudent children, violence, murder and despair. These are
> facts; I am not inventing them. They give point to the cries of the
> preachers for repentance, conversion, and return to the old religion.
> And they challenge, too, the modern educator with respect to his own
> faith and ultimate loyalty. Is the conscientious teacher—concerned for
> the moral character as well as for the book-learning of his students—
> to be loyal first to the supporting myths of our civilization or to the
> "factualized" truths of his science?[1]

Campbell's message is important. In essence he is saying that in spite of
all the titles we may give ourselves and ethical codes we may prescribe

as professionals, there is something deeper which establishes our professional identity and controls our professional and personal behavior. That deeper something—the taboos, ideals, beliefs, creeds, mores—are based upon an internalized, mutual understanding of who we are and how we behave, and that understanding is sustained by a common mythology and is rooted in the concept of community. So it really does not matter whether community or mythology began to disintegrate first in the legal profession. They are part of the same structure and mutually sustaining, and we have lost them simultaneously.

How did the disintegration of professional myths and professional community come about? Why did it happen? There are numerous answers to this from both the standpoint of community and mythology. One of those answers, which illustrates the interdependence of myth and community, begins with the demographic changes in the profession itself. The professional society from which these myths sprung is not the professional society lawyers find themselves in today. The old profession was a society of largely one race, one gender, and one social class. Its prestige, power, and, indeed, its very existence were to a large degree enabled by the social roles dictated by race, gender, and class in the society at large. Founding a professional society upon such distinctions and exclusivity inevitably leads to a type of moral blindness among the society's members toward people and problems that do not fit the old images and roles. Its members tend to become oblivious to the moral movement of the greater culture. In a sense, the larger society changes, evolves, and passes them by, usually without their knowing it.

A good example of this is found in the career of John W. Davis, in an instance that not only damaged his moral legacy but significantly affected his performance as a lawyer. When Davis arrived to present his final argument before the Supreme Court in perhaps the most sociologically laden case in recent American history, *Brown v. Board of Education,* he was largely unaware of the shift in social consciousness concerning racial segregation and was consequently unable to appreciate the possible effect of that shift on the outcome of his case. A lawyer who does not know the social context of his case is a lawyer in trouble. One of his former associates described the scene:

> On December 17, 1953, when Davis strode again into the Supreme Court in his typical club coat and striped pants, he remained as confident as ever that the Court would vindicate South Carolina's position. It was as though the social and political winds that raged over his head did not exist for him, since they were not a part of his

anima. Based upon a thorough study of the history of the adoption of the Fourteenth Amendment and the legal precedents that since construed it, the Davis team confidently predicted that the Court would rule for their clients by a vote of six to three, conceding only Justice Black, Douglas, and perhaps Warren to the plaintiffs. We could hardly have been more mistaken.[2]

A modern version of this myopia affected the recent performance of the Chief Independent Counsel, Kenneth Starr, in his investigation of the various activities of President Clinton. Starr, like Davis a consummate lawyer, became so intently focused upon his legal objectives and methodology that he either failed to see, or neglected to care, how his actions would play in the wider socio-political arena. Given the inevitably quasi-political nature of Starr's investigation, this blindness was more than a failure of political acumen. It was a failing as a lawyer. It is small wonder that Starr was perplexed and offended by the public's negative perception of him.

Such blindness is detrimental to the usefulness of Davis and other mythological giants of the bar as role models for today's lawyers. An essential fact of our present society is that it is deeply immersed in social change. If modern lawyers are to adapt their profession to effectively serve our society, an essential, qualifying skill must be a raised social awareness both of the conditions of society and of its various directions. Thus, a knowledge of the very social factors to which Davis was so blind are today key measures of a lawyer's success as a professional. Perception of those factors will also, I suggest, be an essential characteristic in any hero adopted by an emerging professional mythology.

A frequently heard response to the loss of the old ideals of the profession—particularly by older lawyers and judges who came of age under the old regime—is to lament the passing of the old order with its common understanding of professional standards and values.[3] This reaction is more than impulse. It is part of a cultural reluctance to accept change and to accommodate to it in a progressive fashion—a reluctance which has been psycho-socially documented.[4] It is also exactly what Joseph Campbell predicts people will do when the myths of their society begin to crumble: to cry for "repentance, conversion and return to the old religion."[5] A retired judge from Charlotte, North Carolina, put it this way:

> *Judge Snepp:* If a lawyer doesn't know an ethical problem when it confronts him, that's the Problem. They don't know whether they've got an ethical problem. They just barge ahead. And if they haven't got that gut feeling, "Wait a minute here, there's

something here," and look into it, they can give you all the
courses in the world. It's not going to give you that.

Interviewer: Is it related to education that you were talking about
earlier?

Judge Snepp: I think so. We live in a relativistic world—do your own
thing. There are no . . . accepted, absolute guidelines. If you feel
like doing this, you do it. And nobody can impose on anybody
else. . . . You can't tell me what's moral. Well, there used to be a
consensus. Everybody didn't abide by it, . . . but it was there, and
you got it drilled into you. There were certain things, the moral
code, that you abided by as a human being and as a citizen of
this country. We don't have it anymore.[6]

This frequently heard lament is understandable, but its implicit yearning
for a return to the consensus of yesteryear is a false hope. It is as likely to
occur as history is to reverse itself. Not only is it a largely useless longing,
but it is counterproductive in assisting the profession to face the present
and to reconceive itself for the future.

Nor is it enough to say in response to the racial and gender limitations of the old, professional myths that the ideals they embodied were
noble and that they still apply if we will simply ignore those limitations.
Myths don't work that way. Our connection with them is intrinsic, emotional, and unconscious. As one commentator has said, they speak to
us "phenomenologically, as a felt movement of body and soul."[7] They
speak to us through symbols that engender an emotional connection
and through metaphors that mirror our own experiences and hopes.
Joseph Campbell has this to say about the appropriateness of myths to
particular situations:

> Myths offer life models. But the models have to be appropriate to
> the time in which you are living, and our time has changed so fast
> that what was proper fifty years ago is not proper today. The virtues
> of the past are the vices of today. And many of what we thought
> to be vices of the past are the necessities of today. The moral order
> has to catch up with the moral necessities of actual life in time, here
> and now. And that is what we are not doing. The old-time religion
> belongs to another age, another people, another set of human values,
> another universe. By going back you throw yourself out of sync
> with history.[8]

What sort of symbol does John W. Davis, whose last argument before the
Supreme Court was in defense of racial segregation, provide for a young
African-American lawyer today? What sort of symbol do male lawyers,

whose lives and creeds extolled the virtues of women as homemakers and nonprofessionals, provide for young women trying to establish a place in what has been a largely male-oriented profession? The problem is not that as professionals all of us—including women and previously excluded racial minorities—shouldn't be expected to abstract positive images from the now embarrassing historical contexts in which they gained life and substance. The problem is that the contexts themselves specifically excluded many people we now call fellow-professionals, and on many of those people the metaphorical power of the images that grew from those contexts is lost. It is unfeeling to expect fellow-professionals to overlook and overcome the insulting and degrading connections of these images and stories. Beyond that, it is unrealistic. Stories of the great lawyers of the past may serve as models for some lawyers today and they may continue to inform our professional standards, but they have lost much of their metaphorical power for the profession as a whole and for many of its members. Cynthia Ozick, who has written on the power of metaphor, explains that power:

> Metaphor is the enemy of abstraction. . . . Through metaphor, the past has capacity to imagine us, and we it. Through metaphorical concentration, doctors can imagine what it is to be their patients. Those who have no pain can imagine those who suffer. Those at the center can imagine what it is to be outside. The strong can imagine the weak. Illuminated lives can imagine the dark. Poets in their twilight can imagine the borders of stellar fire. We strangers can imagine the familiar hearts of strangers.[9]

Thinking metaphorically involves an active leap of imagination, which presupposes a desire to make the leap. There must be something in the narrative or in the image created by the narrative that draws us to it emotionally, that engenders a bridge of empathy from us to that which is being portrayed. Where the context of the narrative or image is personally degrading or genuinely repulsive to us, we are not likely to be able to make this leap or to even want to try. Thus it is with many women and racial minorities in today's legal profession when confronted with the old stories of the glorious past. The history of the legal profession was not glorious for them. They were shamefully excluded from it, and they can put little emotional stock in it now. The metaphorical power is simply not there for them. The stories are just old stories; they are not myths.

It is easy to see, then, why women, African-Americans, and other racial minorities in the profession might not draw mythologically on the old stories, and today the embarrassing racial and gender contexts of the old stories probably reduce their power for many members of the profession who are white and male. So in order to heal an ailing profession, we need new stories which will evolve into myths for our professional society. But as we form these new stories, we will be wise to look again at the old ones to recall the abstract ideals they portrayed. Many of those ideals—justice, honesty, civility, a sense of high purpose—are not just nice abstractions. They are ideals essential to the maintenance of a profession. They are at least some of the ideals upon which the new mythology must be built. Part of our work in restoring the profession will be to develop a mythology which embodies these ideals and recasts them in a language which speaks to everyone in the profession.

THE DEVALUATION OF NARRATIVE

But the essential reason for the legal profession's loss of its mythology goes far deeper than the loss of metaphorical power in the old stories. Rather, I think it is largely a function of the devaluing of stories in general and of the narrative function in the profession. And this devaluation is itself the result of economic and social forces within the profession and the greater society. For lawyers, it is a process that begins in law school.

In the curricula of the law schools, the astounding fact is that the devaluation of professional mythology has been systematic and largely intentional because the indefinite character of mythology and the narrative method is conceived as an impediment to the scientific methodology of the law. Return for a moment to the law school story in chapter 2, in which the concept of justice was banished from the classroom. Consider again the myths of lawyers I have outlined in chapter 3, which define the roles of lawyers in relation to society and their fellow man. The ideal of justice is central to every one of those myths. How does one begin to conceive of a lawyer without an ideal of justice? Such a question would have been almost unthinkable fifty years ago. Today, I suspect that many lawyers rarely think of justice other than as an adversarial tool, and a deluge of reports and statistics tell us that the general public does not associate the ideal of justice with the work of lawyers.

In the world of law practice, the devaluation of myths has perhaps been less intentional than in the law schools but just as thorough. It has occurred more through displacement by other priorities dictated by the changing economics of practice and the imperatives of the adversary system: winning cases, making money, and achieving success. And in the profession, the loss of mythology is perhaps more serious than in the law schools because there it is the capacity for mythmaking that has been lost and with it the capacity for self-healing.

The New Public of Lawyers:
The Lost Minstrels and the Dying Campfire

Where and how did the profession formerly maintain its mythology? Again, the answer lies in community. Read it in the testimony of three older members of the North Carolina Bar as they describe practice in Raleigh and Charlotte, North Carolina, in the 1940s, 1950s, and early 1960s:

> The bar itself in Raleigh, and as a matter of fact within the state, was relatively small by today's comparisons. It was a time when all of the lawyers knew each other well, and you spent time talking with each other. There was, I would say, a very high element of trust between lawyers that you did many things, such as continuations, just on a telephone call without going through legal documents. . . .
>
> I think then, because there was less a sense of pressure, that lawyers enjoyed each other and enjoyed their practice more. At that time, the billing was not strictly from the standpoint of billable hours. The tempo was slower, in the summertime in particular it was. But I think, too, that the lawyers knew the judges better. You saw them more often, and there was just time for more relaxed camaraderie than nowadays.[10]

> In Charlotte most of the lawyers were in the Law Building. There were not a dozen lawyers in Mecklenburg County who had offices outside the Law Building. So, lawyers saw each other frequently. Many lawyers you saw every day. Many lawyers you would have a Coke or a cup of coffee with many mornings at Hyman Polier's Snack Bar in the Law Building. You'd see them in the courthouse or on the streets, and the numbers were small, and people pretty well knew something about all the others.[11]

> In those days [1962] you didn't have any practical skills courses. So the bar had to teach you. And these lawyers up and down the hall [in the Law Building in Charlotte, North Carolina] took that seriously, and you could walk into any one of [their] office[s] and say, "Mr. so and so, I've got to do an assignment. Can you help me?" And he would pull out his file, . . . give me forms to work from—very, very gracious, very, very helpful. . . . And you realize, . . . we worked half a day Saturday—everybody came in and worked half a day Saturday. There were opportunities to walk in and find somebody who was not in the middle of something that was important and busy, and they

were most delighted to sit down and chat with you. Every morning
[my two partners] and I and the secretary, Jeanie . . . would go over
to the courthouse and get four Cokes and some nabs, come back
and we would have break time. And we would sit and argue politics
and religion, whatever was on our minds. Then we would go back
to work. And five o'clock was just no different than four o'clock;
whenever the work was done was when you left. You know, it wasn't
a particular hour, and no one worried about overtime or anything of
that nature.[12]

There is more present in these testimonies than merely three examples
of hopeless longing for the lost past. The speakers are recalling lost
ideals, but they are also telling us how those ideals were formed and
maintained. That did not occur through formal structure but through
two elements which are basic to mythmaking and community-building
and maintenance: time and space. Time and space for storytelling and
community-building were once a natural part of the work days of lawyers.
They existed in court houses while lawyers were waiting for cases to be
heard, in tax offices, registries of deeds, and coffee shops. They were
present in lawyers' offices when an associate needed guidance or a partner
needed to consult and at the end of a work day or work week when lawyers
gathered informally to discuss their lives and work. In mythological
terms, these were the times lawyers gathered around the campfire, and by
telling their own stories and those of others—both in words and deeds—
contributed to the mythology of their professional community. These were
the times where "the meter was not running," and these times were valued
because of the human contacts that were strengthened, the stories that
were shared, and the advice given.

In the context of modern law practice, this sort of time and space
is rarely available and certainly not available to the degree it was in
the past.[13] Time and space for myth-building has fallen victim to the
realities of modern practice. One such reality is the increased focus on
the economic bottom line. Harry T. Edwards, a judge on the District of
Columbia Court of Appeals, states:

In my view, the recent past has seen a radical transformation in the
nature of legal practice. The tremendous pressure to create revenues,
which so many of my former clerks describe, is a wholly novel
phenomenon. When I practiced law at a large firm, some twenty
years ago, I felt no such pressure, nor did my colleagues. We enjoyed
our work, because we felt the work was valuable to society, and to
ourselves. The billing of clients was not the single, overriding goal that

it has now become—a compulsion that drains pleasure and honor from the practice of law.[14]

The economic determinism of modern legal practice manifests itself both in an increased emphasis on making money and in a compulsion to measure everything in economic terms, from productivity—and thus the inherent worth and value of partners and associates—to the success of a lawyer, a firm, or a type of practice. A lawyer's work is measured in terms of hours billed, and technology has allowed maximization of the ratio of time-to-task.[15] It does not require great mental acuity to see where this will lead (and, in fact, has led). Under this system one can become more successful in two ways: charging higher fees and billing more hours. The use of both of these methods has increased geometrically in the last twenty years.[16]

A retired judge in Raleigh, North Carolina, identified the driving force behind these changes in the profession as old fashioned "greed."[17] Human nature being what it is, this may be true in part. But the greed driving the legal profession is more than greed in the traditional sense of greed for more money and material possessions. It is greed to be first, to be at the top of the curve, to be better than everyone else. Money, enough of a goal in its own right, is the leading measure of this type of success. And greed for one-upmanship success is another manifestation of the hierarchical thinking that seems so ingrained in the legal profession from law school grading systems to the rating of law schools and law firms. Hierarchical thinking creates and maintains its own dynamic which inherently resists change. In order to be effective at changing the system—to resist the internal dynamic and propose alternative models—one must first excel in the system to gain status within the systematic hierarchy. Excelling in the intense competition engendered by the hierarchical structure requires such a degree of hard work and focus that those who excel in it and are consequently rewarded are not only emotionally and financially invested in the status quo, they are frequently imbued with it. People trained to excel under this paradigm, who have paid the hard price for "making it," are less likely to take a critical perspective upon the greater picture—at least not until it is frequently too late. Under this system, storytelling, mythmaking, and community-building are not activities that move one up the hierarchical scale. They do not produce status and power (as those elements are perceived), and they are not economically productive—at least not in the short run. They are inherently not subject to measurement in economic terms because they operate on another value system altogether.

A second dynamic which has crowded out time and space for story-telling and community-building in the modern law practice is the inherent tendency of the adversary system to drive lawyers to an increasingly more intense and narrow work focus. Much has been written about the effect of the "win-at-all-costs" adversarial ethic on lawyers' behavior,[18] and certainly that ethic is a powerful force in determining how far lawyers are willing to go to skirt ethical rules and win for their clients. But the same competitive forces that drive lawyers to push ethical rules to their limits (and beyond) and to "play hard ball" also drive them to direct their time and energy toward increasingly narrow goals: most often to win, or in a non-trial context, to otherwise maximize the advantage of their client and their case over the other side. A trial lawyer in Raleigh, North Carolina, explains the effect of this dynamic upon his life and practice:

> I think that the problems [which ended my marriage] . . . [were] caused by me, by my overactivity in legal areas and in cases from time to time. I get involved in a major case, and I get tunnel vision. I think about it at night. I can't sleep at night. I think about it on weekends. I think about it on Saturdays and Sundays. I think about it driving to the office and back. It think it's awfully hard to live with people—for families to live with people—when that type of pressure is on them and when they are, perhaps, handling it in a way that excludes, to some extent, family involvement. I hope I'm doing better than I used to do now. I should, but I think it comes and goes. I think I get back to old habits pretty easily.[19]

This intense focus on winning often becomes aligned with the pursuit of financial rewards, and those two measures of success become the consuming interests in lawyers' lives. A New Jersey attorney explains:

> Most lawyers, it seems to me, simply can't balance their energies: the goal of success and money chips away at them until they have succumbed to a dangerous kind of myopia. I want to keep the liberal arts-type thinking and values alive in my vocation of law. Most lawyers, it appears to me, are professional . . . are concerned and genuinely want to relieve whatever tension exists for their clients. But most are too profit-motivated and became provincial to life within the borders of the profession.[20]

What these lawyers are talking about is not errant behavior on their part or an accidental event, but a force—a powerful force—which is inherent in the work of lawyers and which tends to consume their lives and drive the culture of the profession. It is a force which, in its ultimate manifestation, would consume all around it, leaving nothing but the force itself and the "amoral technicians"[21] who wield it with increasing dedication and ferocity. When practiced to its fullest, it leaves no time and space for anything but itself and certainly no time for anything as "impractical" and unfocused as storytelling or mythmaking.

Traditionally, the profession excuses the "win at all costs" ethic by characterizing it as an essential component of the adversary system. That is, we achieve truth or justice (or some other worthy ideal) through the adversary process, where contending forces joust before an impartial fact-finder or judge, and justice (or ultimate good in some form) is achieved.[22] Therefore the aggressive and super-competitive behavior encouraged by the adversary system is morally justified because it is an essential part of the system and is, therefore, socially beneficial and just. Whether or not this assertion is true, and it has been widely debated,[23] it fails to account for the self-consuming dynamic and its effect upon lawyers who practice daily in the adversarial trenches. Thus the early nineteenth-century quotation from Henry Peter Brougham in his defense of Queen Caroline, that it is an advocate's "sacred duty . . . to save [one's] client at all hazards and costs. . . . [even] if his fate it should unhappily be to involve his country in confusion," often cited as one of the founding creeds of the adversarial ethic,[24] misperceives the ultimate danger. Under our system, the country will survive the confusion caused by zealous advocacy, as numerous over-lawyered, high-profile trials and independent counsel investigations have demonstrated.[25] The question is, will the profession survive this increasing intensity, focus, and myopia? The answer to that is by no means certain.

There is yet another force at work in the modern law practice that deprives lawyers of time and space for storytelling—a force which might at first appear to have the opposite effect and which is often touted for its time-and-space-saving benefits. That force appears in the increasing reliance upon cellular telephones, computers, and cyberspace for law office work and communication. In many ways, of course, technology has improved inter- and intra-office communications.[26] With computers, lawyers can access large bodies of information quickly and manipulate that data into usable form. They can communicate with each other efficiently through fax, e-mail, and telephone answering systems without the delays of missed telephone calls and the logistics of in-person meetings. They can access lines of communication from faraway and remote places—communicate with colleagues, clients, and opposing attorneys from motel rooms, automobiles, airline seats, and even trout streams.

Some attorneys are beginning to do much of their work from home by use of the Internet and home hook-ups to inter-office communication systems.

But given the time "saved" by these new and quicker methods of communication, what are the costs in terms of human relations? Lawyers talk to each other electronically, but do they "communicate" with each other as they used to do in in-person conversation? In my experience, most electronic communication, with the exception of the occasional conference call, is one-on-one, between two lawyers concerned with a specific problem. While theoretically electronic communication could be used for reflective, soul-searching conversations between lawyers, in fact it is not being used that way and, in many offices, such "diversionary" use of inter-office systems is discouraged. And even if it were so used, how effective is it for the type of community-building we are talking about here, without the physical presence of the participants?

It seems very likely that rather than improving deep communication between lawyers, the new technology of law practice will substantially diminish it. Prognosticators of future effects of the new technology upon inter-office human relations confirm this likelihood,[27] and one has warned of the "frightening prospect . . . that cyberspace will fade into a mere disjunction of subjective universes as each of us encases himself within a solipsistic cocoon."[28] This is a depressing image for anyone interested in building community. Community-building through the creation of a mutually relevant mythology requires an open and unhurried space where people can transcend the present, where they can meet each other on a deeper level which connects both (or all) parties to the sources from which myths are born and by which they are nurtured. Connection on that level implies an exchange of understanding and empathy. It implies a mutual identity of feeling, a recognition of common humanity, a coming together to identify yearnings, visions, and ideals. That kind of communication cannot be sustained without substantial person-to-person contact. It may be that electronic communication can supplement person-to-person communication on this level, but it cannot replace it. And the real danger seems to be that electronic communication will obliterate it altogether.

So the modern lawyer faces a bleak future in terms of time and space for storytelling and community-building. The forces at work in modern legal practice—the forces inherent in the modern system of practice and being created by new communications technology—are a powerful current against any natural return to more time and place for storytelling. If the professional community is to be rebuilt, it will take positive, conscious efforts. Those must include a recognition of the problems facing the profession, an honest assessment of the forces at work to prevent its being rebuilt as a community, and some hard decisions about what lawyers are willing to commit to in order to save it.

Why the Profession Should Be Saved

What Do We Mean by "Profession"?

I have been talking about "the profession" without specifically defining it. In my experience at numerous bar gatherings, when issues of professionalism are discussed, those of us engaged in that discussion never pause to define what we mean by "profession." I suspect that is so because we are not sure what the term means anymore and doubt our ability to define it. Doing so is not an easy task. Numerous words and phrases have been used historically to define "profession" and "professionals": specialized training and expertise, self-regulating body, high degree of trust, special duty to clients and those served, key role in society, high social standing, etc. But the essence of what constitutes a profession is, I believe, both deeper and much simpler. Roscoe Pound, former dean at Harvard, has given us perhaps the most famous statement of what once made the legal profession a profession in his assertion that "public service is the primary purpose of the legal profession" and a profession is "no less a public service because it may incidentally be a means of livelihood."[1] Justice Sandra Day O'Connor has stated similarly: "Both the special privileges incident to membership in the profession and the advantages those privileges give in the necessary task of earning a living are means to a goal that transcends the accumulation of wealth. That goal is public service, which in the legal profession can take a variety of familiar forms."[2]

Dean Pound's and Justice O'Connor's paeans to service are echoed by senior members of the bar when they are asked to talk about the profession. Some of them, like Chief Justice Henry Frye of the North Carolina Supreme Court, focus upon lawyers' work for clients as the means by which lawyers provide service. Justice Frye described his work as a young lawyer for a poor, elderly widow who came to him for help with her will. He prepared the will for a nominal fee because, he said, as a lawyer, he owed service to the people who needed his expertise:

> This is a little old fashioned, I suppose, but I think of a lawyer as being a person who is performing a service and that your primary interest ought to be in performing a service for someone, realizing that you need to be paid for your work, but that you're working not just for the pay: you're working because you want to perform a service. And whether that's helping someone who needs to have a will drawn or handling their estate or advising them about various things or whether it's representing a big corporation, or whatever it is, that the idea is service. Of course, the servant is worthy of his hire. But the emphasis ought to be placed on service; then the money is another thing.[3]

Others, like legal aid attorney Ellen Gerber, see service in a broader context where lawyer's skills are brought to bear on larger public problems:

> [Being a lawyer] means running for the legislature; it means really stepping out in front and realizing that in addition (and this is the kind of speech that the judges like to give to lawyers, you know), "you owe service." When you get sworn in . . . in most counties, they have a big ceremony for everybody at once in the fall. So . . . forty, fifty lawyers get sworn in at once, and the presiding judge always makes nice speeches about service and stuff like that. Well, that's real. That is real! That is something lawyers, professionals, have— an obligation for service. Maybe everyone does, but I can't speak to everyone. I think we would all have a better country if we all were more community-minded.[4]

What is there about the concept of service by professionals that is different from, say, brick masons or insurance salespersons, both of whom "serve" in their own way? The answer to that is implicit in the myths about the profession, and it is what we have already concluded about the myth of Parcival and the Fisher King. It is a consciousness about the position of the server in relation to what she serves. That is, the professional understands that she serves something greater than herself, that her life is but one small but essential part of a much greater enterprise and that that enterprise, whatever it is or however she conceives it, has eternal significance. Daniel Webster understood all of this when he made his argument before the Supreme Court in the Dartmouth College case, quoted in part in chapter 3: " . . . you may destroy this little institution;

it is weak; it is in your hands! . . . But if you do, you must carry on your work! You must extinguish, one after another, all those great lights of science, which, for more than a century, have thrown their radiance over the land!" This is more than a rhetorical flourish. It presents us the context in which Webster saw his work. He is fighting for something greater than the control of Dartmouth College. He connects his work to other institutes of higher learning, to the historical advancement of science (and learning in general), to the welfare of mankind. This is why lawyers like Webster are often so dejected when they lose a case. For them losing is more than just the loss for a client. It is a rebuke to an element of faith in one's work—that the work serves something much greater than oneself and that, at least in this particular instance, as a servant of that which is greater, the lawyer has somehow come up short. We can see this dejection in the drooping shoulders of Atticus Finch as he walks out of the courtroom in Maycomb, Alabama.

This ideal of service, while frequently directed toward one's client, as the quotation from Justice Henry Frye indicates, is at its heart community-oriented. That is, whatever it is that is greater than oneself, the welfare of the greater community is both an immediate and long-term beneficiary. Thus, even advocates of the adversarial ethic seek to justify that ethic by asserting that zealous representation of one's client ultimately serves the justice system and therefore the welfare of society. But a problem modern lawyers face is that the ideal of service has become hard to sustain in the client-focused culture of law practice. Many lawyers do not take the second emotional and intellectual step beyond serving the client to the concept of service to something greater than their clients and themselves. They do not make the connection that Webster made in his argument in the Dartmouth College case. When service to "something greater" is undertaken by today's lawyer, frequently it is on some project which is ancillary to the lawyer's work, such as service on boards of charities, providing pro bono services for the poor, and running for public office. And it is promoted as "extracurricular" duty, which is ancillary to (or even a form of recompense for) the "real" work for paying clients. For many lawyers, the essential work of lawyers and the ideal of service have become effectively separated.

This should give us a clue to an essential aspect of professionalism. It is more than simply providing service as some component of one's work while the rest of one's work serves selfish ends. It is a faith in the work itself—a common faith among the members of the profession—that their work serves a higher good, a higher calling, something greater than oneself. There is a humility in this approach which precedes the elevated status of professional, a humility in the face of that which is greater, a cognizance of context and one's place in it that makes one feel humble and at the same time important.

What we are describing here is consciousness. Professionals are not only dedicated to service as a fundamental component of their work, they are conscious of the moral significance of that service in their own lives and in the greater public context. They acknowledge and accept the responsibility that consciousness implies, a responsibility which, as we shall see, is for lawyers extremely complex. At the very least that responsibility carries implicit requirements of learning, competence, and dedication. Professionals, then, are people who consciously accept the moral duty implicit in their training and in the use of their skills and expertise, a duty of service to that which is greater than themselves— however they define it—and which results in meaningful benefits to the greater community. They dedicate their lives to the great task of perfecting that service and to the greater and perhaps ultimately impossible task of understanding what that service means. A profession is a group of people, similarly trained and with similar skills, who share this commitment.

WHY THE PROFESSION SHOULD BE SAVED AS A PROFESSION

A current fashion in legal scholarship goes farther than merely acknowledging that the profession is ailing. It declares the practice of law dead as a profession and attempts to compensate the loss by trying to reconceive the legal profession as a business rather than a profession or as some hybrid of the two.[5] This is the type of academic exercise which appeals to some law professors and others gifted at scanning empirical data for startling conclusions and then publishing those conclusions for maximum shock value. It is the idealists and romantics among us who are most easily shocked; and it is the implicit cynicism in this conclusion about the demise of the profession that shocks us most. Commentators who have adopted this stance declare that because the practice of law has virtually ceased to be a profession, as we have traditionally understood the term, and now more resembles a business, we may as well accept this reality and make the best of it.[6] While the encroachment of the business paradigm cannot be denied, it is certainly more true for large corporate firms than for the preponderance of lawyers who still practice in relatively small firms and in small towns. So to some degree the transformation of the profession into a business is overstated. Still, one must admit, even smaller firms operate now more as businesses than they have in the past, and they will, if trends continue, move even further in that direction.

But the key issue as to whether we should concede legal practice to be a business rather than a profession does not lie in whether it operates as businesses operate, "crunches" the bottom line, or bills by the hour, which increasingly more and more firms do. The key issue, I suggest, lies in the nature of lawyers' work. Is lawyers' work something we want to trust to someone who is essentially a businessperson or to someone upon whom, regardless of his business acumen and methods, we have conferred a status which demands higher standards and a higher commitment of oneself (however imperfectly those standards and commitment are met)? Lawyers are not simply selling a commodity or a service. They are dealing with matters that take them deeply into the moral realms of people's lives. Lawyers are trusted with the closest held secrets people have about themselves and the closest secrets businesses have about how they work. But more than this, lawyers possess training, skills, and position (economically and otherwise) which give them immense power and which raise enormously complex moral questions inherent in the work itself. Does a lawyer representing a toy manufacturer retain his client's confidence that a toy on the market is dangerously defective, or does she warn the public? This is not an easy moral issue. Important moral considerations are present on both sides as well as serious legal consequences, and their interrelationships are complex.

Compare the lawyer's quandary in this example with that of her client, who is purely a "businessperson." Both face tough moral issues: How much danger is there to the public? Where are the financial interests of the company? How will the decision affect company employees? What are the interests of the stockholders? Who within the company is aware of this problem and who should be told? There are many others. But the lawyer faces all of these and more: Who is her client in this scenario—the officers of the company, the company as a whole, the owners/stockholders? To whom does the duty of confidentiality lie? How much is that duty worth ethically and morally compared to other interests at stake? What does the fiduciary obligation mean in this context? What is the significance of her client's trust? Do the applicable professional rules give the lawyer any options, and should she consider them? When, if ever, should professional rules be broken? What are the implications for her financially and professionally if she breaks the confidence or refuses to do so? What are the implications for her client? What are the implications for her fellow lawyers in her firm and in the profession as a whole? What is the lawyer's social role here? What does society expect? What does it need? Does any of that matter? The list goes on here as well, but the point is that because of the lawyer's roles as confident, advocate, advisor, expert, officer of the judicial system, and citizen, the moral issues for lawyers are significantly more complex than they are for businesspeople most of the time. This is because of the nature of the work lawyers do and the expectations society imposes on people who do that type of work. The moral issues involved strike at the heart of how we function as a society—economically, legally, and morally. Lawyers' work is inevitably imbued with a very deep and socially significant moral dimension.

What sort of people do we want operating in that complex dimension? Do we want people who are trained primarily to tally the economic risks, or do we want people who, because of their training, experience, and degree of moral consciousness, are expected to be better able to identify and sort through all the risks and interests and arrive at a solution characterized by its justice and integrity? This is the essential nature of the service which lawyers have historically rendered to their clients and society— that is, to understand the heavy moral implications of the work one does and to possess and continue to develop the skills and consciousness to sort through those implications in the most morally conscious way one can. For those lawyers who deal with problems that impact all areas of society and peoples' lives, the moral implications are comprehensive and include economic, social, legal, emotional, and even spiritual questions.[7] Inevitably the issue of business vs. profession boils down to a matter of trust, which relates to the definition of a professional we have just developed. It is not that if lawyers call themselves "professionals" they will necessarily find the best solution to a legal problem more often than if they call themselves "businesspeople." (Though that may well be the case, it is in any event unprovable.) It is rather the degree of dedication and consciousness that society can expect lawyers, as professionals with professional ideals, to bring to their work, the degree of trust that clients and society will place in lawyers' capacity to deal with these very weighty problems, and the willingness of clients, opposing parties, and society as a whole to live with the result.

In a sense the current fashion of saying "good riddance" to the professional status of lawyers is another version of the impulse in legal methodology to discount ideals or anything that smacks of being ethereal and not empirically based. Since we cannot prove that clients and society are better served by lawyers who are professionals than those who are primarily businesspeople, some commentators would have us assume that professional ideals are worthless. This impulse is strengthened by the growing reality that the old ideals of the profession are no longer easily transferable to the new professional environment. But it does not follow that simply because we are uncertain of what our professional ideals should be and cannot prove their worth by reasoned analysis that such ideals are practically worthless. The benefits of leading a life dedicated to ideals are not open to this type of proof. Ideals speak to us emotionally and not empirically.

So perhaps the question we should ask ourselves should be an emotional one: not whether we can prove that society and clients are better off with lawyers as professionals, but whether we would prefer that our most important and personal affairs were entrusted to someone whose morals are grounded in the ideals of a profession or to someone whose morals are grounded in sound business practice. There may be disagreement on which is better, but I for one much prefer the former. Basically I am declaring that ideals are not only worth something, but that they are the most important aspect of lawyers' work. And that presents another basis for redefining what we mean by a "profession": it is a community of persons similarly trained with shared *ideals* of service to that which is greater than itself, where the work and the ideals inform and define the community and guide it to higher levels of practice in fact and in the eyes of those it serves.

A Preface to New Ideals: Coming to Terms with the Historical Masculinity of the Profession

The way to heal the legal profession as a profession is to take our understanding of what a profession is—a community of people similarly trained and with shared ideals, which is consciously in service to that which is greater than itself—and reconceive the meaning of this definition in the context our developing world. This task sounds simple enough, but it is not simple at all, because it is not an intellectual exercise. It is not something we can accomplish by our traditional methods of scientific analysis, empirical reasoning, and linear thinking. It must be accomplished holistically through practice—through a consciously developed practice—which restores community and rediscovers and reconsecrates ideals in meaningful context. A first step in this practice is to look again at our professional heritage and to evaluate its usefulness in reconceiving ourselves for the present and future. Of what use today are our old concepts of the legal profession and of professional goals and ideals?

We have observed that historically the legal profession was exclusive by race and gender and to some degree social class. More importantly, and perhaps as a partial result of this exclusivity, it was conceived as both unified and homogeneous: all lawyers think alike and share basically the same training and values. Whether this conception of the profession was ever true or not, it clearly does not apply to the diverse group of people who are lawyers today. The percentage of persons entering law school and the bar who are women has been steadily rising,[1] and while racial imbalances have been much slower to rectify, that too has changed from what the profession was twenty years ago.[2] In addition, many teachers of law are learning that people entering law school are not as politically and intellectually homogeneous as they were once assumed to be and are more diverse in terms of interests, life goals, and age than some of their predecessor classes.[3] When we look at all this in perspective, it is clear that the old concept of a profession of like persons is not very useful. If the profession is to continue as a profession, we need a new concept—or concepts—much more inclusive than the old one. Let us begin with some of the traditional images of lawyers stated in terms of lawyer's work. In the old mythology, lawyers were most often advocates and adversaries—basically, in positive, mythological terms: fighters, warriors, and champions—and in negative terms: crooks, shysters, tricksters, and bullies. Given the historical male domination of the profession, it is no accident that these are primarily masculine archetypes.

Before proceeding further with the discussion of masculine and feminine aspects of the legal profession, I will pause momentarily and pay deference to the current concern with gender stereotyping. I believe gender stereotyping poses a serious danger to both genders in any context and in the legal profession in particular. I have searched fairly extensively for less politically charged and less jargonistic terms than "masculine" and "feminine" to say what I am embarked upon saying. While some alternative terms convey aspects of the archetypal qualities associated with "masculine" and "feminine," none that I have discovered or imagined convey all of those qualities as well as the traditional terms. I ask the reader to distinguish between the "archetypal" and "stereotypical" meanings of the terms "masculine" and "feminine." I do not intend to value them comparatively in any way or to assign them exclusively, or even predominantly in the case of the legal profession, to one gender or the other. (It is interesting that, in the case of law students, one study has found little difference between male and female students in their use of what have traditionally come to be viewed as "male" and "female" dispositions toward problem solving.)[4] Rather, I use the terms, "feminine" and "masculine" as Jungians and other psychologists and mythologists have traditionally used them: as imbuing the "opposing" qualities of an *individual's* personality, regardless of gender.

As the following discussion unfolds, the nature of those "opposing" qualities will, I hope, be better revealed. For now, I offer the following general working definitions: "Masculine" in its pure form includes: (1) Characteristics that are associated with the rise of *logos*,[5] the ascendance of the rational as a way—*the* way—of problem solving. Its thought is both *linear,* moving carefully step by step to an assumed (or even fore-sighted) conclusion, and *abstract,* which manifests in a tendency or even compulsion to disembody thought from context—particularly contexts which engender emotion. As we have noted, this type of thinking is essential to legal practice and to competence as a lawyer. (2) Characteristics associated with force, physical power, and linear energy—power that can smash through things, overcome them, or drive through them. Often this is the power lawyers feel they need to win. (3) Characteristics that tend to value individuality and independence over relationships, interdependence, and mutual obligation. And (4) characteristics that promote and respect structure—often hierarchical structure—and order.

"Feminine" in its pure form includes: (1) Characteristics associated with the rise of *mythos,* which exalts narrative over abstract logic.[6] Its thought processes and decision-making are thoroughly embedded in context. It is holistic and inclusive and resists pure abstraction and linear delineation. It accepts emotion as an important part—and sometimes the most important part—of the context in which decisions are made. (2) Characteristics associated with accommodation and acceptance rather than raw force and power, and characteristics associated with compromise and conciliation rather than winning. These are also qualities essential to law practice, although they have frequently not been recognized as such. (3) Characteristics that base their power in relationship building, empathy, and mutual understanding rather than independence and use of individual force. These characteristics are elemental in building a profession. And (4) characteristics of inclusion and acceptance and of seeing things as a sometimes amorphous, complex, and interrelated whole, rather than as ordered, logically structured, and ranked hierarchically.

These definitions will sharpen as I apply them to the current context of the legal profession. And I reemphasize: while most people will associate "masculine" characteristics with men and "feminine" with women, in the archetypal sense and for the purposes of our discussion, those characteristics are not limited by gender.[*]

---

[*]There is a great interdisciplinary debate raging over whether such character traits are "essential" (or natural) to either sex or are socially constructed and imposed, and over the implications of those opposing theories. See Janice S. Bohan, "Regarding Gender: Essentialism, Constuctionism and Feminist Psychology," in *Toward a New Psychology of Gender: A Reader,* ed. Mary M. Gergan and Sara N. Davis (New York: Routledge, 1997); Mary Daly, *Gyn/Ecology: The Metaethics of Radical Feminism* (Boston: Beacon Press, 1978); Angela P. Harris, "Race and Essentialism in Feminist Legal Theory," *Stanford Law Review* 42 (1990): 581; Diana Fuss, *Essentially Speaking: Feminism, Nature & Difference* (New York: Routledge, 1989); Luce Irigaray, *An Ethics of Sexual Difference,* trans. Carolyn Burke and Gillian C. Gill (Ithaca: Cornell University Press, 1993); Toril Moi, *Sexual/Textual Politics: Feminist Literary Theory* (New York: Routledge, 1995); Rosemary Ruether, *Sexism*

Historically, the legal profession has been a masculine profession, and at least one legal historian, Michael Grossberg, is of the opinion that it was intentionally structured that way after the American Revolution to glorify and institutionalize characteristics which were traditionally thought to be masculine. Professor Grossberg asserts that the legal profession in America began to institutionalize masculine characteristics after the Revolutionary War when the legal profession became a full-time occupation whose practitioners were no longer men of letters who practiced law as one of several occupations but devotees who made a career of honing ever-sharper skills of reasoning and rhetoric. Lawyers, who had once also been farmers, clerics, novelists, essayists, and poets, were urged to cease such "feminine" pursuits for the more exalted, and manly, pursuit of dialectical, abstract reasoning.[7] The positive images of lawyers discussed above—the lawyer-statesman, pillar of the community, paragon of rectitude, champion of the people, and gentleman-lawyer—are basically masculine images of the lawyer doing good works. In one form or another, they are manifestations of the universal hero myth—albeit in some cases an arrested version of the mythological archetype.

The myth of Parcival provides us with a metaphor for this version of the lawyer-hero, as well as of the arrested nature of the prototype. As we have noted in our previous visits with Parcival, the mythical hero's journey is a movement from birth (and total ignorance and innocence) to ego consciousness which is characterized by an integration of the whole personality—essentially a combination of, and balance between, the masculine and feminine sides of one's personality. To begin the journey, the hero abandons his childhood home (metaphorically killing his parents) so that his quest for wholeness as an adult—basically the formation of his or her fulfilled, adult personality—can begin. This is critical moment when the ignorant child, usually a teenager, leaves the nest and embarks on the journey to adulthood. It is a point of no return.

When Parcival arrives at King Arthur's court as an untutored (and largely unconscious) bumpkin who has little or no comprehension of the ideals of the Round Table or the purpose for being a knight, his first task is

---

and God-Talk: Toward a Feminist Theology (Boston: Beacon Press, 1983). I specifically do not intend to engage in that debate or to make a judgment on who is right or wrong (and, indeed, strongly suspect that when sufficient data is available to make a definitive judgment, if it ever is, both sides may be correct). I deal here with the archetypal realities only. Those realities, however, regardless of their biological, psychological, or cultural origins, are "real" in the sense that they have historically determined how we view and understand the profession. Those archetypal realities may also, I suggest, provide us with the essential working definitions and self-perceptions necessary to reconceive the profession.

to change his status and gain a place at the table of knights. Accomplishing this task is the necessary first step toward consciousness. It will give him a vision of a greater purpose and allow him to dedicate himself, and his fellow knights of the Round Table, to the life-long quest for the grail and for the consciousness to ask the question which will heal the Fisher King. Parcival is advised by Arthur that in order to do this he must fight and defeat the Red Knight, a very powerful and abusive knight who has terrorized Arthur's court, ignored its principles, slandered Arthur, and insulted the queen. Parcival challenges the Red Knight and, by using the skills he learned living in the woods as a hunter, kills the Red Knight and takes his weapons and armor for himself. This is an archetypal moment in the story and a first step by the young knight toward wholeness. In Jungian terms, by defeating the Red Knight, Parcival has conquered the primitive, ruthless, masculine side of himself.[8] He has taken the requisite first step toward controlling the negative aspect of his youthful masculinity—his masculine shadow—in order to make room for the emergence of his feminine side, which will allow him to begin the process of individuation and movement toward psychic balance. On the mythological level, he has demonstrated himself to be worthy of knighthood and membership in the masculine fraternity of knights. In effect he has proved the quality of his character, achieved a measure of social respectability, and been accepted into the firm. Now he is ready to grow as a professional.

A number of the masculine archetypes of the legal profession—the paragon of rectitude, gentleman-lawyer, and champion of the people and causes—are modern versions of the archetypes from Arthurian legends and represent the questing knight bonded with other knights in an honorable and holy enterprise. While the early versions of these archetypes—the professional stories and images portraying them in the early republic and into the nineteenth century—contained characteristics of the feminine, later versions show a more psychically "arrested" model. Under the mounting pressures of practice, increased emphasis on income and personal advancement, and the disintegration of professional community, the archetypes began to revert to masculine methods and motives, untempered by feminine values of civility and service. The work of the profession—practicing law and winning—became ends in themselves. The status of knighthood can be maintained for some time in this arrested state but not indefinitely. At some point, the armor of the Red Knight begins to shape the soul of its new owner, and the questing knight becomes only a warrior, challenging and defeating all who cross his path. In a sense, this is what has happened to the masculine archetypes of the legal profession that we have discussed. Like aspiring knights, lawyers have become locked in the masculine archetype, and masculine ideals have become entrenched and all-controlling. When that happens to lawyers, they lose (or never gain) contact with their own femininity. After a while, without the balance afforded by the feminine side of their natures, the once-conquered Red Knight reemerges in the characters of the bonded knights. Honor suffers; civility suffers; mutual bonds disintegrate. The feminine is further alienated. Growth toward greater consciousness becomes impossible.

The lawyers we have identified in the old myths of the legal profession, whether they appear as warrior, wise leader, socio-political shaman, or patriarch, lived in a world controlled by men doing "men's work." And what has been the men's work of the legal profession? If we look closely at the intellectual essence of lawyer's work as it has been traditionally conceived, that essence is the act and practice of rational judgment. Rhetorical and writing skills are clearly important, but the basis upon which those skills are exercised is a particular type of mental work which has, at least until very recently, been viewed as the *sine qua non* of lawyer's work and is taught from the first day a student enters law school: digging out facts and legal issues; weighing them in terms of relevancy, frequently against each other; discriminating among them by deciding which are worthy and which are not.[9] This is the essence of the mental work that lawyers are taught and which occupies much of their work day. Being accomplished at this type of work is the lawyer's equivalent of Arthur's knights' prowess with the broad sword. Thus we have the image of Justice—a feminine figure to be sure—but holding the masculine symbols of the sword and the scales—the tools of weighing, discernment, and discrimination.

The act of judging as it is practiced in the legal profession is a function of linear, dualistic thinking, which is the hallmark of a traditionally masculine discourse.[10] As has been noted, well-developed, dualistic, linear thinking is a powerful adversarial tool and, I suggest, crucial to the traditional work of lawyering and judging, which inevitably involves making choices (judgments) between or among competing ideas and interests and moving progressively toward a conclusion. Thus, in terms of professional methodology, linear, dualistic reasoning will certainly for the foreseeable future remain a large part of the work of the legal profession, just as jousting and dexterity with sword and spear are a large part of the work of a questing knight. Legal reasoning is a skill which all lawyers should possess to a high degree in order to operate competently as lawyers.

But, as other commentators have observed, the process of thinking dualistically and linearly and rendering judgments is an exercise in which mental powers become more and more intensely and narrowly focused.[11] Feelings, emotions, and other distractions to the rational process are minimized or eliminated.[12] At the end of this process, we have the image, in its most pristine, theoretical form, of the perfect judge, unerringly rational, unencumbered by nonrational influences, and therefore able to make a perfectly rational (and, therefore, presumably fair) judgment: i.e., Solomon's judgment that a dispute between two women claiming to be the mother of a child be settled by cutting the infant in two (1 Kings 4:16–28). But, if we look closely, we can see that Solomon's judgment, while rational to the point of hyperbole, is at first blush not just or even reasonable. And this is the problem with rarified, linear reasoning and oppositional decision-making. It tends to eliminate the other voice— some would say the more "feminine" voice—which roots itself in context and human experience and which makes true justice possible. It is the eventual presence of that other voice which rescued Solomon's child custody judgment and made it a mythological story of wisdom. In making his purely analytical judgment, Solomon had an ulterior purpose—that the true mother of the child would reveal herself by consenting to lose possession of the child to save its life. In mythological terms, Solomon used "masculine" reasoning to call forth the "feminine" voice which ultimately informed his judgment. This is an excellent example of the use of both the "masculine" and "feminine" powers to reach a truly just decision.

It is important to understand the moral implications of eliminating the feminine aspect. In making judgments, lawyers, like Solomon, are exercising immense moral authority. They are assuming the power to make choices between and among facts, evidence, arguments, and human goals. In lawyer's work, those are judgments which ultimately affect the rights, interests, hopes, and dreams of real people. And at some point in the professional lives of lawyers, many of them, through habit or compulsion, begin to apply this judgmental attitude on a moral level toward other people. They apply it toward clients; toward witnesses; toward other lawyers; toward secretaries, clerks and paralegals; and even toward friends and family members. As in Arthurian mythology, where use of the sword means a fight to the death in which one knight is elevated and another debased, the act of judging separates the judge from the judged. Judgment imposes an essential hierarchy in which the judge assumes a higher moral standing, a prerogative of knowledge, intelligence, and power, which places him above the person being judged.

Thus the act of judgment is potentially arrogant. It is fraught with all sorts of danger for the people involved, including both the person doing the judging and those who are being judged. The potential for arrogance is further enhanced because the prototype of the judge, possessing perfect, unencumbered reason—and the penultimate lawyer/judge as the perfect, emotionally unburdened decision-maker—is, I suggest, and as observers from legal realists to postmodernists have argued,[13] an illusion. The act of minimizing so-called "nonrational" considerations is often merely a minimization of "nonrational" influences other than one's own. The purported purveyors of pure reason are blind to their own contextual allegiances and are thus self-deceived. The danger in judging, then, occurs in the sincere but false effort at nonrelatedness, in the fiction that by discounting emotions toward or against others, we render the process neutral. It is in this illusion of neutrality, and in the assumption of authority and rectitude which is based upon it, that the arrogance lies. Feminists and multiculturalists are understandably upset when confronted with the righteousness of those white males who claim to have wielded power objectively, when it is clear to those who have not had and do not have power that precisely the opposite is true. I suggest that the danger of this illusion and the arrogance which it produces increase geometrically as the masculine act of judging becomes further removed from the tempering, feminine qualities of conscious contextualization, empathy, and understanding.

The picture that emerges from this exegesis of the professional mind is that of a very powerful but tragically limited (and potentially limiting) methodology. With judging comes an assumption of and exercise of power. But the act itself, in its purely masculine trappings, creates its own illusion, becomes self-justifying, and thereby inhibits its practitioner's moral growth and increased consciousness. The extent of our consciousness becomes the self-limiting and repeated act of judging. Feelings of masculine power increase. Left-brain mental acuity increases. Confidence in oneself, one's power, and one's methodology increases. Arrogance increases. But self-knowledge and understanding and the facility of empathy toward others and of envisioning a better world do not. Indeed, in many of the "best" lawyers, these faculties seem to atrophy entirely. When that happens, the Red Knight is back in the saddle.

The process of cognitive and moral change I am describing here is very similar to the first-year law school experience I described in chapter 2. And for those familiar with Lawrence Kohlberg's six stages of moral development, it will appear similar to the mental and moral faculties that predicate Kohlberg's fourth level of moral development, the law and order orientation: a focus on rules and authority and on maintaining the status quo and an incapacity to envision general, abstract ideals of justice and reciprocity.* One study of the stages of moral development of attorneys, using Kohlberg's model, indicates that approximately 90 percent of the lawyers tested were at Kohlberg's fourth level of moral development.[14] So there is evidence which is more than anecdotal that through lawyers' training and practice, the act of judging and posture of the judge become ends in themselves and somehow inhibit progression to a more complex level of moral understanding and consciousness. Either this is true, or we must conclude that most people entering law school are simply constitutionally incapable of more sophisticated moral thinking— a conclusion which on its face is very difficult to accept.

In Jungian terms, the commitment of lawyers' mental faculties so intensely to the act of judging represents a psyche out of balance.[15] And, indeed, lack of balance—or temperance and reasonable measure—is at the heart both of the public approbation of lawyers and of the moral and emotional malaise afflicting the profession. The legal method as we teach it, learn it, and practice it; the professional compulsion toward geometrically increased focus and intensity; the pressures inherent in and created by the adversary process; the credo of success at all costs, of expression and demonstration of power only through "winning"; the elimination or marginalization of all aspects of the personality which contextualize and temporize these traits—all work to create and enforce a drastically unbalanced life. It is not surprising that many lawyers are unhappy in their work or that there is an ethical crisis in the profession. The most humane parts of lawyers' characters, the parts which give life meaning, connection, and moral purpose, have been systematically repressed and excluded.

A careful examination of the old myths of the legal profession shows that those early versions of the masculine archetype were less offensive to the feminine and more psychically in balance than they were later to

---

*Kohlberg has come under significant criticism from Carol Gilligan and others for gender bias in his methods and conclusions. Carol Gilligan, *In a Different Voice: Psychological Theory and Women's Development* (Cambridge: Harvard University Press, 1982), 31–63. Without taking sides in that debate, I suggest that the very pro-male bias for which Kohlberg is indicted makes his hierarchy of moral development a useful tool for insights into the historically male-dominated legal profession. For a discussion of the various controversies over Kohlberg's theories, see Steven Hartwell, "Promoting Moral Development through Experimental Teaching," *Clinical Law Review* 1 (1995): 512.

become. Those myths grew from a masculine profession and portrayed
the masculine ideals of the good lawyer or judge, but they showed us a
softer, more humane, and more morally conscious side of lawyers. The
legal practitioner did not have to be totally aggressive, patriarchal, or
judgmental to achieve hero status. He did his most effective work in service
to his fellow man when he tempered his masculine approach with aspects
of the feminine. Thus we see in the ideal of the lawyer-statesman the
paradox of preservation of individual freedom (an essentially masculine
value) through commitment to community (a value which is essentially
feminine). Pillar of the community, Abe Lincoln, preferred to settle or
mediate cases rather than to try them, though he was very good at both.
Daniel Webster employed emotion as well as reason and wept in his most
famous argument before the Supreme Court. Atticus Finch was a good
father—and, in some ways, mother—to his children and a loving member
of his community. Cormac McCarthy's judge—a more modern version of
the archetype to be sure than Owen Wister's patriarchal Judge Henry—
is a compassionate, deferential, and humble man. And even John W.
Davis, who is arguably the precursor to the modern no-holds-barred
litigator of today, was, unlike his modern counterpart, invariably polite
and courteous to everyone with whom he came in contact.

The world from which these old myths sprang was a very different
world from the one facing today's law school students and graduates
and supported a less intense, more balanced, and more holistic life for
lawyers. In the "old world," the lawyer's repeated acts of judging were
performed against a strong tradition of social expectation and obligation.
Legal practice and the education that preceded it were understood in the
greater context of their relation to society and the greater duties that
relationship entailed. They were not goals in themselves.

Prior to introduction of the Langdell case method at Harvard in the
latter part of the nineteenth century, legal education was even less imagi-
native than today. It consisted mostly of lectures intermittently attended
by students and usually no exams,[16] and Oliver Wendell Holmes described the Harvard version as a "disgrace to the Commonwealth of
Massachusetts," representing "nothing except a residence for a certain period of time in Cambridge or Boston."[17] Yet, it was not the all-consuming
trauma it seems to be for many law students today. And in many cases, like
that of Abe Lincoln, insofar as legal education existed at all, it was largely
self-inflicted. Prior to at least the second quarter of the twentieth century,
legal education more resembled a necessary, introductory step toward, or
an interruption to, one's pursuit of his public destiny as a lawyer than it

did an intellectual and moral reorientation. If legal education in the "old world" taught lawyers to be skilled at judging (and given its general low quality, that seems debatable), it did so only to provide a tool for use in the context of greater values accepted by society. As Holmes warns us in "The Path of the Law," we separate law and morality in legal education for the *limited* purpose of "learning and understanding the law"[18] and not as a new way of life. In Holmes's day, legal education encroached less upon one's inner life and less upon one's outer life beyond the law. It never presumed to "take over" one's character.

As we have already noted, the practice of law in the "old world" was also much less intense and less pressured. There was more time and space for building friendships, more time for civility, less emphasis upon winning as the only goal in a case, less focus upon hours billed and the economic bottom line, and more connection between one's work and one's place in the community. These older lawyers were generally more community oriented, more feminine, in their relation to their work than the average lawyer is today. The mental act of judging was not all-consuming. It was a tool to be employed by those skilled in its exercise for the betterment of society, and it was to be employed within the constraints of society's own codes of morality and behavior. Society expected that from its lawyer class. And lawyers were generally members of society first, with the special duties of citizenship that membership entailed for them as professionals, and lawyers second.

What the myths from this bygone era give us, I suggest, which is still useful in teaching us about where we need to go as a profession today, is not heros we can all emulate (though they may serve that purpose for some) but something more abstract than that which we can use in building a new mythology. That gift is an ideal of balance, which is itself based upon a more holistic concept of power. As we have noted in chapter 6, the context in which these old ideals arose—the exclusive, all-white, all-male profession—make it difficult to extrapolate the images from these old myths into useful ideals for today's more diverse profession. They are limited by the masculine context in which they arose. But we can learn from those old myths why they worked as myths in the context in which they evolved. And that is because they spoke to a comprehensive view of the total lawyer in the social and legal context of his time. They portrayed a lawyer whose life was so integrated and balanced that other aspects of his character, aspects other than the purely masculine, were brought to bear in his work. They showed us lawyers who understood intuitively that power comes in more than the purely masculine form, that true purpose arises in a union of work and soul, and that soul requires the exercise of feminine and masculine power in our everyday lives. When we come to understand what the possibilities for that broader ideal of power are, we will begin to understand how to begin to tell our new professional myths.

Realizing the Feminine in Lawyers' Work: Conceiving a New Ideal of Power

The Red Knight is alive and well in today's legal profession. Either he has never been defeated or he has been resurrected in the lives and characters of many of today's lawyers. He still swaggers about the court houses, law offices, and bar conventions at will, insulting the principles of the profession, punishing openness and compromise, intimidating the profession's feminine capacities, and inhibiting chances of professional growth. The untempered power of the Red Knight is an oppressive and morally limiting power. As in Arthur's court, where Queen Guinevere's voice is absent because of the Red Knight's insult to her, the voice of the Red Knight mutes other voices in our profession. It asserts that its version of power is the only operative currency and that the person who wields that power most effectively will win. And since that voice speaks the loudest, we tend to believe it. Certainly in the past twenty years this version of power has been the dominant ideal of power in the legal profession, so dominant, in fact, that women and other people entering the profession who might find other alternatives to the Red Knight have often accepted his definition of power and adopted his demeanor.

This phenomenon is revealed in a remarkably insightful and productive panel discussion at the Buffalo Law School in 1984.[1] The panelists, including Carol Gilligan of the Harvard School of Education and Catherine MacKinnon of the University of Michigan Law School, discussed the imbalance of power between the sexes as illustrated by Professor Gilligan's now classic study of an eleven year-old boy's (Jake) and an eleven year-old girl's (Amy) different approaches to problem solving and to communication with others (and with each other).[2] In the Buffalo talk, Professor Gilligan makes the point that where voices (and methods of reasoning and problem solving) are different and there is a power imbalance, the owner of the dominant voice can win any argument by simply not listening to the other, less powerful, person.[3] In the case of gender differences, men have traditionally held the positions of power, and women, who speak in what Gilligan calls "a different voice," have consequently not been heard unless they learn to speak and reason like men.[4] Later in response to a question from the audience to Professor MacKinnon about the political implications of Gilligan's articulation of the plight of women's different voice, MacKinnon replies, and an interesting exchange occurs:

> *MacKinnon:* . . . I am—it will shock you to hear—ambivalent about it. On the one hand, I feel excited by the strong and elegant sensitivity in [Gilligan's] work. There is something deeply feminist there: the impulse to listen to women. . . . On the other hand, what is infuriating about it (which is a very heavy thing to say about a book that is so cool and graceful and gentle in its emotional touch), and this is a political infuriation, is that it neglects the explanatory level. *Why* do women become these people [who speak in a different voice], more than men, who represent *these* values? This is really very important. For me, the answer is clear: the answer is subordination of women. That does not mean that I throw out those values. Those are nice values; everyone should have them. I'm not saying that taking these values seriously would not transform discourse, which would be a good thing under any circumstance of gender. . . .
>
> What bothers me is identifying women with it. I'm not saying that Carol does this expressly in her book. I am troubled by the possibility of women identifying with what is a positively valued feminine stereotype. It is "the feminine." It is actually called "the feminine" in the middle chapter of the book. Given existing male dominance, those values amount to a set-up to be shafted. I am particularly worried about the legal impact of this. Take what Carrie [Menkel-Meadow, Professor of Law at UCLA and another member of the panel] said. If Jake and Amy converse, what happens? Well, we heard if Jake does not listen to Amy, he wins. There is something gendered about that. What happens if Amy doesn't listen to Jake? She loses. You see what I mean. The reason I put it out like that is because I think the power issues are crucial and unignorable. If it is male dominance that has created people in these images, then *recognizing that* really matters for the applications. . . .
>
> *Gilligan:* Your definition of power is his definition.
>
> *MacKinnon:* That is because the society is that way, it operates on his definition and I'm trying to change it.

Gilligan: To have her definition come in?

MacKinnon: That would be part of it, but more to have a definition that she would articulate that she cannot now, because his foot is on her throat.

Gilligan: She's saying it.

MacKinnon: I know, but she is articulating the feminine. And you are calling it hers. That's what I find infuriating.

Gilligan: No, I am saying she is articulating a set of values which are very positive.

MacKinnon: Right, and I am saying they are feminine. And calling them hers is infuriating to me because we have never had the power to develop what ours really would be.[5]

What is striking here is Professor MacKinnon's inability to see—or envision—power in any other guise than the masculine model, or to see impotence in any other guise than the feminine archetype (she would, I assume, say "stereotype"). This limited vision is disturbing because as a leading voice of feminism, she was, at least at one time, in a position to help us all to higher ground. But what is perhaps more disturbing is the image of Professor MacKinnon in this debate. She not only sees power in terms of the male definition, but she articulates it in those terms as well. The relation between Jake and Amy appears for her only in terms of Jake's dominance of Amy through his exercise of masculine power ("his foot is on her throat"). Amy is a complete victim who has no power because Jake has subdued her, and power is per se defined as a predominance of male force. All MacKinnon can do in response to this is to be "infuriated" and to rail against the heavy foot of the oppressor. Her response is to demand that men "take their foot from women's throats" and we will see what sort of power women have.

This response is archetypically masculine.[6] It treats Amy and Jake as total opposites: one is total victim—the other is total oppressor; one is weak—the other is powerful; one is good and deserving of empathy—the other is evil and undeserving of empathy—in fact, deserving of anger and hatred. The interaction between Jake and Amy is thus "deconstructed" into dualistic stereotypes of the powerful (and therefore oppressive and evil male) and the helpless, victimized female. (Note that MacKinnon's solution is not to find the strength in Amy and call her to action to use it, but to demand that Jake take his foot off her throat.) This model is ultimately too limited to be either helpful or hopeful for those seeking gender equality and justice. It seeks to fight the Red Knight by becoming more like him. It is a response born out of justifiable anger, but the anger is so intense it has consumed the antagonist and blocks hope for other answers which might lead to healing and reunion. Anger holds no vision, and, while it may serve temporarily as a useful tool for change, ultimately it provides no salvation.

The salvation, I suggest, lies in coming to understand power in terms broader than the traditional, masculine definition portrayed by the Red Knight and which Professor MacKinnon so abhors, yet emulates. The physical and psychic power of the sword-wielding, judgment-delivering warrior is one type of power and the one by which we have primarily defined ourselves in the legal profession. And, indeed, as MacKinnon correctly and repeatedly states, it is the power that has made the most *visible* difference in defining our lives. In its more aggressive manifestations, this power is frequently fueled by masculine anger,[7] and MacKinnon gives us a demonstration of that in her argument with Gilligan.

But where does this narrow definition of power lead us as a profession? It has led many of us—mostly white males who have aspired to this power, achieved it, and used it successfully—to become a profession peopled in large part by dominators and manipulators. Others who have been victimized by it and those who have not achieved it, or at least not until recently, like Professor MacKinnon, have been led to their own type of fury. As long as this narrow understanding of power inheres in our discussion of what our profession should be, our current tailspin will continue, because, as a power of dominance and control, it admits, as every trial lawyer knows, only one type of resolution: winning or losing. Power that admits only winning or losing is not a basis for sustaining community, and a professional community which idolizes only this kind of power will dig its own social grave. That is precisely what is happening in the legal profession.

I agree with Professor MacKinnon's assertion that the values and methodology Professor Gilligan labels as "feminine" are examples of weakness rather than of power—as weakness and power are traditionally defined in our society and in our profession. But I dispute MacKinnon's assumption that there is only one viable definition of power. I do not accept that the values and methods she sees as weak are, in fact, weaknesses only.[8] The "feminine" power described by Gilligan is, I suggest, a deeper and more pervasive power than the masculine power enshrined by our social mores and conventions. It is at heart a creative power—the power to build and sustain relationships—and a persevering power—the power to survive and ultimately triumph over the vicissitudes of life, many of which are brought on by the masculine compulsions to self-reliance, independence, dualistic thinking, and relentless competition. This power is based upon the value of community, the capacity to empathize, and the need to bond with other human beings.[9] It is power for the long term, marathon power, which binds groups and societies together, nurtures its members and allows them to grow. It is power that allows people to look inside themselves and examine their souls and their relationship to the rest of the world. It is power that has been traditionally wielded more by women in our society than by men, and it has thus been lacking in the legal profession in part because women have been until recently excluded from the profession, but primarily because increasingly the dominant ideal of power in the profession has been the purest form of the masculine image.

Jung asserts what many people have come to accept as psychic reality, that all human personalities—male and female—encompass masculine and feminine archetypal traits. Jung says that these traits are potentially in conflict and develop and express themselves in varying degrees.[10] The "feminine" side of men Jung labels the *anima;* the "masculine" side of women he labels the *animus.*[11] In the healthy psyche where self-realization and social consciousness are possible, the opposing sides are integrated in harmonious balance. For men, this means that their *anima* is actively engaged and a powerful force in their lives which tempers their masculinity. For women, it means that their *animus* is engaged as a companion to and counterbalance to their femininity.

In Jungian terms, the central problem with the traditionally masculine legal profession is that, in regard to its methodology and mind-set, it has become so intensely masculine that its anima has been overwhelmed and largely lost. The dual sides of its professional personality are not balanced nor integrated. Applying this analysis to the context of a dual gender profession, the anima is understated for men and the animus overly encouraged (perhaps demanded) and emphasized in women: the masculine in all its forms simply crowds out the feminine. In Gilligan's terms, the profession has stopped hearing its feminine voice. The Red Knight has silenced the queen. Though the strength of the feminine voice in the masculine legal profession has always been insecure, I believe that the profession—even when it was exclusively male—once heard (and spoke in) its feminine voice better than it has in the recent past.[12] (As I have stated, the archetypes of the lawyer-statesman and pillar of the community, for example, both included strong, relational ideals associated with feminine values.) In addition, while more potentially feminine voices (usually, but not necessarily, women) are entering the legal profession, the feminine voice has not yet been restored to its former tenuous place nor has it achieved anything near the equality of volume necessary to put the profession in psychic balance. This imbalance continues because of the increasing masculinization of the concept of power in the profession; the use of that power to repress not just women, as MacKinnon asserts, but the feminine voice from all sources; and the virtual elimination of space and time for feminine power to operate.

An example of the "masculinization" process experienced by women entering the profession is related by attorney Mary Ann Tally, formerly one of North Carolina's leading public defenders and death penalty defense lawyers, in her description of becoming a trial lawyer:

> There was a judge one time who told me this—it was a judge who was here during the first six months or a year . . . that I was working. He said to me one time, "Mary Ann, the first time I came through . . . I can remember a case you were trying. And I can remember seeing you crumpled up in the hallway in tears after the case was over." And he said, "And the next time I came through, which was about a year later, you were hard as nails and just as cynical as you could be." . . .
>
> People tell me now, once they get to know me, [that] I'm a very intimidating person and that people are afraid of me, which just comes as a huge shock to me, except every once in a while somebody will say it, which will reinforce that that must be true. . . . But I suppose that I started to have to be hard. I learned early on that this—and certainly it was more true then than it is now—that the legal profession is clearly a male-dominated profession, and that if you fall into any stereotypical behavior, that you'll be in trouble.
>
> So I learned very early on—don't do things with your voice that are stereotypically feminine, and don't let anybody see you cry.[13]

How do we begin to find psychic balance? How do we bring the Red Knight in our profession under control? Again the Parcival myth provides metaphorical guidance. Parcival, the innocent fool, poorly armed and untested in battle, defeats the much larger and physically stronger Red Knight by hurling a javelin into his eye, the only place on the Red Knight's body not covered by armor. Parcival does this after being knocked out of his saddle by the first blow from the Red Knight. Clearly Parcival cannot match this giant blow-for-blow. He relies instead upon the skills he learned as a youth hunting alone in the forest, and he strikes the point where the Red Knight is physically the most vulnerable and psychically the weakest—his eyes. Like the Red Knight, untempered masculine energy has sight but no perception and no vision, and it recognizes only the skills possessed by the Red Knight. If masculine energy is to be brought to heel in the legal profession, that must be accomplished by some method other than the use of more, unchecked, masculine power.

A more feminine myth which suggests "other" ways to deal with masculine power appears in the story of the trials of Psyche.[14] Psyche, the most beautiful woman on earth, has offended the goddess of beauty, Aphrodite, because Psyche is the more beautiful. To compound the insult, Psyche has caused Aphrodite's son, Eros, the god of love, to fall in love with her and has, through a series of misadventures, caused Eros physical injury and great pain. Aphrodite is enraged and requires four tasks of Psyche in order for Psyche to redeem herself. The second of these tasks requires a confrontation with masculine energy. Psyche is ordered to steal golden fleece from the royal rams, which are symbols of masculine energy and which will kill her if she approaches them directly. While Psyche is sitting by the river near the pasture of the rams, despairing over how she will obtain the golden fleece, the reeds of the river speak to her. They tell her that this is not a task to perform by left-brain, masculine direction, in which she locates the rams and approaches them in broad daylight to take the fleece. Rather, it is a task which calls for indirection. So she should wait until evening when the rams are asleep, slip silently into the pasture, and collect the remnants of fleece left on the bushes and brambles. Psyche goes by moonlight and performs the task. By understanding the nature of sheep, by relying on the gifts of darkness and moonlight, and by taking advantage of nature's own wool gatherers—the bushes and brambles— and the gifts they offer, Psyche accomplishes more than she could have by purposeful confrontation. It is a story of the success of the feminine method in a world that appears to be dominated by masculine power. And it illustrates that what appears to be an unassailable dominion may not be so if we will look for other options.

And those other options are there. They appear to us all the time if we will look for them and recognize them. Much of Parcival's journey, after his defeat of the Red Knight, is confrontation in one form or another with these options. He frequently does not recognize them, so engrossed is he in the work of the quest, and when he fails to heed them, he inevitably pays for that failure. He actually finds his way to the Grail Castle at one point and is too engrossed in his own self-importance and his work as a knight to recognize it. He fails to ask the necessary question and departs in the morning, a failed knight. All he can do is to once again take up the long quest. As the quest continues and his failures increase, his missed opportunities reappear in more frightening and shaming forms— weeping damsels, dead warriors, rebuking crones, drops of blood in the snow. These signs tell him that he is still undeveloped as a person, that he is does not sufficiently honor the feminine in his nature, and that he is not worthy to meet the Fisher King and save the kingdom. Gradually we begin to see, as Parcival eventually does himself, that the real enemy is himself—Parcival. It is he—or the masculine bent of his character— which is preventing him from honoring the feminine in his nature. He needs that aspect of his nature to temper his masculinity and bring him to a psychic balance and spiritual wholeness that will allow him to value other people and act responsibly toward the greater community. The story of Parcival's quest is ultimately the story of the long and difficult process of bringing one's feminine power into proper balance with masculine power in a profession which has traditionally rewarded masculinity. It is that balance which creates a morally mature person, able to serve her community and therefore to save herself.

So, I echo Professor MacKinnon's cry for deliverance, but I cast it differently and direct it at a different source: If we (all of us) will listen to our internal feminine advisers and broaden our concept of power and learn to use all of our power in different ways, we will learn to take our masculine feet off our own feminine throats. We will then be able to save our relationships to each other, which are the basis of community, which is the basis of a profession. And this salvation is likely to occur, not through *logos* (masculine, reasoned analysis), or by a reactive flexing of masculine strength through anger—though both of these may help in the short run—but through *mythos*,[15] through the rediscovery and reactivation of the power of stories, narratives, myths, and dreams as part of our psycho-professional mentalscape. That is how feminine power will emerge—is emerging—in the legal profession. That is how masculine power will be tempered and brought under control so that the profession can grow and lawyers in the profession can grow in a more hopeful and holistic fashion.

Beginning the Lawyer's Inner
Journey: New Models and Heros

The revival of *mythos* in the legal profession will not just "happen"—not in a profession which has cultivated a methodology that marginalizes and destroys it. It will take a conscious effort—an effort which has, I believe, already begun. And it will take conscientious practice. In order to foster that practice, we will need to establish new structures for creative time and space in which a new, expanded, professional mythology—one that is *in*clusive in terms of both culture and gender—can emerge and develop. We must, in a sense, rekindle the campfires and create new circles in which our new stories can be told. Then we can begin to tell the new professional stories and develop a new professional mythology with new heroes and heroines that draws upon a broader concept of power. With the new mythology will come new professional ideals—ideals which transcend the traditional masculine images of the lawyer-statesman and the other professional myths we have discussed above. And if we follow the teachings of the Parcival myth, on an individual level our new ideals will be more psychically balanced and socially connected with a proportionate life at the center.

I will have much to say about the structural changes necessary in the bar and the legal academy in chapter 13, and for now I would like to focus upon the changes necessary in the psyche of individual lawyers. While new structures must provide the framework and opportunities for developing a new professional mythology, it is individual lawyers who must do the hard work of creating that mythology and changing themselves and the profession. This work requires lawyers to rediscover the concept of individual calling, to recommit to its fulfillment, and to develop a renewed vision of professionalism. And these new attitudes must appear not only in public statements and actions but in how lawyers think and do their work. They will involve both re-dedication and re-education, a coming to both individual and communal consciousness about the lawyer's role in relation to his work, the role of lawyers' work in the framework of the larger community, and the effect of that work upon other people. This is a moral journey and of necessity a long one. It is born out of desire and sustained by a vision of an ideal. And it begins with the individual lawyer.

CREATING DESIRE AND FINDING VISION

Such a deep, personal commitment needs a driving force. In the Parcival myth, the young rube, Parcival, sees a vision of knighthood and sets out to find the Round Table and become a knight. He gains initiation into the order (by slaying the Red Knight) largely through luck and audacity, and, like any young lawyer who has just passed the bar, he is pleased with himself. He thinks he has arrived. But the work has just begun. The remainder of the Parcival story is the long and arduous quest for the grail in which Parcival encounters and eventually overcomes one obstacle after another. It is a journey of hard lessons, and it is fraught with failure and missed chances. Yet Parcival continues, persevering in his quest until finally he arrives at the Grail Castle (for a second time) and this time asks the question that heals the king.

What is it that keeps Parcival in the saddle through the many trying and turbulent years of the long quest? Basically it is the vision of an ideal, an ideal of himself. His first encounter with the knights of the Round Table as they ride by his woodland home has planted a very childlike vision in his head. In fact it is hardly a vision at all, but rather a flashy, romanticized image of what a knight must be. Parcival has no real idea of what it takes to be a knight. He is dazzled by his image of knighthood, and it is powerful enough to cause him to leave home, find his way to the Round Table, and there to challenge and defeat the Red Knight. With that act, he takes on the status and burden of knighthood. Then the true learning can begin.

Any lawyer who has passed the bar and begun to practice knows a personal version of this story. Somewhere either before or during law school, he has formed a vision of what an accomplished lawyer looks like. He has seen attractive images of lawyers in movies or on television, or he has felt the energy from watching real lawyers operating in a courtroom or before an investigative committee, or he has been dazzled by the mental dexterity of his law school professors grappling with legal problems in class. These visions are, like young Parcival's image of the passing knights, often inaccurate and highly romanticized (and they are frequently mangled in the relentless mill of legal education). But like Parcival's image, they serve a purpose. They bring the young lawyer through the initiation process—through law school and studying for and passing the bar—and into the profession. And there, as with Parcival, the real education begins.

As most young lawyers soon learn, when you enter the pressing realities of day-to-day practice, the old, romanticized image of lawyering (or whatever is left of it after law school) dissolves as quickly as the brief euphoria over law school graduation and admission to the bar. Suddenly you are working on cases that are real and that have real consequences. The people around you, if you are lucky enough to have joined a firm where there are older lawyers around to help, are all much more skilled at what they are doing than you are, and they go about their work with a vigor and assurance that you do not have. The lawyers you deal with as opposing counsel are more skilled than you are and quick to take advantage of it. Judges, courtroom clerks, and bailiffs are apt to treat you with either indulgence or condescension. You feel constantly off balance. The work load mounts quickly. You labor for hours over problems which, if you had more experience, would not be problems at all or would take only minutes to solve. You scramble to make up for lost time and oversights. And you make mistakes, mistakes which in hindsight seem stupid and which you are afraid any competent lawyer would see as the work of a bumbling fool.

This is a tough time for many young lawyers, and it is a very crucial time in the formation of a professional life. The romantic vision which brought the novice attorneys through law school has been exposed for the fantasy that it was. The hard reality of the working life of a lawyer has set in. What will sustain the young attorney through that? What will help her to persevere through the hard times and grow in the process? Unfortunately, many lawyers are unable or unwilling to find a new vision in the rubble of the old one. Rather, faced with the hard choices of a real life in the law, with the long hours and unremitting pressure to excel (and fear of failure), they abandon any idea of vision altogether and settle for something more immediate and recognizable. We have talked some about these "substitutes for vision" in chapter 6, and there is nothing new or surprising about them. They are the usual suspects: money, success, winning, power. These all may be goals to drive a lawyer's life, but they are not visions of fulfillment as a professional. They are not goals which will heal the ailing king and save the ailing kingdom.

How do lawyer's form the vision for the long quest? Once again, the Parcival myth provides a useful analogy. When Parcival has defeated the Red Knight and prepares to begin his career as a knight of the Round Table, the first person he encounters is Gournemand, an elder knight in Arthur's' kingdom, who invites Parcival to his castle where he instructs the young knight in the art of arms and the chivalric code and offers practical advice on how to get along in the world. Gournemand is himself a model knight, and Parcival learns to emulate him in his knightly bearing and his unfailing courtesy and generosity toward other people. We will have more to say about the Gournemand role as mentor in a subsequent chapter, but for now it is important to see what Gournemand provides for the young Parcival. In essence, Gournemand gives him a vision of what it means to be a knight. It is not the flashy, romanticized image which enticed Parcival from his woodland home to the Round Table, an image created out of ignorance and fantasy. Rather the vision Gournemand provides is an ideal grounded in reality and founded upon experience and hard-earned knowledge. It is a *moral* vision born out of the travails of the legions of knights who have gone before and given their lives to their profession. It provides something to strive for which engenders desire and a yearning for moral perfection, which supports moral courage and renewed effort after failure, and which ultimately drives moral growth. The formation of this vision is essential to Parcival's perseverance in the great quest.

MODELS FOR PROFESSIONAL VISION

A vision of professional excellence is as essential in the life of a lawyer as it is in the life of a mythological knight, and it must be perceived in the same way. We will talk in the next chapter about an abstract ideal for lawyers, but for now it is important to understand how lawyers begin to perceive an ideal. And that is done primarily through images of the ideal as they appear in the lives of other lawyers—lives which we witness through story and myth, lives which we witness first hand in courtrooms, law offices, and places where lawyers are in action. Even where a strong professional mythology is in place (which is not true of the modern legal profession), living models of the ideal are necessary to introduce the ideal to young lawyers. The mythology of the ideal is merely the sacred text of the profession, the heritage of the ideal that is passed from generation to generation. It is the living models of the ideals—the Gournemands, the professional elders, and "real life" heros—who must keep it alive and pass it down. These models provide the inspiration to achieve the ideal; they create the *anima* and *animus* necessary for new members of the bar to persist in their efforts to attain the ideal through the long, difficult, and sometimes heartbreaking quest. They initiate the internal voices which say, "I want to be like that someday," or, when confronting a difficult moral problem, "How would so-and-so deal with it. . . . What is the professionally honorable thing to do?"

It is very important, then, for young lawyers to meet their Gournemands and to find inspiring models of professionalism. Without those models, it will be very difficult to form a vision of what it means to live a fulfilled professional life. Who are the heros we should be recognizing and emulating in today's legal profession? One difficulty which today's young lawyers face, and which the young Parcival eliminated, is that in the round table of the legal profession the Red Knight is still the loudest and most visible of all the knights. The Red Knights of the legal profession are not models of a professional ideal. In fact, as was true in the Parcival myth, they will slay it. And it is very easy for young lawyers, who by training and practice are used to applying primarily masculine, left-brained skills and are taught to be wary of humane impulses, to fix upon the Red Knight as the person to be emulated. It is even more complex than that, because in some respects we *do* need the skills of the Red Knight to succeed as lawyers. But we need those skills to be fixed in the context of a greater vision so that we use them in conjunction with other skills and capacities which allow for self-reflection and moral growth. The key, again, is balance—in Jungian terms, balance where the masculine and feminine parts of the personality are integrated and harmonious and where moral reflection and understanding temper energy and action. Where that sort of balance exists, there is opportunity for moral growth, increased consciousness, and perception of an ideal. Looking for the Gournemands who can teach balance should be the first task of the aspiring young lawyer. Making those Gournemands the heros to be emulated should be the task of the profession.

The good news is that there are a lot of Gournemands around, though we don't see very much of them in the public image of lawyers. But they are there in the law offices and courthouses doing their work and living dedicated and fulfilling professional lives. My students and I discovered them among some of the most successful lawyers in North Carolina in our efforts to record the oral histories of lawyers and judges. In the process of gathering these life stories, my students and I also learned a mythological truth: there is a Gournemand in each of us, just as there is a Parcival in each of us. When we saw the type of balance I am describing (and most frequently it would appear in a student's report to the class on a lawyer or judge he or she had interviewed), the effect upon the class was both heartening and soothing.* "It was encouraging," said one student, "to speak with and hear about people who *do* believe in what they are doing and who can help us to see the value of what we are going to do as lawyers."[1] "We saw," said another, "how these individuals incorporated their beliefs and values into the practice of law . . . and how these beliefs and values sustained their faith in the law and their love for the practice of law." And another: "My beliefs and values were reaffirmed by a man whom I respect greatly. Not only did I gain knowledge of the law, but I also gained by the friendship we developed."

The following excerpts from some of the oral histories recorded by UNC law students illustrate the balance I am talking about. These are voices of people with integrated professional personalities who are able to approach their work in a holistic fashion which opens them to moral reflection and moral growth. All of these lawyers are very accomplished attorneys and highly successful in the line of work they have chosen.

Roger Smith, noted criminal lawyer in Raleigh, North Carolina:

> I think that humans hunger for stories. . . . And I think that what stories do is . . . they teach us several things. One thing they . . . teach us [is] that there . . . are countless ways for events to unfold and for lives to be lived and for decisions to be made. . . . They open our eyes to the possibilities. They give us experience without our having to have the experience. They teach us without our having to learn from experience. We learn from seeing other peoples' experiences or reading other peoples' experiences. . . .
>
> I think that jurors, like all of us, are taken by, are fascinated by what happens to other people when events come along. And so I do think that . . . words, how you put them together, . . . it's obviously what lawyers do for a living. . . . And so, . . . I'm absolutely fascinated by all of that, and I don't understand much of it. But as I get into this part of my life now, I certainly want to explore what it is about stories that has such power and that draws [us to them].[2]

Katherine Holliday, trial lawyer and former lobbyist and advocate for children:

> I do think one's effectiveness and one's ability to be able to . . . get one's message across is in large part dependent upon relationship

---

*I describe in more detail my student's reactions to the oral history seminar in my discussion of changes in law school curricula in chapter 13.

building. . . . I've seen how important it is to have integrity in your relationships with people and to treat people with—this sounds real basic—but I've been really focusing on manners the last few weeks and noticing when people exhibit manners and when they don't. And so just the whole notion of being courteous and treating people with respect and being willing to listen has long been looming large for me. . . .

Hopefully, [ways of solving disputes in our society will change] once women are more comfortable with asserting some of the values and ways of dealing with conflict that I think are more typical of women in our society because of what our historical roles have been. I see frequently women who go in and adopt a male style. And I really struggled with this personally when I first started practicing law, because, . . . being the first woman in my law firm, I was surrounded by men who played hardball. And so I felt that the way of being an effective attorney was to do it the way they did it. I had some real discomfort around that, . . . and it took me a while to realize that my own natural problem-solving style and attempting to get people to the table to discuss issues was an effective style and one that I could use much more effectively than very aggressive tactics.[3]

This sort of multifaceted, multi-leveled understanding of one's work, in which all the parts of one's personality are engaged in a way that brings real meaning to work and practice, is a different model from the dominant model of the legal professional today. It is a different story of what it means to live the life of a lawyer. Yet very successful lawyers practice this holistic model, though maintaining that type of practice is not always easy. As the following testimony from William Thorp, one of North Carolina's most successful trial attorneys reveals, the old, masculine archetype has a very strong pull:

And in the law practice . . . —the adversarial system makes it very difficult to be holistic, and yet the adversary system is a good system. But we've got to figure out how to keep from polarizing and how to recognize that we are all working for the right solution rather than working to beat the other guy's butt, which is really the way it gets sometimes. And I feel that way; I get polarized. And the worst mistakes I've made practicing law [were] from being polarized, without a doubt.[4]

It is remarkable how similar these sentiments regarding the polarizing effects of the adversary system (and the oppositional, binary thinking it requires) are to those expressed by leading feminist legal scholars.[5] The antidote to the harmful effects of binary thinking and polarization lies within the individual lawyer. It involves a rediscovery of and validation of the *whole* self. That undertaking is a spiritual journey sustained by practice. Two lawyers relate how that journey has unfolded for them. William Thorp, again:

> When I was a kid in my teens, and I'd go to the beach and lie in the hammock and look at the gulls flying over the ocean, I just had this sense of yearning, and it was a yearning for wholeness. And, of course, part of wholeness is . . . integrating your own masculine and feminine parts of you, and part of wholeness is being in touch with your left brain and your right brain, . . . and part of it is being visionary and grounded with a balance between vision and groundedness, and part of it is learning to see the divinity in every person, which is pretty presumptuous for me to say, perhaps, but we can strive for it.[6]

Ben Bridgers, general practitioner and former counsel for the Cherokee Nation (discussing the effects of his learning about Native American spirituality and Zen meditation):

> It tended to free me and to let me sort of try to strip away those things that are there that shouldn't be there—other people's expectations, society, and so forth. So, . . . the best way I know to describe it is it got me so I could just let go and do what I want to do and be what I want to be, and then, eventually, I began to think about that in terms of how that worked with what I did for a living, how that effected me as a lawyer and that sort of thing. In the last two or three years in particular, I've sort of calmed down. When I was a young lawyer, I used to love litigation, used to love going to court. I liked nothing better than whipping somebody in the courtroom, especially the lawyers you don't care much for. There's a great sense of satisfaction in all of that. I just have a completely different sort of attitude now. I'm not attached to all of that like I was. I don't care if I go to court or if I win this case or get written up, or whether it's something I can add to my list. Now it's what it is you are trying to accomplish. So I find during the last five or six years that I litigate much less and spend more time trying to get people to talk to each other and to really talk—not take positions, not posture, not . . . to get the other guy to say "yes" and all that game stuff—but to just say, "What is it we're trying to do here; how do we get there?" I found it's a lot easier to do.[7]

An important result of psychic balance is perspective on oneself and one's life in the profession. Attorney Wade Smith:

> I think it was about age forty that I began to realize how short life is, that we're here for just a very, very short time and we're gone, that it's gone by in such a hurry. It's only a moment that I was in law school. Just a moment. I remember every day, every class, every person, every face. And it's been thirty years. It went by [Smith snaps his fingers] just like that. The next thirty will go the same way, and I'll be gone.
>
> The other thing to remember is my cases—no one will remember them. The little moments that I build to create cross-examinations— they'll be gone. No one will remember. And I have to keep that in mind, too, as I go about my work. After all, while I might think that I'm the greatest trial lawyer who ever lived, there'll be better ones. There will be much better ones coming, and we will not be remembered. We may be remembered for a very short while, and then we'll be gone. So for me the meaning of life is, stay up as late as you can, get up as early as possible, laugh as much as you can laugh, tell as many funny stories and collect them, and be a good sport, and be a good friend.[8]

The above quotations reveal lawyers in a mode of reflection and self-examination. This *is* the inner work of the long quest of a professional. Implicit in the voices of these lawyers is a recognition of self in relation to other people and to something greater than themselves. Roger Smith appreciates the power of stories in shaping lives and events. He understands that his own life is a story and that stories provide moral perception and give us a greater context from which to measure our own lives and those of others. Katie Holliday learned how to live a relational life in the law— a life that focuses upon helping people through relation-building rather than upon "winning" though the adversary process. Bill Thorp sees his quest as "a yearning for wholeness," which drove him to seek his own sense of selfhood until he came to "see the divinity in every person." Ben Bridgers' journey led through Zen meditation to a deeper understanding of himself and his relation to others that allowed him to be a different kind of lawyer—one that shunned posturing and gamesmanship for a sincere effort to help people solve problems. Wade Smith describes coming at age forty to a change in life-perspective, where he began to see the relative importance of his work in the greater scheme of his life and in the years to come after he is gone. All of these attorneys seem to have attained a high degree of balance between their masculine and feminine qualities.

That balance gives them a perspective which places them and their work in purposeful context with their communities and their universe.

If we are to promote "heroes" in a renewed and renewing profession, these are the types of heroes who should become Gournemands—people who undertake the work of an extremely demanding profession and maintain through the practice of it a life of true purpose, meaning, and integrity, a life which promotes personal growth and increased consciousness, a life which builds community. This is a new concept of the hero—or at least a radically different one from the masculine superman currently in vogue. It is true heroism in the context of our present lives and professional reality.

As we have noted previously, Parcival's hero's journey is the metaphorical story of the journey of our individual lives. In our own version of that story, we are the only possible, real-life heros. We are questing for our own souls. The Parcival myth teaches us that if the quest is to be successful, if our journey is to truly be a hero's journey, it must lead each of us to the type of self-discovery described above. And that means, in particular, becoming aware of both the masculine and feminine aspects of our natures, honoring them both, and bringing them into complimentary balance in our lives through practice. It means coming to a deeper understanding of our own character and recognizing its potential. It means becoming aware of our contextual relation to the people and the world around us and of our dependence upon each other and upon the greater community. It means understanding and accepting moral obligation. Finally, it means accepting the transcendent nature of that obligation—that its undertaking involves service to something greater than ourselves, however we define that something and however it manifests itself in our lives.

What the Parcival myth teaches and what all of these lawyers learned is what we mean by the phrase, "coming to greater (or deeper) consciousness." Gaining consciousness is the essence of the long quest. So when Parcival has faced and overcome the repeated challenges of his journey and has grown in moral consciousness enough to see himself in proper perspective in his relationship to others and to something which is greater than himself, he is able at last to ask the, by now, anticlimactic question: "Whom does the grail serve?" And instantly the ailing king is healed and the ailing kingdom set on the road to recovery from its desolation. The moral development of Parcival to full individual and social consciousness is the key to healing the king and the ailing kingdom. In a sense, his developed personality is the holy grail. The moral development of the individual lawyer to full individual and professional consciousness is the key to healing the profession. It is no mythological accident that the holy grail is a vessel. As such it is a symbol of what we all become to our fellow lawyers when we have taken the road to consciousness. We, the individual lawyers, are the vessels of professional ideals from which others can drink. We are the Gournemands. We carry within us the secret to professional redemption. The more lawyers who take this path, the more the profession will be healed and the more Gournemands there will be to help others along the way.

11

Something Greater than Oneself: Envisioning a New Ideal, Understanding Lawyers' Faith

Parcival teaches us that the professional journey—the lawyer's quest—proceeds on two levels. The most obvious level is the outward journey of the questing knight, the "daily grind" of the mythological world—rescuing damsels in distress, relieving besieged castles, ridding the land of dragons and demons. In the world of lawyers, these tasks appear in the form of cases undertaken, wills and deeds transcribed, deals negotiated, cases tried, and appeals argued. But in the metaphorical world, the questing knight is embarked upon another journey as well. The signs and messengers which appear to Parcival along his way—the weeping maidens, dead warriors, haranguing crones, drops of blood—arise from another world and call him back to his inward journey of the soul. They remind him that the outward journey alone will not lead to salvation for him or for the kingdom. So on he goes with both his outward and inward journeys, growing in character, as his external journey leads him closer to the barely perceived but yearned-for ideal while the inner journey prepares him to achieve it.

But what, really, is that ideal? What is the holy grail for lawyers? What is it that unifies our inward and outward journeys? The answer to these questions lies in the relationship of lawyers and lawyers' work to other people. It is significant that from the outset, when Parcival leaves his forest home to follow the flashing knights to King Arthur's Court, hoping to join the Round Table, he is pursuing a life of service. That is what knights of the Round Table and other mythical seekers do. They go out into the world on quests in which they help others in need, restore communities, and pay respect to the world around them. If they do this conscientiously, they find themselves and eventually find God in the process.

As a fledgling knight, Parcival is instructed by his tutor to ask the question, "Whom does the grail serve?" when he meets the ailing king. Though Parcival does not understand it at the time, that question points to a life of service. He pursues that life of service on faith (because it's what knights do, and he wants to be a knight), and in so doing, comes slowly to understand, after repeated trials and failures, the full meaning of the question. Because, as we have seen, in the final analysis Parcival is the grail. He holds the divinity of God in him, and he perceives his divine potential (and duty) when he grows in consciousness enough to understand that his years of service are not for his own glory and advancement but for the advancement of others and the salvation of the kingdom. *Then* he is able to understand the question and ask it in its true meaning. And of course the answer is obvious: "Something greater than oneself," of which Parcival's life has become, by that point, a living symbol. Parcival is the instrument of divine purpose, and he finally sees himself in this greater context. This simple tale with its multi-leveled meanings is the quintessential story of a life of service depicted in mythology. And, if we believe the truth of the myth, we must understand that service to others is the means by which we as professionals find the meaning in our lives and our own salvation.

So, to envision new ideals for lawyers, we might begin by asking the essential question: "Whom do lawyers serve?" A cynical response today would be that they serve themselves, and for many lawyers, as for the young and ignorant Parcival as well as for the Red Knight, that may be true. But that type of service is not idealistic, and it is not a basis for professionalism. So we ask again, "Whom do lawyers serve?" And to the repeated question, there can be only one other answer: They serve other people. If that is so, how do they do that in an idealistic way?

We can begin to answer that question by examining the concept of lawyers' service in its two different, though related, manifestations. The most obvious of these is lawyers' service to individual clients: to people, groups, businesses, institutions, and governments. This is a traditionally recognized form of lawyer service. It is the day-to-day work that lawyers do. It is the kind of service Chief Justice Henry Frye is talking about in his story about helping the elderly widow with her will, quoted in chapter 7. The ideal of service to clients has suffered significantly under the new "law-as-business" mentality. In its most crass interpretation, the "law-as-business" approach views clients primarily as sources of revenue and the lawyer-client relationship as a business arrangement for the benefit of both parties. Law firms become structures for maximizing opportunities for such business arrangements, and the more potentially lucrative those arrangements are, the more desirable they are. Thus lawyers with skills for sale in the more profitable legal markets become themselves "hot commodities," and rich firms "raid" each other for revenue-producing lawyers. The ideal of service to clients becomes smothered in this atmosphere of white-hot competition and pursuit of the dollar. Where it exists at all, it appears as something resembling a creed of prideful competence—"We provide the highest quality of work for our clients"— rather than a commitment to actually serve (to give of oneself) to help others in need.

A second way in which lawyers practice an ideal of service is through "public" service to the greater community. This type of service is part of the vision of the lawyer-statesman and pillar of the community. It is service on a macro-scale, which facilitates, and perhaps ensures, the working of our democracy. For the sake of this discussion, because American lawyers are licensed under our democratic system of government, I take the "greater community" to be American society in its many manifestations (though service to community can also occur beyond our national boundaries, as many lawyers now demonstrate). One of the most obvious forms of this macro-scale service to community is service by attorneys in community organizations and the various levels of public office.

We often call this service "public" (and thereby attempt to distinguish it from service to clients) because it is accomplished by participation in the public institutions which form and support our social structure. But service to community may also come from the day-to-day work of service to clients. When Chief Justice Frye assisted his elderly client to prepare her will, he served not only her but the greater community because a democratic community is stronger if everyone who needs legal representation is able to obtain it. The community is stronger because Chief Justice Frye's service increased the degree of fairness among community members in terms of access to power. The community's contract with its individual members was reaffirmed.

But Chief Justice Frye's example is an easy one. We can readily see how his pro bono help to one of the elderly poor is a service to society. The harder question is whether representation of a large, wealthy, corporate client whose business pollutes a vital river is service to the public through service to the client. I believe the answer to that is "yes" and "no." Yes, it is a service in that even large corporate clients who pollute rivers deserve representation under our legal system, and, if that system works fairly, the entire truth of the client's effect on the greater community—both bad and good—will come out. No, it is not service if that representation takes advantage of an unequal and unjust legal system to give to the corporate client an undue advantage, which is a detriment to both the system and the public it serves. Thus, service must be weighed in terms of some ultimate good, and that ultimate good must be connected to something greater than the server and is not necessarily coterminous with the interests of the client being served.

Whether one's service qualifies as a professional ideal depends also upon what is in the heart of the server. If one who engages in sincere, moral self-reflection honestly feels that service to one's client is service to "something greater than oneself," then at least for that person his service qualifies as professional service and provides a professional ideal. This may occur, and frequently does, where service to the client is detrimental to another party and perhaps even the public at large. But that detriment must be honestly weighed in the context of the greater public welfare. That broad consciousness, that realization that one's actions must ultimately be weighed in terms of their effect upon the lives and relationships of other people, is what gives service moral weight and makes it idealistic. This is a central theme of the Parcival myth: the necessity for personal consciousness about one's dependence upon and duty toward the world around him. Does service to the client rise above self-interest and, if so, how? What is the greater interest that is served?

In 1976 Professor Charles Fried of Harvard Law School wrote a seminal article which helped greatly to define what we mean by morality and service in the legal profession.[1] Essentially, Fried's thesis is that lawyers serve clients as "special purpose friends" and that, regardless of the client's goals or motives, the lawyer's work is morally justified if it is within ethical rules because, under our legal system, every client is entitled to take his rights and interests as far as they will go. As "special purpose friend," the lawyer helps the client fulfill this entitlement to autonomy within our political system and thus serves the greater society. This is another, more intense version of the "adversary system excuse" discussed in chapter 6, and while I will have more to say about my fundamental differences with Fried later, he has at least provided a clear line of demarcation for lawyers to examine the moral bases for their work. Essentially, Fried rejects the notion that in order to assess the morality of the lawyer's role, one must "weigh" service to one's client against disservice to the greater community. Fried believes that though our legal system permits lawyers to help their clients achieve ends that may be harmful to others, because the system ultimately serves a laudable end—expression of and protection of individual freedom—we do not have to worry about harm to others or society in assessing the moral worth of the lawyer's work. The help to the client alone, as part of our "good" legal system, provides a basis for moral prerogative. And as long as the lawyer acts within the rules of the system in behalf of his client, he acts morally.

Without quarreling over the fine points of morality at this juncture, I believe that service involves more than this, and I believe professionalism demands more than this. Essentially professional service involves a moral consciousness about the effects of one's acts upon others. This includes consciousness about the benefits and harm of one's acts to one's client and to other parties, and ultimately to the community at large. I will concede, and in fact applaud, Fried's recognition that, for a professional, duty to one's client carries fundamental moral weight. But I reject the notion that the moral inquiry stops there. As professionals, lawyers occupy an important socio-political status which they in part earn and which they are in part granted by society. That status carries with it both privilege and responsibility, and the responsibility includes an obligation of devotion to the common weal and a vision of how one's life's work serves or harms the greater society. It is not a status which gives license to ignore the effects of one's work upon the society in which one lives. It is rather a status of heightened moral responsibility.

Professionalism demands that we face that moral responsibility seriously and make deliberate choices that utilize our capacity to serve. Our ultimate goal as professionals, like Parcival's ultimate goal, should be to heal the kingdom. Thus, in my view, both service to clients and "public" service in governing bodies and charitable organizations must ultimately be *public* service in order to provide an ideal for lawyers. And while service to clients is itself a form of public service and is a basic moral obligation society has conferred upon lawyers, service to clients must be weighed in the greater context of service to the whole. Does work for a client, in its totality, provide more service than harm to other people? Often this will prove to be a very difficult question which may not yield a clear answer. Yet it is the act of seriously asking the question which is important, and the question provides a moral scale upon which individual lawyers may weigh the virtue of their work. It is a complex scale with many different weights and measures needing constant adjustment. And lawyers must tend to it constantly in order to maintain an ideal of professional service.

I would like now to begin to imagine a vision of what the ideal of service in the legal profession can look like in terms of the two manifestations of service I have identified. In a sense, this is a first step in our journey to ascend, as Parcival eventually did, to a higher level of consciousness. What can we identify which is "greater than ourselves"? What special skills and talents do we have as lawyers that lead us to serve that greater reality? I will begin with this caveat upon the discussion to follow: it will lead us into some fairly abstract questions. But ideals are abstract, a fact we frequently forget as we pursue the mundane work of trial preparation and preparing wills and merger agreements. I will proceed with a discussion of the broader manifestation of service first—the lawyer's macro-scale service to the community—and will try to define an abstract ideal that explains in broad terms the particular nature of the lawyers' service to American society as it is currently evolving.

THE LAWYER'S IDEAL OF MACRO-
SERVICE TO THE COMMUNITY: A MODERN VERSION
OF THE LAWYER-STATESMAN/PILLAR OF THE COMMUNITY

In order to envision an ideal of how a lawyer's work may benefit the greater society and to understand why the old ideals of the lawyer-statesman and pillar of the community may provide guidance toward, but not a formula for, this vision, we first need to talk about community. I begin with the assumption that effective community is desirable both on a national (and local) political level and within the profession itself. But desire doesn't make it so, and given the conditions in modern society, it is difficult to imagine what community should look like either for society as a whole or for the mini-society of the profession. As a group, lawyers have lost their ideal of what an effective professional community should be,[2] and their loss mirrors a similar loss, among American citizens, of a coherent vision of national community. The disintegration of community in America is now well documented by Robert Putnam and others,[3] and it is a startling state of affairs. As Putnam has demonstrated, that breakdown appears in virtually every aspect of modern life. But the true injury may be even worse. Some of our most perceptive thinkers believe that not only is our national community in a confused and decrepit state, but that we have lost the power to rebuild it because we have lost our capacity for moral reason and are therefore unable to form the moral consensus necessary for a coherent national community.[4] This is a dark view, and if it is true, it presents a daunting challenge to the rebuilding of professionalism— not only in terms of rebuilding a community of lawyers but in terms of reconceiving the nature of the lawyer's service to the greater society.

It has not always been so. In the era of the early-day lawyer-statesman, the problems of community-building and maintenance were, at least as then conceived, relatively one-dimensional. Essentially they were problems of how the individual related to the republican state and how the balance between individual freedom and state prerogatives would be negotiated and maintained. Politics, law, and the legal profession were modeled to address these issues. A common understanding of what was moral and good was assumed, and the political apparatus was assumed to embody and promote that understanding. The participatory model employed to that end was civic republicanism, which defined the relationship of the good citizen to the state. Essentially, the good citizen pursued individual interests in the context of the greater good, and the essence of the good citizen's "goodness" was his capacity to perceive and maintain the balance between the two. This capacity is frequently referred to as "civic virtue,"[5] and it was practiced through effective deliberation about the common good. The ideal good citizen not only participated in the political process in an informed and committed way, he felt bound to the process because he was an essential part of the system. He "belonged,"[6] and he expected the system to secure that sense of belonging and to reward his commitment by ensuring both his freedom to participate in public discourse and by cultivating in him the virtues needed to participate meaningfully and positively. Freedom meant more than uninhibited pursuit of private ends. It meant freedom to participate fully and effectively in public affairs in pursuit of the *common* good, in which each citizen had a fundamental stake.

Within this vision, however, lurked conflicting individual needs and interests—the individual need to survive, the need to prosper, interest in private property and accumulation of wealth—all of which clashed with similar interests of others and, potentially, with the vision of common good. Ideally, the practitioner of civic virtue was able to weigh these competing interests against each other without upsetting the balance between them or doing permanent damage to any of them. He resolved the conflicts between them with reason and temperance, and the resolutions maintained and strengthened the common good. On the macro-scale, disputes were resolved though reasoned public debate and political compromise. On the individual level, competing rights and interests were settled through negotiation or, ultimately, through civilly conducted combat in the adversary process. On both levels and on both sides, differences were resolved with an awareness of one's relation to and duty toward the common good.

The hero in this process was the lawyer-statesman/pillar of the community, who, as public servant, assumed the offices which negotiated the balance between private interests and public good, and as advocate, advanced the rights of his client only in the context of the greater good of society. As commentators on American society recognized as far back as de Tocqueville,[7] because lawyers were the trained elite of the new society, they were the ultimate practitioners of public virtue and the high priests of civic republicanism. They served as administrators, interpreters, and caretakers of the system. They were all white and all male, steeped in the philosophy of the Enlightenment, imbued with notions of public service, and confident in the ultimate beneficence of the patriarchal and racist social order which they were helping to design, build, and maintain.

The lawyer-statesman/pillar of the community/practitioner of republican virtue was a function of the society in which he lived. As we have seen, many of the assumptions which underlay that social order are no longer valid either in regard to the structure of our society or the direction of professional growth. If lawyers are to serve our modern society on the level which the lawyer-statesmen and pillars of the community served theirs, they must understand a new reality. Our society is infinitely more complex than that served by the lawyer-statesmen. It is far more pluralistic—a social fact which has been apparent for some time but which many Americans are just beginning to accept. And our pluralism includes not only racial, ethnic, religious, and gender diversity, but, most importantly, an over-riding value pluralism with, as political philosopher William Galston puts it, "conflicting and incommensurable conceptions of human good."[8] The primary philosophical and ultimately political question facing democracies now is how (or whether) a national community can be envisioned which will transcend that value pluralism and bind people together in a social context that is compatible with basic democratic principles.[9] If we are to construct a new ideal of public service for lawyers—an ideal worthy of the legal profession—it should be based upon the answer (or answers) to that fundamental question.

A magnificent debate on that question rages among political philosophers today. That debate is intricately complex, and as fascinating as it is, it would take us places we don't need to go for purposes of the present discussion. At the risk of oversimplification, however, there are aspects of that discussion which it will help us to know. First, to illustrate the profound nature of the problem of value diversity as it relates to formation of community, let us look at one aspect of the disagreement over the common good. Not only is there now no common understanding among members of our society of what is good, a common moral code (a "consensus" as the retired judge says in chapter 6), there are numerous versions of what is good and some people who resist the idea of a common good altogether.[10]

For example, feminist political philosophers such as Nancy Fraser are suspicious of efforts to define a common understanding of what is good in a society which they see as "stratified" and predominantly patriarchal. They specifically object to the old, civic republican ideal of the lawyer-statesman as a "common good that transcends the mere sum of individual preferences,"[11] because it assumes a common definition of good that does not work for people outside or on the periphery of the socio-political power structure. It is, as Fraser says, "tainted by the effects of dominance and subordination."[12] Fraser and other feminist political philosophers believe that adherence to a "common" definition of what is good limits discussion and silences expression of real difference and a search for divergent definitions of good. Given what we now acknowledge about the legal profession's systematic exclusion of women and racial minorities and the similar patterns we perceive in other social institutions, it is not surprising that women and others would be suspicious of any talk about a "common good" and would prefer public deliberation that admits and honors differences and seeks a way of protecting them.

Philosopher Alasdair MacIntyre, among others, believes that the problem is more pathological and ominous than mere incompatible notions of the common good.[13] He believes that our society has lost the capacity to reason toward a moral consensus:

> The most striking feature of contemporary moral utterance is that so much of it is used to express disagreements; and the most striking feature of the debates in which these disagreements are expressed is their interminable character. I do not mean by this just that such debates go on and on and on—although they do—but also that they apparently can find no terminus. There seems to be no rational way of securing moral agreement in our culture.[14]

If MacIntyre is correct, this loss, which Professor Tom Shaffer calls a loss of capacity for moral discernment,[15] is profound indeed. It means that our society has lost the ability to maintain itself as a coherent moral community. It has loss the capacity to *practice* community-building and maintenance. This is a vision of a truly ailing kingdom. It is a political-scape in chaos, with innumerable voices competing to be heard and no one listening, with, as MacIntyre says, "conflict and not consensus at the heart of modern social structure," and modern politics reduced to "civil war carried on by other means."[16] Capacity for healing and compromise atrophy. Vision of a common good is lost. National community is no longer possible.

Social and political thinkers have addressed the problems to community posed by social pluralism from two basic perspectives, and an understanding of those perspectives and the essential difference between them is important to our envisioning a new ideal of service for lawyers. One approach, represented most notably by the work of John Rawls and others,[17] seeks commonality by focusing upon what many lawyers would call "procedural" and what Rawls calls politically "neutral" principles—principles which all members of society can accept and which are necessary for a functioning democracy. Because of the inherent conflicts between groups having different value perspectives and different understandings of public good, Rawls believes that government must function on some basis other than the premise that it advances a particular moral scheme. That basis is justice—for Rawls, essentially fair participation—for all citizens. And justice is insured by a political domain which is "free standing" and not based upon or ruled by any subgroup's understanding of what is good.[18] Society functions—maintains social unity—on the basis of "overlapping consensus" among subgroups regarding the preeminence of those "neutral" political values (such as, for example, freedom of speech and the concept of due process of law) which permit society to function to produce a maximum of justice and fairness. These principles, though they appear to be "good" for the maintenance of society and may spring from religious and moral beliefs of the consenting subgroups, are essentially functionary and do not themselves comprise a comprehensive moral scheme.[*]

Rawls admits that his scheme will not achieve community, if by community "we mean . . . a society governed by a shared comprehensive religious, philosophical, or moral doctrine."[19] In a sense, faced with the realities of value pluralism, he searches for a "neutral" common ground upon which democratic societies can survive. He finds it in the principles of justice and fairness and the procedures necessary to ensure both. And

---

[*]Rawls's view is individualistic in the sense that it retains a fundamental reverence for and deference to individual rights as the basis upon which social debate and interaction proceed. Yet, his view differs from more traditional liberal models of a functioning society in that the interests he would bring into play are not limited to private, self-oriented interests but include notions of common good cherished by participants in the political process and which, as part of their individual freedoms, they might seek to advance. Among reasonable participants, some of these notions will certainly "overlap" so that a political consensus may be achieved which ensures justice and a functioning society. But Rawls specifically rejects any goal of a comprehensive moral consensus. He prefers instead a "well-ordered democratic society," in which "everyone accepts, and knows that everyone else accepts, the very same principles of justice." Rawls, *Political Liberalism* (New York: Columbia University Press, 1993), 35–43.

I think it is fair to say that by justice and fairness Rawls intends primarily principles that guarantee equal access to and participation in the political process—in a pluralistic society, freedom to agree and disagree—rather than any ideal of justice as good will and charity toward one's fellow man.

It is the divide Rawls constructs between the political process and a search for moral consensus which concerns his most ardent critics. And their fears are based upon a different view of what people need in order to participate effectively in the business of society. Rawls's leading critics are communitarian, while Rawls is a political (some would say "procedural") liberal. They feel that the relation between the individual and society must be more than a mutual bond to ensure political tolerance and participation. Justice to them means more than procedural fairness to secure basic political rights. It must include some ethic of care which weighs not only political freedom but "respect for the richness of social life," economic fairness, and personal security,[20] and which values the "internal goods"[21] individuals bring to the work of community-building (what some later-day Aristoteleans would call "virtues"). It may be an exaggeration (on both sides) to say that where liberals yearn for individual freedom, communitarians yearn for mutual love, but it is no exaggeration to recognize the emotional aspect of the communitarian model. Ultimately, for the communitarians, the bond between an individual and a morally coherent community is an emotional commitment. And that level of commitment can only come from a moral identity with the community as a whole. Michael Sandel describes that moral identity:

> To say that members of society are bound by a sense of community is not simply to say that a great many of them profess communitarian sentiments and pursue communitarian aims, but rather that they conceive their identity—the subject and not just the object of their feelings and aspirations—as defined to some extent by the community of which they are a part. For them, community describes not just what they *have* as fellow citizens but also what they *are,* not a relationship they choose (as in voluntary association) but an attachment they discover, not merely an attribute but a constituent of their identity.[22]

Alasdair MacIntyre portrays it in terms of patriotism—once a virtue because it once included moral identity with one's government, but no longer:

Patriotism is or was a virtue founded on attachment primarily to a political and moral community and only secondarily to the government of that community; but it is characteristically exercised in discharging responsibility to and in such government. When however the relationship of government to the moral community is put in question both by the changed nature of government and the lack of moral consensus in society, it becomes difficult any longer to have any clear, simple and teachable conception of patriotism. Loyalty to my country, to my community—which remains unalterably a central virtue—becomes detached from obedience to the government which happens to rule me.[23]

Where such detachment is present, Sandel warns, the individual need for emotional commitment to community does not vanish. Then the yearning for "larger meaning" in public life "finds undesirable expression," as narrow and intolerant views of the common good, which are anti-communitarian and frequently *ex*clusive, invade the public square.[24] The communitarians revere the "formative politics" of civic republicanism, "a politics that cultivates in its citizens the qualities of character that self-government requires."[25] And yet most of them admit the difficulty of achieving that in the modern world, where political bodies are increasingly pluralistic and political allegiances increasingly globally dispersed and where, as MacIntyre claims, moral reasoning is no longer practiced. There is in their writing a yearning for an ideal kingdom in which everyone comes to understand, once again, the value of community,[26] or a searching for salvation in the concept of smaller, more contiguous communities within the national body politic.[27]

So what service, comparable to that of the lawyer-statesman and pillar of the community, can modern lawyers render to their morally incoherent society, where community is in decline and a myriad of groups and subgroups compete and clamor for power? This is a difficult question, and the answer requires a vision beyond that held by most modern professionals. We might begin by focusing on the professional, legal community itself, and say that the first thing lawyers need to do to serve the greater society is to stop emulating it. What is a profession? Is it simply a body of people with similar training who band together for self-regulation and financial and political advantage? Or is it a community, in which shared values bind members together in a mutual, moral commitment—a professional "patriotism"? If we look at the Rawlsian and communitarian ideals for social cohesion discussed above, we can see that many lawyers today do not live by either one—not even the more procedural model proposed by Rawls. They have given up altogether on the ideal of a professional community in any form. They have reverted to a radically individualistic model which does not recognize a need for or obligation to a professional community or the obligation of the professional community to the greater society. This attitude is an abnegation of professional responsibility more profound than any violation of the Model Rules of Professional Conduct.

To serve the greater society, the legal profession must resurrect its own community. It can do that by reaffirming its values and reconnecting those values to a higher purpose of service to the greater society. The two tasks—self-reclamation and envisioning a service to the greater society— are interdependent. We need the vision of service to the greater community in order to develop a moral consensus on professional values, and we need a professional community bound by common values in order to envision a higher purpose.

Implicit in the task of envisioning a higher purpose is an emotional step which, at least on the level of service to individual clients, is an anathema to many lawyers: the possibility of another "god" to displace the credo of total devotion to the client's cause. That other god, as conceived by the practitioners of civic republicanism, was the public good. Yes—public good was ultimately superior to the interests of individual clients. Lawyers sought offices of public responsibility and advancement of their clients' interests in that context. Tempering a client's options by notions of public good was ethically sound in the republican society because under the assumptions of civic republicanism, the client, too, had a vital stake in the public good, and the lawyer implicitly understood that. There *was* a national community which had moral importance for everyone—lawyers and clients alike. And lawyers, as the educated, trained elites of society, were presumed to have the skills to reconcile first-level conflicts between individual rights and freedoms and the common good which ultimately protected them.

To do that takes lawyers who conceive themselves as something more than legal technicians. It requires something closer to what Professor Milner Ball calls the "learned artist,"[28] an old professional model which may, however slowly, once again be gaining favor.* Instead of teaching lawyers and law students that client's interests must always trump other

---

*The Professionalism Committee of the American Bar Association recently defined the professional lawyer as "an expert in law pursuing a learned art in service to clients and in the spirit of public service; and engaging in these pursuits as part of a common calling

considerations, we need to develop lawyers who are not afraid of their own morality and are morally equipped to measure and to assist clients in measuring the value of the clients' interests in the greater context. This is a big step for many lawyers, and it will not occur overnight. It will require both a new attitude, a broader concept of lawyers' work than now inheres, and a new approach to legal training. It will require lawyers who are willing to reassert the moral prerogative of a professional in the lawyer-client relationship.

In order for lawyers to undertake such a task with competence and humility, they must be part of a professional community that promotes the ideal of public service and articulates the public good which is served. The professional community must support lawyers in negotiating the delicate balance between duty to client and public service. That means that the profession through which lawyers serve must be, at least on some minimal level, a morally coherent community, one in which basic values are shared, nurtured, and understood. And those values must form at least a part of the moral character of each member. The emotionally based connection which the communitarians recognize as essential to such a community should be at the center of a professional's relation to her profession. Professional membership should, as Sandel says, be a matter of "belonging" and "identity," in the civic republican sense. And the profession itself must both demand and foster that level of commitment. The profession must actively cultivate the qualities of character necessary to sustain it.

But once again, assuming we can recreate such a community of lawyers, how can they serve a public good in a radically pluralistic society which itself is unable to agree on a common good? First of all, let us note that "public good" is not necessarily the same or coterminous with "common good." Common good, as most political philosophers use the term, implies a common understanding of what is good for society and all those in it. In the Aristotelian sense—as practiced by civic republicans— it meant a good in which the needs and aspirations of the individual and of the community were inseparable and in harmony: what is best in my life is also best for the life of the community as a whole.[29] It implied a common moral understanding of what is good—and, as Alasdair MacIntyre notes, included a process for reaching moral consensus. Public good does not necessarily go that deeply. It may merely connote what is

---

to promote justice and public good." American Bar Association, *Teaching and Learning Professionalism*, Report of the Professionalism Committee, ABA Section of Legal Education and Admission to the Bar (1996).

good for society as a whole—in a public as opposed to an individual or private sense (without addressing whether or to what degree that good is in harmony with individual needs or aspirations). Whether public good benefits a private individual depends upon that individual's relationship to the public community.

Let us invert the question which began the last paragraph: are lawyers, as a community, limited in their concept of public service by society's ability to perceive a common good? I believe they are not. It is the social prerogative of a true profession, I suggest—a profession which is itself a morally coherent community seriously devoted to service to the greater good—to propose its own ideal of public good and to pursue that as service to society. They may do that without necessarily reconciling that ideal with any of the various notions of common good favored by the various factions of society. A great profession cannot be limited by the debilities of the society it serves. Its province and duty is to lead, and in the early days of the republic, that was the role of the legal profession. It was easier then because service to the public good was starkly defined by the times, and lawyers were the best people to render it. Now the need is just as great, though the society is more complex and the nature of the service less clear. But opportunity for professions to lead and serve is still there.

So what is the public good to which the legal profession can dedicate itself? It is a good to which lawyers have, ideally, always dedicated themselves; a good which lawyers are uniquely qualified to pursue; a public good upon which they all should be able to agree. It is the very ideal which was banished from my first year torts class in law school: Justice. Justice is easy to propose as an ideal, but achieving justice in our increasingly complex, pluralistic society is and will continue to be the leading socio-political challenge of our age. Even under John Rawls's limited, rights-oriented concept of justice, how does one ensure equal political access and fairness in a society as complex as ours, where a constantly shifting Babel of groups, widely varying in size and resources, compete for influence and power? How are "smaller" voices heard? How are competing claims fairly decided? How are compromises formed and implemented?

A more vexing question deals with the meaning of justice itself. What does it mean in our society? What should it mean? Even the rights-oriented model proposed by John Rawls is a much more complex undertaking in today's society than that faced by the early civic republicans. Present issues of justice include many questions which were either not present or not recognized in the early republic—gender and racial equality to name but two. And if recent history has taught us anything, we should know that for many Americans the concept of justice has expanded beyond entitlement to basic political rights. As communitarian thinkers are telling us, any new ideal of justice must include concepts of fairness in other areas—social security, physical security, economic security.[30] And fairness itself may be a fluid and relative concept, depending upon availability of resources and individual or group need.[31] It is not an exaggeration to say that much of recent American history has been a great debate over the expanded meaning of justice. That debate grows more intense and complicated every day.

Lawyers and the legal profession should be leading this debate, and they should be leading it toward the reality of a broader and more inclusive ideal of justice, which incorporates not only principles of fair political participation but economic and social justice as well, in which the intrinsic worth of each citizen is connected to the welfare of society as a whole. The broader concept of justice looks to the future of our pluralistic society and provides our best hope for a new national community. Whether such a community is ultimately possible, we cannot know, but it is something to strive for. Striving for it—helping to envision and shape it, helping it to come about—is work worthy of a great profession.

It will not be easy, but lawyer's work is rarely easy. And this is quintessentially lawyer's work. Their natural ideal is the promotion of justice. Their heritage has been directed toward that end. They are trained and intellectually equipped to negotiate between the various factions of society and to devise structures for resolution and compromise. They are (or should be) trained to understand principles of fairness and equal voice. Serving justice in our society will draw upon the legal profession's traditional function as social engineers and will demand the lawyering skills of analytical reasoning and advocacy. It will engage the increasingly revitalized lawyering skills of counseling, mediation, and reconciliation. It will require a comprehensive understanding of history and democratic principles (formerly endemic in the lawyer-statesman), knowledge of the mechanics of society and the evolving political system, an ability to comprehensively grasp the issues of the present and to imagine the future, and the energy and pluck to undertake such a daunting task.

Lawyers not only have the training and expertise for this undertaking, they have the disposition for it. As Michael Sandel says (in a passage that sounds remarkably Rawlsian), "The civic virtue distinctive to our time is the capacity to negotiate our way among the sometimes overlapping and sometimes conflicting obligations that claim us, and to live with the tension to which multiple loyalties give rise."[32] For a profession, I think it goes a step further. Lawyers must do what Sandel envisions while at the same time forging a vision of public justice that transcends the management of conflicting obligations. The "tension" present in such an undertaking will be substantial and will impose both emotional and spiritual costs. The emotional costs lie in the inherent uncertainty of a process in which so many voices compete in never-ending debate. Such debate is ultimately inconclusive; it is impossible to guarantee or predict finality, direction, and outcome. The result is a persistent feeling of indefiniteness, uncertainty, and unease, which, if heeded, either smothers action or intensifies it, making the action more aggressive and the actor unopen to compromise. The spiritual cost lies in the lack of consensus on the common good—a spiritual cost which, if Alasdair MacIntyre is correct, has reached the point of crisis. Why are we engaging in this increasingly cacophonous discourse if it leads only to more disagreement? If there is no hope of moral consensus, no hope of a moral justification in the greater society, then the tendency is to seek it elsewhere, particularly in one's own moral judgment and in that of people similarly disposed. There is no faith in a greater community to supply it.

Lawyers face this kind of emotional and spiritual uncertainty daily in almost all they do. And while that type of uncertainty is present in much of human undertaking, it is a central factor in lawyers' work, which is, as Holmes so succinctly put it, "the prediction of the incidence of public force" upon the interests of one's client.[33] Whenever lawyers accept and pursue a case, they begin a process—the legal process (a formal method of "reasoned" deliberation)—in which the issues are frequently unclear, the way uncharted, and outcome almost always uncertain. Alasdair MacIntyre's description of the current state of moral and political discourse as "interminable disagreement" and "civil war carried on by other means" are characterizations very familiar to any lawyer who represents clients in disputes with other parties. Sides are frequently entrenched, impatient, and unyielding. Empathy and moral understanding are absent. Reason and compromise seem impossible. Good lawyers nevertheless undertake such cases with a commitment to pursue them through the legal process and to persist in that process until the best conclusion for their clients is reached, conclusions which frequently involve compromise and in some cases a form of individual or bipartisan reconciliation.* When the lawyers are dedicated professionals, their undertaking is made as a matter of professional character and personal commitment and is based on two assumptions which underlie the lawyers' faith.

First they assume a basic integrity in the justice system. This requires faith because lawyers are exposed to the imperfections of that system every day. But beyond those imperfections, lawyers expect and assume a basic and ultimate level of integrity—enough integrity so that they can put their trust in it.† It is the closest model we have in this country to Rawls's "free-standing" political domain, created from values derived from an "overlapping consensus" of diverse groups and thus unpolluted, at least theoretically, by the moral agendas of various constituencies.‡ It has integrity because it is a deliberative process which presumes, however imperfectly, to insure fairness and render justice: to be open and inclusive and to give everyone an equal voice. It is this hope—this expectation that, if one is conscientious in preparation and skilled as an advocate, one will be heard and listened to and taken seriously—that gives lawyers faith in the justice system. Their faith is further supported by the knowledge that in our system the subjects appropriate for discussion are radically open. That is, part of the deliberative process may include a challenge to the fairness of the process itself.

A second basis for the faith of the conscientious lawyer in pursuing a case derives from a perception of something greater than themselves. They perceive that a greater good results from the process itself. This greater

---

*It is true that cases do have conclusions—decisions for one side or the other—and in that sense are not "open-ended" like the deliberative process within the public sphere envisioned by Rawls, Galston, Fraser, and other commentators. But the conclusions of cases at law are not foregone, and, as any good lawyer knows, cases—any case—can for any number of reasons take a very different direction than one expects it to take. It is that aspect which requires good lawyers to be nimble on their feet.

†The practice of courts to avoid involvement in "political questions" is one of the safeguards employed within the justice system to preserve public perception of the system's integrity. A number of commentators have claimed that that perception was endangered by the action of the Supreme Court in *Bush v. Gore,* the decision which ensured the outcome of the 2000 presidential election, because the decision took the Court into the arena of presidential politics. See Ronald Dworkin, "A Badly Flawed Election," *The New York Review of Books* 48, no. 1 (January 11, 2000): 53; Larry D. Kramer, "The Supreme Court v. Balance of Powers," *New York Times,* March 3, 2001, A13; Jeffrey Rosen, "Judge Not," *New Republic,* December 12, 2000, 16; Jeffrey Rosen, "Disgrace," *New Republic,* December 25, 2000, 18.

‡There is, of course, ample evidence of moral and emotional pollution of our justice process. But where that occurs, it is seen as a failure of the system and not characteristic of it. It is not what we expect of it.

good is nothing less than the maintenance of relationships between people and entities and the basic functioning of democracy. Without lawyers to take cases and pursue them through a justice system in which some minimal level of integrity inheres, we would indeed have civil war—multi-sided and chaotic for as long as the sides lasted. Avoiding that prospect is a public good which transcends value pluralism. In its best guise, that good is more than simply making the machinery work for society. It is a moral commitment to society which assumes that society is worth committing to, that it has hope and a future, and a coherence on some level which is worth sacrificing for. The problem is that many lawyers forget that they serve such a good or that it even exists, so focused are they on winning the case at hand or making the monthly billing quota. Good lawyers who practice as serious professionals take time to reflect upon the "greater" purpose in what they do. They practice their faith that their work serves a greater good. And they identify themselves and their profession by that faith.

This faith can sustain the work of lawyers both as practitioners in the justice system and as servants of justice in the broader public sphere—making democracy work under the realities of a pluralistic society. But in order for the profession to assume that greater role, in order for lawyers to rise to that level as professionals, in order for professional faith to be more than a sham, the profession as a whole must seriously undertake the pursuit of a broader ideal of justice. That includes giving voice to the voiceless in our current system. It includes refashioning the old myth of champion of people and causes and rededicating it to a vastly more diverse society. It includes a renewed professional commitment to represent political dissidents and persons who are challenging the system, in order to ensure that all voices are heard. And, above all, it includes serious, profession-wide commitment to represent poor people.

Because of the failure of the legal profession currently to meet these commitments in our society, our legal system is fundamentally unjust and unfair. It is unjust under the more limited, rights-oriented concept of justice as well as the broader, socially expanded concept of justice that should inform the new justice ideal. And much of that injustice and unfairness springs from a failure of the profession itself to provide representation for poor people and people of moderate incomes. The chief ethical failing of the American bar is the fact that only approximately 20 percent of the legal needs of the United States' 35 million poor people are being met by the legal profession.[34] The legal needs of the lower-middle class fair little better.[35] More litigants now appear in court without lawyers than those represented by counsel.[36] These are not new phenomena. They have been true for a long time. The excuse offered by some lawyers that the failure is society's and not a failing of the legal profession is an astounding repudiation of the most basic professional responsibility. Indeed, poverty is society's problem, but lack of fairness in the legal system is the problem of the profession which, as Professor Deborah Rhode points out, has been granted by society a virtual monopoly on providing legal services.[37] And unlike medicine and the construction industry (as examples), which also provide services crucial to society, the legal system is adversarial. It is the nature of the system itself—not merely the exigencies of life in society—which makes fair access to legal services so important. Thus, for lawyers, fair access and representation are not simply laudatory hopes for society. They are essential components of the justice system over which we have almost exclusive control. It is therefore our responsibility to see that fair access and representation are implemented. This is a professional responsibility of the most profound sort. Should pro bono work be expected of lawyers as professionals? If there are poor people who are unrepresented, then of course it should. Should it be mandated? It is shameful to think it has come to that, but if lawyers will not willingly accept pro bono work for poor people as a matter of their professional status (as many lawyers now do),[38] then it is the profession's responsibility to see that they do, and state bars should enforce that requirement as a matter of professional duty. Unless the legal profession earnestly undertakes to solve this basic problem of access to the courts and the legal system, its hopes of serving the greater society by leading the struggle for justice in the broader sense, will fail. The hypocrisy is simply too great to support such leadership.

The legal profession can, in the process of reclaiming itself as a profession, help lead our society back toward faith in itself. It can lead by demonstrating faith in the legal-political process and by practicing that faith, by working to make the process just and fair. In so doing, the profession will fulfill its moral duty toward society and ultimately demonstrate the beneficence which flows from the work of a dedicated and compassionate professional community. Yes, we live in a complex, pluralistic society in which differences are many and often deep. But do we want a politically functional society or don't we? Do we want one based upon fairness and justice or don't we? Do we want the strength that comes from moral coherence or don't we? If we want these things, then we need compassion more than ever before. And to find that compassion in a chaos of different views and voices and in a political landscape which is weighted toward wealth and power, we need seekers who are used to making order out of chaos, who can recognize injustice and inequality and work to correct it, and who can find the thread of our commonality and weave it into cloth. Lawyers know how to do this. And they have faith—even before they approach the task—that justice is real and that the thread is there.

I do not know whether the legal profession can ultimately restore society's capacity for moral discernment and perception of a common good. Certainly it cannot do so alone. But it can restore that capacity in itself. It can work to restore that capacity in society. And it can do so by concentrating on the things it does best and by reconnecting with the moral, community-based reasons for why it does them. Practice is the key—practice of law and life as a moral undertaking—practice which is sustained by a vision of moral purpose and faith in one's work. Lawyers can perceive a common good—justice and fairness to all. And they can learn the practice of moral discernment which will enable them to pursue it.

At the end of the movie, *Night Falls on Manhattan*, the young district attorney, Sean Casey (played by the actor Andy Garcia), who has just triumphed over the forces of crime, evil, and injustice through his courage and skills as an attorney, welcomes a new group of assistant D.A.s on their first day on the job. They are sitting in the place he sat only a year or so before. He gives them a preview of where they are headed: "You're going to spend most of your time in the gray areas," he tells them. "But out there, that's where you're going to come face to face with who you really are. And that's a frightening thing to ask of you. And it might take a lifetime to figure out." The "gray areas" are the domain of the lawyer. Leading the society through the gray areas is the continual work of the lawyer-statesman. The difference between the gray areas today and those of the early republic is that today those areas are more gray than ever. They are inhabited by more and more people and groups of people contending over more difficult choices. What this means is that today lawyers need faith in what they do and the courage to rely on that faith more than they ever have. And the first step in securing that faith is to practice the ideal of community service which sustains it.

THE LAWYER'S IDEAL OF SERVICE TO CLIENTS

In addition to "public" service, lawyers provide service to individual clients. For purposes of the following discussion, I am setting aside for the moment incidents in which service to clients serves the greater public good by insuring fairness in our justice system, equal representation, etc. I am focusing here on the attorney-client relationship itself. In the context of our present-day society, is this inherently moral service? Can it be moral service when the lawyer does not condone the client's objectives or, worse yet, when the lawyer views those objectives as harmful to society? Is it service to something greater than oneself? Does it provide an ideal of service for lawyers?

As I have noted above in my discussion of the lawyer's ideal of service to the community, Charles Fried attempts to answer these questions affirmatively by describing the lawyer as a client's special purpose friend who helps the client achieve his deserved autonomy in the legal system and therefore in society, regardless of whether the specific goals of that autonomy are harmful to the society's welfare. I like very much Fried's notion of a the lawyer-client relationship as a special form of friendship based upon the client's need for services and the lawyer's capacity and willingness to provide them. I have, however, three specific objections to the premises that underlie Fried's attempt at moral justification of a lawyer's work for clients.

First, Fried's thesis does not recognize or attempt to deal with the inequities in the legal system—inequities which are substantial and largely based upon wealth and power. Some clients have much more money to spend on lawyers and legal services than others and more resources to help them manipulate and even abuse the legal system. As we have noted already, a substantial number of people cannot afford lawyers (and as a result often do not even attempt to enter the legal system to seek redress). By not dealing with these inequities, Fried's model does more than ignore them. It exacerbates them because it gives lawyers who represent wealthy and powerful clients carte blanche to use those inequities to their clients' advantage.*

Second, by placing the legal autonomy of the individual client at the pinnacle of what is good, Fried's thesis does potential damage to the concept of individual autonomy as a whole. Under Fried's formula, the client's legal autonomy trumps all other interests, and it is the single, consistent value upon which Fried bases the morality of service to clients.

---

*Thomas Shaffer has warned that, given the inequities present in American society, "the liberal ideologies of freedom and equality that lawyers protect 'in the end . . . make freedom a principle that members of the ruling class should not be interfered with in the use of their privileges, and equality a principle that no differences count except those that characterize the ruling class.' " Thomas L. Shaffer, "The Christian Jurisprudence of Robert E. Rhodes, Jr.," *Notre Dame Law Review* 73 (March 1998): 737, 746, quoting Robert E. Rhodes Jr., *Pilgrim Law* (Notre Dame, Ind.: University of Notre Dame Press, 1998), 68.

But if I manipulate the system (legitimately) for my client and prevail for him, I may destroy the autonomy of numerous other people and institutions in the process. My client's legal autonomy will be vindicated, but autonomy in general will be *dis*-served.

My third objection to Fried's thesis is that it promotes a limited, traditional, and somewhat patriarchal view of autonomy and thereby blocks a fuller understanding of autonomy which includes a deeper moral dimension. True autonomy in the context of the attorney-client relationship, I suggest, involves informed moral choice as well as exercise of legal rights. It is more than merely an aggressive pursuit of a prechosen legal option, but an opportunity for personal and mutual moral growth for both the client and the attorney. Thomas Shaffer, former dean of Notre Dame Law School and noted legal ethics scholar, has written much on the moral duty the lawyer owes the client, which Shaffer characterizes as the "ethic of care."[39] Like Fried, Shaffer views the attorney-client relationship as a type of friendship, but Shaffer's version of lawyer-client friendship is not a morally static one. Rather, Shaffer's attorney-client friendship, which incorporates a caring ethic, is open to mutual reflection which can result in new moral direction for both the lawyer and the client. Prechosen legal goals, while they may form the basis for the relationship, are subject to reexamination in light of the moral predilections of both parties to the relationship. And certainly the tactics used to achieve those goals, regardless of whether they are permitted by the ethical rules, are subject to moral reconsideration. Under Shaffer's model, moral reflection is part of the work of the lawyer; moral conversation is part of the work of the attorney-client relationship; moral change and growth are possible for both parties.

The most often voiced objection to Shaffer's model (and others who have made similar arguments supporting an attorney's right and duty to second-guess a client's moral agenda),[40] is that it imposes a lawyer-dictated moral filter on the client's autonomy (interpreted as the client's freedom to exercise individual rights through the legal system). One commentator has famously referred to this lawyer-dictated moral filter as "an oligarchy of lawyers," which arrogantly imposes its moral vision on society by taking and rejecting cases based upon the lawyer's judgment of their moral value.[41] A more crass statement of this position is attributed to Elihu Root: "The client never wants to be told he can't do what he wants to do; he wants to be told how to do it, and it is the lawyer's business to tell him how."[42] In this version of lawyer's work, the lawyer is essentially an "amoral technician"[43] who has no moral prerogative in his work other than those dictated by his client and prescribed by the ethical rules.

It is not surprising that the legal profession, in which a large number of members—and some of its more prominent ones, including some of its leading academicians—take this morally minimalist attitude toward their work, has serious problems with its professional image. It is difficult to imagine a true professional, one who values the moral heritage of his professional status and his image in the eyes of his fellow citizens, beginning his work every day by first blocking out his own moral consciousness. And it is arrogant to imagine that one can do that without serious personal (and ultimately professional) costs. As numerous lawyers and commentators have testified, the true danger in practicing law as an amoral technician is that, when that course is rigorously followed in the hyper-competitive world of legal practice, it becomes more than a professional role. It becomes a way of life. The blocking out of moral compunctions soon changes from a temporarily induced state by which lawyers avoid moral qualms about their clients and their work, to a permanent mind-set that colors almost everything they do.[44] The potential harm from this attitude to lawyers' personal lives is obvious. And ultimately, it will affect their capacities as professionals as well. The old stories about good lawyers amply demonstrate that one's humanity is essential to one's ability as a lawyer. Absence of it can be debilitating. Virginia Woolf has had this to say about the professional's loss of humanity:

> [This makes] us of the opinion that if people are highly successful in their professions they lose their senses. Sight goes. They have no time to look at pictures. Sound goes. They have no time to listen to music. Speech goes. They have no time for conversation. They lose their sense of proportion—the relation between one thing and another. Humanity goes. Money making becomes so important that they must work by night as well as by day. Health goes. And so competitive do they become that they will not share their work with others though they have more than they can do themselves. What then remains of a human being who has lost sight, sound, and sense of proportion? Only a cripple in a cave.[45]

The "oligarchy of lawyers" critique of lawyers who bring their moral selves into the context of the attorney-client relationship overstates the dangers in doing so and fails to credit the dangers in leaving one's moral self out. And that critique also fails to credit the possibilities in what Shaffer is proposing. It is true that when lawyers undertake moral conversation with clients, there is danger of manipulation—of the lawyer steering the client into doing what the lawyer thinks is the right thing rather than raising moral issues so that the client may face them and make moral decisions. In order to raise moral issues with one's client and to bring the lawyer's own sense of morality into the professional conversation, it is not necessary to act as moral autocrat or manipulator, laying down the moral law in the case or refusing to take the case if the client's goals do not square sufficiently with the lawyer's sense of morality. Shaffer's vision of a moral conversation between lawyer and client, in which the lawyer raises moral issues and helps the client understand them, keeps the lawyer in the adviser's role. Ultimately, the client makes the moral decisions about what he wants to do. This sort of advice is—or should be—an essential component of legal assistance,[46] and lawyers are—or should be—well qualified to give it. They are certainly trained to foresee consequences and to advise their clients accordingly. As a group they are intelligent and highly educated. They should be as morally aware as any other group of citizens and could be even more so if their training was improved to include broader and more innovative courses in ethics. Basically, the lawyer's moral job in this context is to raise moral questions which bear on the client's case, be open to such questions when they are raised by the client, help the client (and perhaps the lawyer himself) to define those moral issues, and *engage* both the client's moral qualms and his own in finding solutions. This may lead to a change of goals or tactics, and it may not. It may result in a change in moral perspective by the client, and it may not. It may result in a change in moral perspective by the lawyer. It may even lead to the point that the lawyer cannot in good conscience continue to represent the client, though I would suggest that given the lawyer's professional duty of loyalty (which is also a moral duty of great weight in a professional context) and the danger of manipulation in the lawyer-client relationship, withdrawal on moral grounds should only occur in extreme cases. But the important point is that the moral faculties of both the client and the lawyer will have been engaged in a mutual undertaking that involves a mutual risk of change and therefore presents an opportunity for moral growth.

I argue that this possibility for moral growth is true autonomy, and that a lawyer who structures her relationship with her clients in order to provide that opportunity in the context of legal service is providing a deeply moral service as well. This is, I would argue, inherently good in a way that transcends traditional notions of good and bad. A lawyer who makes this kind of commitment to her client truly deserves to be called a "special purpose friend." This is ideal service to something that is greater than oneself—the chance to help another person (and perhaps oneself as well) achieve, not only legal objectives which are based upon moral reflection, but ultimately a deeper moral understanding.

The model for this type of lawyering is present in all of the positive myths of the profession we have visited, but it is perhaps most present in the ideal of the pillar of the community. In that context, it is the notion of the lawyer who practices with an eye to the moral status of his clients in their communities. Thus a lawyer may say to a client, "Before you go through with this land purchase to build a new shopping mall, have you considered the effect the mall will have on the people in that part of town and how they will feel about it and you when it is completed? You have a lot of good will in this community; do you think this project will risk that good will and is it worth it? You and your family have deep roots here; is this the direction you think this community should be taking in terms of economic growth?" Perhaps the client's intent to purchase the land for the shopping mall will not change with these questions. Perhaps the client has thought of them already and answered them to his satisfaction. Perhaps he will think further about them and make some modifications to his plan that will make the project less offensive to the project's neighbors. But whatever the outcome, the important factor in this scenario is that the lawyer will have actively brought moral issues to the table where they can be addressed and the client's moral liabilities can be openly acknowledged and resolved. The lawyer has not recommended that the client do anything other than consider the moral issues. He has not even stated his own moral preference, and because of the potential for manipulation, he should be careful about doing so even if the client asks. This will be a different relationship from one in which the lawyer merely takes the client's plan and, without further reflection or inquiry, does all he can legally to bring it to fruition. There is more opportunity for change in this relationship. There is more integrity and more chance for true, mutual respect. There is more freedom.

But what about lawyers who represent clients who do not wish to engage in moral conversation and are unwilling to risk moral change and growth? How does Shaffer's model work with them? What about, in particular, criminal lawyers whose clients are frequently so repressed or angry or psychopathic that the suggestion of moral conversation with them seems ludicrous? And what about, in criminal cases, the constitutionally ordained duty of the lawyer to do everything he legally can to keep his client from being convicted regardless of the immorality of the crime? As anyone who practices criminal law knows, criminal cases present a very different set of ethical problems for lawyers. And the more open and sometimes aspirational goals of the attorney-client relationship in civil cases often do not apply well in a criminal law setting.

I suggest that an extended version of Fried's model may be more appropriate for criminal cases than Shaffer's. A good criminal lawyer may be a criminal client's "special purpose friend" at a time when, quite often, no other friends are available. But the "special purpose" served by the criminal lawyer contains a moral purpose beyond that posited by Fried: merely winning for one's client, in whatever form that takes. The "special purpose" of the criminal lawyer is to give of himself to his client, to guide his client through the criminal justice process as carefully and skillfully as possible, insuring that the client's rights are fully protected and that the client's opportunities for regaining personal autonomy and reconciliation with his community are fully explored. This may mean "beating the case," and it may not. What it means will depend on the context of each case and the question of whether any form of moral conversation is possible between the lawyer and his client. (And by "moral conversation" here, I mean "conversation" in its broadest sense: conversation by words and conversation by example and simply through relationship.) At a minimum, though, the lawyer's moral service to his client means that the lawyer will himself have a vision of the moral possibilities for his clients and his work and will stand by his clients to see that those possibilities are fulfilled to the highest degree possible.

In most criminal cases, the client will see only the opportunity for freedom from the charges he faces and could care less about moral change and growth. This should not mean, however, that in the cases where some sort of moral reflection is possible, it should not occur. And the criminal lawyer is in a position to see that that can happen. But even in the hardest cases where the client is the most unreachable, the criminal lawyer may provide a model of moral friendship that in itself provides a form of moral conversation. That model should include loyalty to client, integrity in task, moral vision and openness to moral reflection, and the capacity to find something in one's client that inspires one's compassion. This is not easy in an area of the profession where lawyers are grossly overworked and clients are often themselves hateful people. But it can be done. Three of the leading criminal lawyers North Carolina have this to say about their work:

> Think about what I do, the kind of work I do. More sad and hurt
> people come through my life in a year than come through the life

of a minister. . . . So over and over, I'll bet if you took all the people we've dealt with in thirty years, and you take all the people most any minister . . . has dealt with in thirty years, and you . . . go interview the people we represent, and go interview the people the minister has worked with, and then you go see the people affected by those works, and the ripples that came from that, . . . you would see that we are like ministers. We do the same. . . . We make good things happen. The difference is that ministers . . . deal with the reconciliation of human beings with God. We deal with the reconciliation of human beings with each other, with their families and their loved ones, with their communities, with their governments. . . . What we are doing in this profession is we're making the world better. We're making people feel better. That means, for me, it's a dignified, wonderful profession that we should feel good about.[47]

I've practiced law for forty-three years, . . . and I have seen very few criminal defendants whom I would say were basically mean and vicious people. Very few. The great majority, even those involved in serious crimes, are people who are misguided, who get in emotional jams or other type jams beyond their control. I've seen very few really vicious, mean people, although I have seen some. . . . But by and large, they're just ordinary people who are caught up in emotional crises and they get out of control. . . .

Some of the clients I haven't liked. Most of them I have liked. I found something likeable in almost all of them.[48]

Well, I've represented lots of people who I knew were guilty. I represented lots of people who I thought were frightening, mean, and had done terrible things. I've got a friend down in Charlotte, who's a great trial lawyer, named Jim Cooney, and Jim says every client, no matter who it is, there's something about them you can put your arms around. And so that's the way I look at it. No matter who the person is, there has always been something that I can put my arms around. So, I've really not been in a position of representing someone and hoping that they lost. I've never felt that way. I've always wanted to win and felt like it was the right thing for them to win.[49]

These are criminal law examples of Shaffer's ethic of care. The lawyers speaking are criminal lawyers who care about their clients because they recognize a common humanity with them. That capacity to perceive humanness under layers of social and psychological malfunction permits them to treat their clients as fellow human beings with a moral as well as a legal dimension. Thus the work of these lawyers becomes more than winning or losing cases. Their vision of their work contains the possibility of moral connection and attendant moral responsibility. And with those elements comes the blessing of moral purpose.

LINKING THE TWO LEVELS OF IDEALS:
PERCEIVING PERSONAL DIVINITY

A complete picture of the ideal for lawyers involves a composite of the two levels of ideals discussed above. The truly idealistic lawyer will see herself as both a special friend of her client and a servant of the greater community. In some cases this will be a relatively easy rational deduction: a lawyer who represents people in a neighborhood suffering from the health affects of a toxic waste dump can easily extrapolate service for her clients into service for the community, and further, to service for the country as a whole where important precedent is set for legal work in behalf of other victims of toxic waste. Robert McMillan of Raleigh, North Carolina (one of the lawyers quoted above on the humanity in criminal clients), links service to his criminal clients with service to the community because by representing his clients well, he protects basic rights for all of us. His work for his client is related to his vision of the common good:

> I feel a high sense of calling when asked to defend an accused. It is my belief that Christ speaks to us when we stand with one who is alone and afraid. I know that we are doing God's will when we demand due process under the law. I know that without the efforts of criminal lawyers, mistaken convictions, as the one reported in Orange County recently, would be commonplace. I know that without the efforts of criminal lawyers, Governor Martin would not have spared the life of Anson Maynard recently. I know without the efforts of criminal lawyers, we would have a most efficient criminal justice system which ignores the Magna Carta, which ignores common law, which ignores the Bill of Rights, and which bans Bibles, burns witches, and hangs heretics. So that's my position, and that's my belief. I'm not just, as they say, "whistling Dixie" when I say that.[50]

Robert McMillan has successfully linked the morality of service to clients with his role as lawyer-statesman and pillar of the community. But what about the harder cases? What about lawyers who represent clients whose legal goals seem detrimental to the community? In those cases, reasoned efforts to define a moral purpose that encompasses both service to client and service to community—efforts such as Charles Fried's—almost always fail (a failure which frequently leads to cynicism by and against lawyers). The reason they fail is that, as a rational matter, it is difficult to reconcile propositions which seem to be in direct conflict. If there is to be a morally idealistic linkage between a lawyer's service to her client and service to the greater community—a linkage which has any degree of universality for lawyers—it must be on a more emotional level. Now, I realize there is danger in this assertion, but bear with me for a moment.

When Robert McMillan tells us, as he does in the above quotation, that he is doing God's work when he "stands with one who is alone and afraid" and "demands due process under law," he is not just, as he says, "whistling Dixie." He is connecting his work to "something greater than himself," which for him is divinely inspired. And his statement, though humble in a traditionally Christian way, is also an unabashed declaration of his own divinity in the limited way humans can try to claim divinity. Basically, Robert McMillan sees his work as a ministry—a ministry to his client and to his country. He sees himself as the servant of that ministry, and he finds great dignity in that service. He speaks to us from emotional, inspirational conviction, not trying to persuade us of the moral basis for his work from a rational standpoint, but by testifying for it. He is telling us the story of who he is and who he perceives himself (and other criminal lawyers) to be. These are hard-earned, reflective assessments—assessments which come through honestly facing one's own motives and shortcomings, accepting one's place in the greater context of society, and evaluating one's work against one's vision of a common good. They are not cheap rationalizations. They represent an act of faith and an emotionally and deeply held belief which, for Robert McMillan, is stronger than any rational syllogism.

It is this kind of emotional conviction that nurtures an internal and external ideal—an ideal that sustains lawyers through the long quest of a professional career. It may not be for everybody, and it may be much more difficult for lawyers engaged in an arduous and time-demanding civil practice than it is for Robert McMillan. How does a lawyer who is billing 2,500 hours a year for corporate clients he never sees and over whose objectives he has no say develop either an internal or external ideal for what he is doing? For me, I will admit, that would be impossible, though exceptional members of the bar appear to do it. But as expectations in large law firms continue to rise and work becomes more impersonal, it will certainly become more and more difficult. Tom Shaffer has suggested that lawyers serving primarily corporate business clients may be emerging as part of a new managerial class more united with the managers they serve that with any notion of professionalism.[51] Professor David Wilkins has raised the prospect of different categories within the "profession" for lawyers engaged in different types of work which impose different professional demands.[52]

While I am not yet willing to concede that corporate lawyers in elite firms are a distinct class with either different or reduced professional inclinations and obligations, it is hard to envision a professional life which is not consciously devoted, both personally and professionally, to public good. At the very least, I believe, with Milner Ball and Robert Gordon, that a lawyer must maintain enough independence from clients and their power to "serve the higher purposes of law,"[53] and that "a part of a lawyer's professional persona must be *set aside* for dedication to public purposes" (emphasis added).[54] Taken to its logical extreme, rather than uniting the two levels of service we have discussed, this rather minimalist approach allows them to remain separate and allows the individual lawyer to view only one of the levels as public service. There is great danger in that separation for the professional soul. It will take exceptional people to manage that kind of life, and I, for one, could not do it. I also believe it is not necessary, because by realigning their priorities, even large corporate firms can make space for lawyer-members to pursue professional lives devoted to something greater than themselves (see chap. 13). And there is plenty of pro bono work to go around for lawyers who wish to find a way to serve justice outside the routines of their basic practice. In the meantime, the profession cannot continue to call itself a profession when a large number of its most prominent and gifted members lead lives devoid of a professional ideal. Unless that changes, some version of what Professors Shaffer and Wilkins envision may formally come to pass if the profession is to survive as a profession. Reclaiming the profession will be hard enough if everyone pitches in to achieve it. It will be impossible if a large portion of its most powerful and prestigious contingent does not participate.

12

Pursuing the Lawyers' Faith: Reconvening the Campfire, Creating Storytelling Models for a Broader Ideal of Justice

Like the formation of moral consensus, formation of ideals is difficult in a complex society. The ideals tend to be complex as well. Their purity dissipates. They are harder to see, harder to imagine, harder to feel. People tend to either give up on them or to revert to a simpler version which suits individual needs and tastes. The legal profession faces a daunting task in constructing and serving an ideal of justice in a society as complex as ours. Even within the community of the profession itself, it will be difficult. And while it may help to pass ethical rules to assist in that process (rules such as those requiring lawyers to devote time to pro bono work for the poor), the profession will not establish an ideal of service to justice by simply passing rules to micro-manage lawyer behavior. The problems of profession-building are deeper and broader than that. They are not left-brain problems, and they will not yield to the profession's standard, left-brain solutions.

The young Parcival learns early in his life-journey the hard lesson that ideals are more than image and status. He is dazzled by the image of the glorious knights as they ride past his woodland home. He wants to be like them, so he follows them to Arthur's court, where he assumes all he will have to do is join them. There he finds that becoming a knight is not quite that simple. First he must prove himself worthy, which he does by fighting and defeating the Red Knight, the mythical equivalent of finishing law school and taking the bar exam. Next he must appear before King Arthur and be sworn into the company of the Round Table. He has the accouterments of a knight, having taken the defeated Red Knight's armor and horse. Now, under oath and in the saddle, he can call himself a knight of the Round Table. Parcival has entered a noble profession, and he has done so as unwittingly as many law students today enter the profession of the law. He soon learns that with his new image and status come huge responsibilities—responsibilities for which he is ill-prepared. Being a knight means proving himself further, stepping up to "a higher, more differentiated form of the warrior," where he is expected to behave as a "nobler and more disciplined human being."[1] He is expected not only to be highly skilled in the work of knights (defeating evil and defending good) but to be a noble practitioner of the knightly virtues of courage, loyalty, and humility. And above all, he is expected to pursue for a lifetime the knightly ideal—becoming the perfect knight, who is aware of himself and his imperfections and conscious of his duty toward others and toward the greater community. Of course Parcival cannot perceive this ideal when he begins his quest. He is not conscious enough to do so. But as a member of a community of knights, he can perceive the symbol of it—the grail—and, with the support of his fellow knights, he will have sufficient faith in the worthiness of the ideal to set off in quest of it. That community-based faith will sustain him through years of hardship, failure, and practice until he finally understands that the ideal exists on earth only insofar as he (and other people) are the embodiment of it; until he understands, as some would say, his own divinity; until he knows that the grail and the questing soul are one.

For the questing lawyer, this presents another "chicken and egg" situation, and it raises a number of very important questions: First, do we have to live out our professional lives before we find what our professional ideal is? The answer to that is "no, but": no we don't have to live our entire lives before we *perceive* our professional ideal any more than Parcival had to live his life before he *perceived* the grail, but we will only come to understand the full meaning of that ideal by living it and practicing it. How do we begin to perceive it, then? How do lawyers begin to perceive a notion of justice which is broad and deep enough to serve our complex society? And, perhaps more importantly, what will sustain the lawyer through the long quest for that difficult ideal?

The answers to these questions lie in three aspects of professionalism which we have already visited in one form or another: community, faith, and practice. These are not separate aspects of professionalism; they work together and supplement each other. We need to practice justice in order to perceive the ideal, build community, and sustain the faith. We need community to practice justice and support faith in the ideal. We need faith in a common and worthy ideal in order to build community and to endure the hard work of practice.

We have discussed the lawyers' faith and the ideal of justice in the preceding chapter. I would like to focus now upon the roles of community and practice (particularly the narrative aspect of practice) in the lawyer's pursuit of the professional ideal. Turning first to community, how will lawyers reform their professional community in order to pursue the broader ideal of justice, and to what additional communities should lawyers look in search of the lawyers' faith? There are numerous structural and consciousness-raising steps which bars can take to strengthen professional community, and I will discuss those in more detail in the final chapter. For the present, I would like to examine the function of community in profession-building and the types of community necessary to support lawyers' practice of lawyers' faith.

The one axiom on which most social philosophers seem to agree is that the larger and more diverse (and dispersed) the community, the less functional it tends to be as a community. Thus, on the level of the national society, commentators such as Robert Putnam and the authors of *Habits of the Heart* see community in decline in America, and philosophers such as Alasdair MacIntyre see public discourse in our pluralistic society as divisive and anti-communitarian. In a modern world in which impersonal methods of communication are increasing in speed and availability and individual mobility is vastly easier than only a decade ago, communities are expanding and dispersing rather than shrinking. The advocates of community-building thus face a very difficult problem. The only answer, other than some sort of diluted redefinition of community, is to seek community on a more localized or coherent level, on what Alasdair MacIntyre calls the "small scale."[2] On that level, communities may practice moral discourse, may achieve some degree of moral coherence, may reach an effective level of moral consensus. They may still serve the essential purpose of community—particularly in the professional setting: they may serve, as Tom Shaffer has noted, as "communities of moral discernment,"[3] which support individual members as they reflect on moral issues and grope for moral consciousness. If the profession, as a whole, wishes to reclaim itself as a moral community, it must be supported by functioning smaller communities of lawyers where the lawyers' faith can be practiced, where stories can be told, where a mythology of greater purpose is formed and nurtured.

Shaffer suggests five possibilities for such communities in the lawyer's life: the civil community (the lawyer's town or city, and one assumes, the smaller the town, the more opportunity there might be for effective community); the accessible members of the bar (local and state bar

associations and lawyers with whom one communicates in everyday practice); other lawyers in one's firm (and, again, the smaller the firm—over
a minimal number—the more opportunity for effective community; also,
in "firms" where the practice itself has a more coherent, moral focus—
legal aid offices and public defender offices are examples—there tends
to be more opportunity for natural communities to form); the lawyer's
clients (if the lawyer effectively practices moral discourse with her clients
in her practice); and communities of religious faith to which a lawyer
may belong. We have seen, in one form or another, examples of lawyers
working in these communities in the old stories we have examined. We
have also seen how the adherence of these communities and their effect
upon the lawyer's life has dissipated under the compulsions of modern life
and modern practice. In order for lawyers to rebuild their profession into
an effective moral community, they must find a way to restore effective
community in their lives. They must find communities to which they can
go to practice moral reflection and, together with other members of the
community, moral discernment. They must find communities which are
open to the narrative process as a way of envisioning ideals and measuring
the lawyer's life.

I urge lawyers to begin to direct their organizational thinking to the
question of what size and make-up of groups and subgroups best promote
communities of moral discernment. What is the optimum size of a law firm
in order for it to promote the moral growth of its members? What should
the firm's members have in common? How should they be different?
What is the optimum size of a department within a firm in order for
it to practice moral discernment? What sort of formal and informal
communication would assist that sort of practice? When would it be
advisable to form a group of lawyers from different firms or different areas
of practice? When groups, within firms or otherwise, are identified and
established, what should link them to the larger community of lawyers?
How can the practice of moral discernment be part of the culture of the
greater profession?

Many lawyers I know now are members of firms and departments
within firms which meet periodically—weekly in some cases—to discuss
ethical issues which are plaguing one or more of the lawyers in the firm.
This is a start. But, having taught legal ethics to law students and lawyers
for over ten years, I know the danger when lawyers gather to discuss any
issue with legal overtones: frequently the discussion focuses only upon
the legal issue and legal solutions. In order for such meetings to support
effective moral discourse, they must be meetings of the heart as well as the

head. They must be open to deeper moral concerns of lawyers as human beings. And above all, they must be directed toward a greater purpose of a life in the law, toward individual growth to consciousness and perception of that greater purpose. This means that the professional life as a whole must be important to community members. They must be morally invested in their own life stories and understand how the life story of each of them affects the others and contributes to a professional ideal and a coherent moral community. The lives of the community members and the life of the community itself must be seen as inextricably entwined. This is what we mean by a truly effective moral community.

We have seen glimpses of such communities among lawyers in the stories from the past, particularly in our discussion of the failure of community in chapter 6: the judge's lament over loss of moral consensus; the Raleigh, North Carolina lawyer's account of the local bar when he practiced in the period after World War II (when, "all of the lawyers knew each other well, and you spent time talking with each other . . . [where] there was . . . a very high element of trust between lawyers"); the Charlotte, North Carolina lawyer's description of Saturday mornings at the office where lawyers visited with each other to discuss problems and where work breaks were taken to "sit and argue politics and religion, whatever was on our minds." Two small-town lawyers interviewed by the UNC Law School Oral History Project, D. J. Walker of Graham, North Carolina, and Judge Sam Ervin III, of Morganton, described the courthouse communities in which they began their practices.[4] Everyone— lawyers, judges, clerks, registers of deeds—knew each other intimately and were invested in each other's lives. Many of them were kin or related by marriage. Many of them were second or third generation members of the legal community. Young lawyers were taught both the ethics of practice and the ethics of community membership by their elders in the community—by both lawyers and lay elders—and they watched as their elders practiced those ethics and heard them tell the stories of the community ideals.

Some of this atmosphere still exists among bar members in smaller North Carolina towns, but as communities grow and become more fluid it will be more difficult to maintain. When I practiced law in Charlotte, North Carolina, fifteen years ago, I could leave my office and walk up the street to the Equity Building Snack Bar, find a table of familiar lawyers eating lunch, sit down and be assured of at least an hour of intense conversation on subjects ranging from the behavior of certain judges and lawyers, to the ethics of taking a default judgment against an unrepresented party, to the theological basis of infant baptism. These sessions varied in tolerance for moral and personal subjects, but when the right people were present, they were remarkably open. People felt, or should have felt, able to raise moral issues and receive moral guidance—sometimes much more than they bargained for. And underlying it all was a common understanding—loose, I will admit, from time-to-time—of a common moral purpose. We were doing the work of lawyers because ultimately it was good work and was essential to the welfare of society.

But the Equity Building Coffee shop is gone—bulldozed for a more modern office building. Lawyers lives are more rushed than they were fifteen years ago. Communities of moral discernment among lawyers are less likely to "happen." If they are to exist in the future, they must be planned and formally organized. And given the changed demography of the profession, they must include the different voices within the profession if they are to succeed in building a new ideal of justice and a new professional mythology. The community of the profession and the "smaller scale" communities which will form its day-to-day matrix will not succeed as effective communities unless they build a true moral consensus among the people who are in them, unless the process of community building is an inclusive effort which binds all individuals together under a mutually forged and mutually admired ideal.

It is the job of the individual lawyer to help build these communities. It is the job of the individual lawyer to recognize the old truth understood by the civic republicans: for the individual to practice virtue, he must do so in relation to a community which nourishes that practice and flourishes because of it. The practice of professional ideals is more than believing in them. It means living them in one's work. It means taking the time to promote them, enhance them, reflect upon them, and mythologize them for future generations of lawyers. This sort of work can only be done in community. Therefore, lawyers need community to be professionals. They need community to perceive professional ideals, to have faith in them, and to bring them to life through practice. They need the stories of practice and of the lawyers' faith to build a mythology which will pass those ideals on to the profession of the future.

The narrative process is the way we honor ideals, revere the practice of those ideals, and create a professional mythology. It is a creative process which is accessible to everyone (given appropriate time and space). It is contextual and inclusive. It is not consciously directed or preordained and is, therefore, an ongoing enterprise, constantly open to further information, rejuvenation, and change. Further, narrative is a natural inclination:

that is, we will do it anyway; it's just a question of how constructively (and consciously) we will undertake it.

But if the old narratives of the profession which we have identified are not the answer (or, at least not all of it), what sort of stories should we look for in the legal profession to rebuild our mythology? This is not an easy question. And it is difficult and in fact self-defeating to try to project or plan what is basically a creative process. There are, however, a few guidelines which may help us free ourselves to be as truly creative as we need to be. I hope the following suggestions will be taken as liberating rather than directive.

First, it is important that we attempt to tell true stories about the profession and about the ideal of justice. By this I do not mean *factually* correct as in courtroom testimony, but stories that are not false about the realities of the past or present or about hopes for the future. We need to face the truth about our profession's treatment of women and racial minorities and its current failure to serve justice for all Americans. That is not to say that our new narratives should not be aspirational. But there is a difference between honest aspiration and deceptive fantasy. The ideal of the lawyer-statesman can be both, depending upon the reality of the context in which we view him and upon our honesty about who in fact he was and what he represented to *all* people. The same is true of the other, old ideals—the pillar of the community, the champion of people and causes, the paragon of virtue and rectitude, and the gentleman-lawyer. To effectively rebuild our community, our renewed ideals must derive from an honest understanding of our professional history and from the realities of modern day society, not from our impulse to see only what we want to see. Building ideals by ignoring history and the realities of the present will only lead to false ideals.

It will also be helpful in creating our new mythology to begin to tell complete stories about lawyers' lives. The stories we have seen in the past—the lawyer-statesman, pillar of the community, etc.—present one facet of a lawyer's life. The more complete myth—a myth like the Parcival myth—addresses a life in its entirety. Where the grail we seek is something as complex and elusive as social and legal justice for our society, it is ultimately the entire lives of questing lawyers which will illustrate the struggle for the ideal. Mythology gives us heros and triumphs, but it does not shirk the darker side of reality. Parcival fails over and over in his quest for the grail and his mission to save the kingdom. Even some of his triumphs over various foes and obstacles turn out to be false trails leading to hubris and ignorance of self and others, trails he must finally recognize as false—often painfully—and renegotiate before he can proceed on the path to true consciousness. And we must not forget the presence of the trickster archetype in our professional mythology. The trickster in some form will follow us into the future. He will be part of the story of the legal profession. Pretending he is not there will not help. It is obviously important to recognize the heroic potential in what we do, that we see, for example, the brilliant and courageous champion in Daniel Webster. But would it help us also to see that Webster was not always so heroic, that he had a dark side and that there were areas of his life in which he struggled and failed? Would this more complete story about Webster show us how heroism occurs in the broader context of one's life, and that heros are not demi-gods but people like us? Would it help us to see the ambition, doubt, and depression in Abraham Lincoln to fully appreciate what it meant for him to be a pillar of his community? These more complete myths are, I suggest, true hero myths. They show us men and women who perform heroically in their finest hours but are still men and women like the rest of us with the same problems, failings, and shortcomings. Only after reading or hearing the complete story are we able to understand and appreciate what true heroism is. Only then are we able to see the hero—or the potential for heroism—in our imperfect selves. It is such heroes who can help us understand the true meaning of justice.

The seminar which I taught at the University of North Carolina Law School, entitled The Oral Histories of Lawyers and Judges, showed me the value of life-stories about lawyers. In that seminar, students would research the life of a lawyer or judge, go into the field with a tape recorder and record, from the judge's or lawyer's own lips, the story of his or her life. Then the student would reflect on that story and try to find and present to the class the meaningful lessons which the story taught. Students who listened to the life-stories of leading members of the bar saw human beings, much like themselves, who had become heros and heroines in a very difficult profession. They had not become heros through some sort of magic, but by the hard work of preserving their own integrity and developing their own characters. The life stories also revealed a "human" side to the lawyers we interviewed. Listening to an older lawyer talk about her childhood can be a very moving experience which brings one much closer to the person talking. Judge Elreta Alexander Ralston, the first African-American woman to serve as a judge in North Carolina, told us a story from her earliest childhood. As my students and I heard that story from the student who interviewed Judge Ralston, we empathized with the judge and shared in her triumph as a heroine of the bar:

> The only thing I can remember about [my childhood in] Smithfield [North Carolina] is that I was in a carriage, and my mother was crying. She was pushing the carriage, and my sister—I was the youngest of three children— . . . little sister was at the rear at the . . . foot of the carriage. And my brother was holding onto the arm of the carriage. And mother was crying. I can remember this. I was a mere infant.
>
> They always said I couldn't remember it until I had a case down there. . . . And I told Dad—Dad was living then—I was going to show him the house I was born in in Smithfield. And . . . I remember that railroad, she was pushing the carriage across the railroad track, across the track in the street. And I remember it. . . . I'd never been back until I was fifty years of age. And Daddy was riding with me, and I had a person drive me. We went down into town, and we presumed to turn left. I could see it all just as if it was just happening. After we got to a certain corner, I said, "Go across that track. That's where Mother was pushing the baby carriage." And I was lying there. I was a baby, just a few months old. . . . Mother was crying, and I remember her crying. And I said, "Two more blocks." And I said, "Turn left there." And I said, "Dad, that's the house I was born in right there." There was a horse grazing in the yard that day that we went there before I went on to the courthouse. . . .
>
> And I know what happened now. They interpreted it for me as I grew older. . . . What it was, my father had purchased that house. He hadn't had the title searched. And it turned out to be somebody else's, and he couldn't pay them off, and we lost the house. And that's what she was crying about.
>
> But it affected me. . . . And later, of course my first husband, who was a surgeon . . . , said children are affected when they're in their mother's womb by what goes on around them. . . . When you're in your mother's stomach, you're aware. . . . You're very much aware of the trauma.[5]

This story tells us a great deal about Elreta Ralston, the future lawyer, and it tells us a great deal about justice. We see her first experience with the law. We see how law affects children and families and the particular vulnerability of African-American families in the society in which they lived. We wonder if this experience spurred Ms. Ralston to study law at Columbia and return to North Carolina to practice. We ask if it is justice that the legal rights that cost Ms. Ralston's family their house were vindicated? Or, is justice something more? Later in Elreta Ralston's interview, we learn that when she attended Columbia Law School in 1943, she struggled under the knowledge—stated to her directly by the dean— that the admissions office would be watching her performance to determine whether other black women would be considered for admission. We learn the difficulties she had as a young, female, African-American attorney trying to establish a practice in the South in the first half of the last century. We understand the heroic nature of her life because we see how hard it was, that she nearly broke under the pressure of it from time to time, that she was able to find other lawyers and other people to help her along the way. This is a true heroine's journey, and she has emerged from it as a highly respected member of the profession and mentor to numerous women and black attorneys who came after her.

From the life story of Judge Dexter Brooks, a Lumbee Indian and the first Native American to become a Superior Court judge in North Carolina, we understand the obstacles he faced growing up in racially segregated Robeson County, North Carolina, a pluralistic society composed roughly of one-third whites, one-third African Americans, and one-third Native Americans. As a child, he was told that the professions were closed to Indians, and he saw that the only Native American who even tried to go to law school from his community had been denied admission by the University of North Carolina. From the life stories of Wade and Roger Smith, two of North Carolina's leading trial lawyers who grew up in relative poverty in rural North Carolina, we learn that heroism is often nurtured by other people. In their case it was nurtured by their parents, cotton mill workers, who devoted their lives to their children, and despite poverty and lack of education beyond high school, raised two sons who won UNC's most prestigious academic scholarships, were captains of the football team, and later clerked for one of North Carolina's leading Supreme Court justices.

Heros do not have to be leading statesmen like Daniel Webster or saviors of the Republic like Abraham Lincoln. Heros are people who live their lives honestly in dedicated pursuit of noble ideals. Everyone has the capacity to do that. Professionals have both the capacity and additionally the duty to follow the ideals of the profession. Stories which show us how to do that, which give us an account of a professional life well lived, of a life of integrity and moral growth through failures and hardships, are stories which can inspire heroism in all of us. These are the kinds of stories we should be telling each other and memorializing in law schools and among members of the bar.

This idea of telling complete stories of lawyers' lives as part of our mythology also more directly addresses some of the deep morale problems in our evolving professional culture. It addresses, for example, the recurrent problems almost all lawyers experience in balancing the demands and expectations of career with the needs of families and their own personal needs. One of the first questions I want to ask when I read about how successful a lawyer has been in a case or in his career is what the costs were. What were the costs to personal life, family, and friendships? What was neglected? What was "put on hold"? What was given up? How did he or she achieve what has been achieved and still take care of the basic, personal needs that make life worth living? Stories that do not deal with these questions are incomplete and often misleading stories. They provide images similar to Parcival's image of the knights passing his woodland home. They appear glorious and immensely attractive but tell us nothing of the deep, hidden costs of the life-long quest. Historically in the legal profession a lot of these costs were patiently (and sometimes not so patiently) borne by the spouses and children of successful lawyers. Now there is less inclination by the people around lawyers to bear these costs. And frequently, spouses of lawyers are themselves lawyers or are engaged in some other very demanding career. In a complete life story, the professional is not viewed only as a professional. She is viewed as a person with multiple roles to fill who, as a means of livelihood and job focus, chooses a professional career. To find heros among these "new" professionals, we will need to see more than professional accomplishments. We will want to know how they live as human beings.

It will also be very important in learning to tell our truthful and complete professional stories to open the structures of our dialogue beyond anything we have imagined before. By this I mean that traditional narrative models by which we have imagined and defined our roles in patriarchal social structures may no longer be adequate for a broader and more inclusive deliberation where the ideal in question is a broader and deeper understanding of justice. One example is the form of our traditional, professional story. It is largely masculine, developed and consecrated by a patriarchal profession with a very rights-oriented concept of justice. The stories we visited earlier of the lawyer-statesman, pillar of the community, champion of the people and causes, paragon of virtue and rectitude, and gentleman-lawyer are essentially variations of or based upon the archetypal story of the hero's journey. They posit a lone lawyer, guided by an ideal of honor, living a heroic—even a chivalric—career, doing good works along the way by vindicating basic rights and serving in other ways to save his community or society. The life journey is viewed as linear and essentially progressive, with the lawyer as questing knight leaving his band of noble brothers and venturing into the world to face opposing lawyers, uncooperative judges, and obstreperous parties— the evil knights, sorcerers, and dragons of the legal profession. At the end of each such foray lies the grail—a favorable verdict, an appeal well argued, a merger successfully completed, a job well done—and at the end of a life of such work lies the grail of a lifetime: status of senior lawyer, revered practitioner, honorable member of the bar—a life, as Holmes says, lived "greatly in the law."[6]

The metaphor of the heroic quest is particularly appropriate for a primarily masculine profession, as the law has traditionally been. But while the quest format has produced noble stories, it may not work mythologically for everyone, and it may not suffice for a more complex and inclusive ideal of justice. There is growing evidence that the traditional hero's journey does not provide a metaphor which speaks to the lives of many women. In a recent interview, novelist Lee Smith said of a raft trip she took with some female friends down the Mississippi River thirty years ago:

> Increasingly I'm seeing that the prototypical male heroic journey is unsatisfactory for women. . . . I thought about going around and talking to each woman who was on that raft [trip] and saying, "How did you envision your life at the time we went? What did you think that it would be like? How has it been?," with the obvious motif of the journey. And I thought that was real interesting, but when I thought about it myself, I realized that for *me,* the journey doesn't even work; the notion of the journey doesn't even work as a plot anymore in my writing. I can't go from point A to point B to point C as a way to think about my life. I can't think about it like that. It just doesn't work. I don't know how I think about it, but not as a journey.[7]

Other women have explained the inappropriateness of the quest myth for women in psychological terms:

> To argue, as many would do, that the hero's quest is only a metaphor for an inward, spiritual journey is not satisfactory: from a gynocentric perspective, which does not dichotomize between the two, [the journey] is necessarily both inward and actual; both bodily and spiritual. In contrast to the reductive, dualistic tendencies characteristic of androcentric theoretical structures, those inherent in gynocentric

thought are relational and holistic. Consequently, from a gynocentric perspective, this traditional quest of the hero cannot adequately fit the needs of a woman attempting to develop the selfhood appropriate to her sense of herself as a woman.[8]

What forms will new professional myths take when they do not follow the traditional quest format? What types of stories should we look for? It may well be that one key to envisioning a new profession for the twenty-first century is for lawyers—men and women—to begin to see their lives and work in a less linear mode and more open to change and *in*direction. Some scholars have suggested that the heroic journey itself can be reconceived as less linear or even as circular.[9] A modern literary example of such a heroine's journey, told in a nonlinear fashion, is Toni Morrison's novel, *Beloved*. Others have suggested that women will benefit from a different, female-oriented and "gynocentric" or "matrifocal" mythology altogether.[10]

Given the nature of myths, almost certainly all of the above will happen. Women lawyers will tell, and will have told about them, stories which fit many archetypes, and, as the profession becomes more open, perhaps men will as well. But the important point is that those stories have to be given room and acceptance as valid stories about lawyers and about the profession and must not be rejected because they do not fit the traditional archetype of the linear, male journey. The story of the hero's journey has validity as well, but it is no longer—if it ever was—the only story which explains the lives of lawyers.

It is frequently overlooked in the myth of the Fisher King and Parcival's quest for the grail, and I suspect in other "masculine" myths as well, that though the narrative appears at first blush to be linear, neither the external journey of the questing knight nor the internal journey of the questing soul is entirely so. Parcival repeatedly comes upon people and images which take him back to episodes in his journey which are in some manner incomplete. Indeed, the visit to the grail castle itself fits this model, as Parcival visits the castle fairly early in the narrative before he is conscious enough as a knight or as a person to know where he is or what tasks he should perform. He has to find the castle a second time, when the masculine and feminine aspects of his psyche are more in balance, before he can ask the crucial question and heal the ailing king. His journey, like most journeys of the soul, is, if not circular, certainly something of a spiral. On each revolution, Parcival's character achieves more balance and his soul achieves a higher level of moral consciousness, but he keeps going through essentially the same cycle. It is much like the message near the end of T. S. Eliot's *Four Quartets:*

> We shall not cease from exploration
> And the end of all our exploring
> Will be to arrive where we started
> And know the place for the first time.[11]

This is the process of increasing psychic consciousness, of growing as people, and of learning our roles as professionals. We cannot be expected to get it right the first time, but we can be expected to learn from and grow morally from our experience. Whether we conceive of this as being done linearly, circularly, in a spiral or holistically, or through some other yet unimagined model, it is the undertaking professionals must assume in order to be professionals. And the stories we tell ourselves about that undertaking, if they are to assume the healing properties of myths, must above all be stories of moral development. The new ideal of justice will require that. The new ideal of justice requires lawyers who, like Parcival, are willing to undertake the long quest toward deeper consciousness about themselves, their society, and their relation to their fellow man.

The Roles of Law Schools and the Bar in Conceiving a New Profession

LAW SCHOOLS

In order to restore ideals to the practice of law and rebuild the profession as a moral community, the legal academy must find ways to recontextualize its educational process. This does not mean abandoning the teaching and practice of rigorous legal analysis. Rather, it requires undertaking something far more difficult: continuing to teach rigorous legal analysis as well as other lawyerly skills, such as the emerging curricula in alternative dispute resolution, while making all of it morally relevant. Mary Rose O'Reilly, who has written an inspiring book on education for the twenty-first century which indicts much of the current pedagogy, says of the type of change needed:

> I will conclude by conceding that although hierarchical systems may not always be, of their very nature, depraved, I consider them to be on moral notice. And though consensual systems and the banal processing of insights around the feminist campfire often make me nervous and bored, I am willing to gnash my teeth a little for the sake of advancing consciousness. . . .
>
> If we take the long view, it seems apparent that the movement we call feminism is part of a much larger reorganizing process at work in human consciousness. The task is not to replace the male system with the female but to increase the range of humane problem solving strategies available to us all; to bring intuition into the critical process, for example, but not to exclude rational ordering; to articulate a reasonable closure but to allow within it an element of gentle tentativeness.[1]

In legal education, instituting this degree of change will involve the same process that is necessary to reconstitute the profession: development of a moral community that practices the ideals of the profession and that tells the stories which promote those ideals and which explain the moral purpose for lawyers. The first step toward making the legal academy operate as a moral community is for it to begin to perceive itself as a community that is part of the larger moral community of the profession. For many law faculties and faculty members, this will require a reorientation on the purpose of legal education. An essential purpose of legal education should be to teach the Holmesian skills of legal analysis and prediction. But it should also be to teach and practice professional ideals. Both law students and faculty should feel the presence of those ideals in the work of law school. At present, ideals receive intermittent attention in law school, and some aspects of legal education actually work to defeat ideals and the promotion of community.

The current scaled grading system in most law schools, which is based solely upon comparison to and competition with other students, is not a system designed to promote either community or the broader ideal of justice. It is a prime example of the hierarchical systems Mary Rose O'Reilly places on moral notice in the quotation above. It is entirely individual-focused and rights based. It is judgmental and exclusive rather than compassionate and inclusive. It is essentially designed to rank students in an important but limited area of legal skills (while ignoring other important indices of qualifications as a lawyer) for the convenience of firms who are in the job market. If it has a pedagogical purpose, it is only to spur students to study for grades in competition with their fellow students, a "benefit" which is lost on many students after the first year when they see where they stand in the class and give up on trying to rise any higher. The competitive grading system is a primary instrument separating students from faculty in law schools and separating students from other students. It is a central impediment to construction of an effective law school community.

Other impediments exist as well. The inaccessibility of faculty to students has long been a major problem in legal education, though it has broken down some recently through the efforts of younger faculty and motivated older faculty to make the law school experience more humane. There remain two very strong counterforces, however. One is the high faculty/student ratios in law schools, ratios which were once justified as well suited to the dominant methods of law school instruction: the lecture and the Socratic dialogue. Until these ratios change—and that will not happen without a very serious reevaluation of law school teaching methods—there is a limit to how much time students can expect for meaningful contact with faculty members. A second counterforce to accessibility of faculty is the attitude of many faculty members that they have little in common with students who are not on an academic track (as in other graduate schools) but are headed into the "real world" of law practice. Meeting with students becomes a burden rather than an opportunity for learning or for mentoring in professional values and culture. This attitude is a byproduct of the more basic posture of academic superiority toward the profession itself, a posture which in some cases reaches the level of disdain.

Aside from its use as a justification for high faculty/student ratios, reliance upon the lecture and Socratic dialogue as the primary methods of law school teaching serves to impede community in law school in another significant way. These teaching methods physically and emotionally separate students and teachers. Both of them place the professor at the front of the classroom, frequently on a different physical level from students, in a distant and sometimes adversarial posture. As a former beneficiary of the Socratic method, I readily admit its value as a teaching tool in legal analysis when it is used by someone who is skilled as a lawyer and a teacher. In the best hands it can work as a fine chisel with which the professor helps the student chip away the stone of a problem to reveal the lines of a true legal analysis. But, as almost everyone who has been in a law school classroom knows, in less skillful and caring hands it can be used more as a bludgeon against students. There is a slowly growing movement among law professors to investigate new methods of teaching which attempt to open the classroom and involve students more in the teaching and learning process.[2] But the resistance to such a movement is strong. The legal academy has traditionally viewed the Socratic method as superior to all other forms of teaching for law students, with the lecture method used as a fall-back technique to be employed when it is necessary to save time and cover material faster. Innovation and introduction of other methods are often resisted, almost to the point of contempt, particularly when the suggestions come across the campus from the Department of Education.

Making structural and substantive changes in law school grading policies and faculty/student contacts and opening teaching methods to allow more student participation will take time and a fundamental attitude shift among law school faculties. The good news is that some of this shift has begun to occur as law schools have developed clinical programs, instituted arbitration and mediation programs, developed cross-disciplinary training, and developed innovative approaches to teaching legal ethics and law and literature. For these "structural" changes to have meaning in the effort to restore the profession, they should be seen as part of a larger effort to reconnect legal training to the great professional ideals of public service. That can only be done by placing what we now call legal training—essentially learning to think like a lawyer—in contexts that make it purposefully relevant and something more than an end in itself, contexts that are emphatically present in the law school curriculum. It means taking the second step after Holmes's admonition to banish moral language from the *study* of law by bringing moral reasoning *back into* the study of law and doing so in a way that Holmes understood as part of his own professional outlook: the study of law may best be mastered by divorcing it from moral language, but it is relevant *only* in terms of its reference to a greater moral context.[3] And it means making discourse in the greater moral context, in a manner that gives purpose and definition to lawyers' work, a central part of legal education.

The pedagogical tools for accomplishing this curriculum revolution are currently being developed in the academy, and those are most often in the form of reintroduction of narrative into the educational process.[4] While these efforts have, in some settings, extended to traditional law school courses,[5] perhaps the most dramatic and widespread introduction has come though the clinical programs now in place at most law schools. Clinical education for lawyers essentially began in the 1940s and 50s as a method of teaching law through hands-on experience and providing legal services for the poor.[6] Clinics represented a very different approach to legal education from the formal and highly structured classroom experience. The cornerstone of that new approach—at least in the clinical programs which served real clients rather than teaching through simulation—was the reality of practice. And the essence of that reality was the stories brought to the clinical programs by real clients.

The most important lesson for clinical students to learn—and the most difficult for some of them—is that, unlike the traditional classroom, the focus in clinical education is no longer upon them and their mastery of the material for the course. The focus in clinical education is upon the needs of the client. It is the client's story which must be listened to, understood, researched, analyzed, and advocated. Student performance is measured by how well the student works for and with *someone else*. In addition, in many clinics, students are required to work together in teams to better serve clients, and frequently clinical students attend a clinical class as a group where they cooperate to address problems and exercises which arise in some of the real-life cases they are handling. This is essentially an inversion of the traditional, narcissistic approach to law school education, and it is no accident that in clinical settings one frequently finds the closest thing in law school to a real community among students.

Perhaps the most encouraging recent development in clinical education is the recognition that the real-life narratives generated in clinical case-work provide useful classroom teaching exercises. Whether that recognition is viewed as a part of the narrative movement in legal education or not, it is a very natural and highly effective method of bringing students face-to-face with real legal issues in a close-to-real-life context. Narratives from clinical work and from other sources are especially effective tools for teaching professional responsibility and addressing issues of professionalism, and an increasing number of law schools have engaged in innovative efforts to perfect ways to do this, including team problem-solving and simulated law offices.[7] These efforts, which include use of narratives and case-studies from various sources and which are sometimes presented in the form of simulations, have now spread beyond the relatively small populations of clinical students to reach nonclinical students as well and are in some places being employed as early as the first year.[8] The prospect of a continuation of this trend is encouraging indeed.

Two of the most effective ways I have found for contextualizing legal education are the seminar I have described in preceding chapters, called the Oral Histories of Lawyers and Judges, and a mentoring program where students from a class in professional responsibility were matched with lawyers and judges in an intense year-long mentoring experience.[9] In the seminar, students selected a lawyer or judge as a subject to interview, researched the life of that person, and then went "into the field" (homes, courthouse, and law offices) of their subjects and recorded their life stories. Students brought these stories back to the seminar in the form of oral presentations and seminar papers which reflected on the professional life the student had studied and upon how that life informed his/her own life story. In the mentoring program, which was part of a class in professional responsibility, students were matched with a lawyer or judge as their mentor, attended a law-school-sponsored weekend workshop on the profession with their mentors, and spent the remainder of the academic year meeting with their mentors and visiting their mentors at work. In both the seminar and mentoring experience, students were exposed to the moral contexts of professional work through examples and stories of real people who have led lives of both triumph and error in the law. This contact presents an opportunity for "deep" learning, reflection upon one's life and purpose, and practical advice about practicing law, professionalism, and ethical responsibility. The effect upon students was to reassure and inspire them and open their eyes to their chosen profession.

Trying innovative courses and techniques in law school teaching is hard work and emotionally draining, but the rewards can be tremendous. At the first meeting of the oral history seminar in which a student made his oral report on his interview subject, I sat nervously waiting to see how it would go and how the other students in the class would respond to it. I had never tried to teach such a course before, and while I believed in the idea behind it, I did not know how my students, who had spent two years in more traditional law school courses, would relate to the real-life lawyer stories they were uncovering. The student making his report had interviewed Robert McMillan, the renowned criminal lawyer from Raleigh. He gave an inspired report. He had clearly been deeply affected by McMillan's devotion to his work and reverence for his professional calling and impressed by McMillan's unabashed pride in his status as a lawyer and member of an honorable profession. When the report ended, there was a profound silence in the seminar room. I was so pleased with what I had heard that I was afraid to say anything which might detract from the effect of it. But we couldn't sit there silently forever, and I was in charge. I was preparing to say something to begin a discussion when another student suddenly began to talk about her interview, and how inspiring it had been for her. The attorney she interviewed, she told us, had said that lawyers were the most honest and honorable people he knew, and he was proud to be a member of the legal profession. And then other students began to speak of moments in their interviews where the lawyer or judge in question had revealed pride in the profession or dedication to his work or a vision of professional service. I had never heard anyone talk about such things in law school other than the occasional guest lecturer or in isolated conversation, and from the effect the interviews were having on the students, it was clear that they had not either. Suddenly they felt connected to professional ideals. They had met people who believed in those ideals and who practiced them, who tried to be good lawyers and sometimes failed and admitted it. There was hope for the soul in what they were hearing. There was a purpose beyond making grades, finding a job, passing the bar, and paying off law school loans.

Recent legal educators have talked about "disorienting moments" in classrooms which present opportunities for teaching and learning—"when the learner confronts an experience that is disorienting or even disturbing because the experience cannot be easily explained by reference the learner's prior understanding."[10] The responses of my students to their contacts with lawyers in the oral history seminar and in the mentoring program at UNC Law School indicate that student experiences in those settings were *re*orienting. They brought students *back* into the larger context of their lives and required them to address basic value questions about what kind of life they wanted to lead as a professional and what a well-lived professional life might look like. Those are the questions which must be dealt with before students can be expected to understand and accept the ethical and moral responsibilities of a professional.

Other teachers of law have achieved some of these effects through courses in law and literature, which have gained stature recently as second and third year elective courses.[11] The law and literature course at UNC Law School, taught by Professor Patricia Bryan, raises tough issues of ethics and professionalism and takes a hard look at images of lawyers and other professionals in such works as Herman Melville's *Billy Budd,* Leo Tolstoy's "The Death of Ivan Ilyich," and Kazuo Ishiguro's *Remains of the Day.*[12] Professor Mark Weisberg at Queens University Law School in Kingston, Ontario, has developed particularly effective, pioneering law school courses which draw upon literary sources. One of those courses is co-taught to law, medicine, and nursing students by Professor Weisberg and a member of the medical faculty.[13] There, not only are law students required to reflect upon their own responses to ethical problems, but they see those responses in comparison to ethical responses of other profes- sionals. It is unfortunately true that law and literature courses have been frequently viewed as "soft" courses by more traditional law professors and are currently most often elective courses or seminars in the second or third year of law school. But as part of the new emphasis upon narratives as teaching tools for law school classrooms, they represent another step toward bringing more context into courses in the "core" curriculum.

The following story, offered in contrast to the description of the first- year torts class I described in chapter 2 of this book, is an example of how the integration of more context into core curriculum courses might work: The scene is a classroom in a law school in the first quarter of the twenty- first century. The twenty students are seated at tables arranged in a circle, and the professor sits in the circle with the students. This group is the "context component" of a much larger torts class that has met during the first part of the year under a more traditional lecture/Socratic format in which students were taught the substance of tort law and *guided* (instead of embarrassed or frightened) in learning legal reasoning and analysis. At least one wall of the classroom is composed of large windows which can be opened to let in air and sounds from the outside. There are five guests in the room also seated at the table: two lawyers, a judge, and two lay people. They were all participants in a complex legal action that has been completed and which the class has studied through various out-of-class assignments since the beginning of the semester. Students from the class have researched the law in the case, interviewed these participants and others involved in the case, and have in the last few weeks made oral and written reports to the class on their findings. The class has examined the conditions that lead to the filing of the complaint; the economic and policy decisions that lead to those conditions; the actions of the lawyers in investigating the case; their actions in attempting to negotiate, prepare for trial and, finally, to litigate; the actions of the judge during the entire court process; the results of the trial and the positions of the parties after the trial. The class has questioned the actions of the lawyers and judge particularly as to motive, purpose, and result.

Now the class will hear in person from these participants and ask them questions about the case, their roles in it, and its effects upon them. The breadth of their inquiry will be open and inclusive. The student questioners will ask specifically about the context of the legal action and the conditions leading up to it. They will examine whether and in what manner race or gender affected the parties, their treatment in the system, or the outcome. The class will try to measure not only the legal results of the case but the emotional costs as well. Class members will ask questions about the purpose and effect of the legal action in terms of public policy, and look for the principles of justice and fairness in the case and determine how well those principles were honored. They will examine particularly the lawyers' and judges' roles—not only in that case but in the greater contexts of the justice system and the political structure. They will study the ethics of the participants and their professional behavior and analyze the nature and parameters of the lawyer-client relationships. And they will examine the human dimension—the effects on the participants in terms of emotional costs and opportunity for moral insight and growth, and the effects on the participants' families and personal lives.

The a priori assumption underlying this study will be the desirability of community, including the greater community outside the windows of the classroom, the community of the legal profession, and the community of the class itself. The need to build effective community and the roles of the case participants in the effort to fill that need will provide the standards by which the actions of the participants in the case are understood and ultimately assessed. That assessment will include questions about how and to what degree justice was achieved and about public good and common good. Part of the work of the class will be to develop the skills of listening, speaking, and reflecting necessary to discuss those difficult questions. In this very complicated undertaking, many of the answers students find will be based upon subjective judgments. But it is the process of finding those answers in a morally serious and reflective way, gently guided by their teacher, that counts. And the class's study of the case and the conduct of the class itself will be presented as an exercise in community-building and civic responsibility, including the profession's responsibility to the greater society and the professional obligation of each lawyer to the education and edification of all fellow-members of the profession.

At the end of this course, if the students do their work thoroughly and are competently lead by their teacher, they will have a relatively complete story of an important legal case and the people in it. They will have exercised their new-found skills of legal reasoning and analysis, but will have done so in a context that demands that the exercise of those skills be related to greater questions of justice, morality, and the lawyer's role in society. Each of them should then be competent to write a comprehensive, analytical paper that critiques the quality of the legal work and the outcome of the case in terms of overall social purpose. Each of them will also write three short papers: one from the standpoint of the average citizen which critiques the lawyers' roles and the ideals of justice as they manifest in the case; one from the lawyers' standpoints defending their actions on the same basis; and one fictional account of themselves as an operative lawyer or judge in the case, explaining how they would have dealt with various tactical and ethical issues and how that would affect their growth as a person and a professional.

The use of a fictional account here is important. It calls upon students to exercise the right side of their brain (as well as their left) in dealing with ethical problems. It encourages them to *envision* and *imagine* themselves in the role of lawyers dealing with real problems and finding solutions which square with an ideal image of themselves and their work. The noted short story writer, Flannery O'Connor, has said:

> The beginning of human knowledge is through the senses, and the fiction writer begins where human perception begins. He appeals through the senses, and you cannot appeal to the senses with abstractions. It is a good deal easier for most people to state an abstract ideal than to describe and thus re-create some object that they actually see. But the world of the fiction writer is full of matter, and this is what the beginning fiction writers are very loath to create. They are concerned primarily with unfleshed ideas and emotions. They are apt

> to be reformers and want to write because they are possessed not
> by a story but by the bare bones of some abstract notion. They are
> conscious of problems, not of people, of questions and issues, not of
> the texture of existence, of case histories and of everything that has
> a sociological smack, instead of with all those concrete details of life
> that make actual the mystery of our position on earth.[14]

Approaching ethical issues in a moral universe "full of matter" is the
only way to deal with those issues realistically. This is done in miniature
every time a law professor poses a hypothetical problem. But fiction adds
another dimension to reality. Through it students can be asked to imagine
themselves in a material context and, further, to imagine themselves
acting in that context in an idealistic way. It causes students to project
themselves into their own future and to begin to conceive a heroical
image of themselves. This gets very close to mythmaking on a personal
level and is a process which should be endemic to a professional life. For
lawyers, that process should begin in law school and continue for the rest
of their lives.

And law professors should not be exempt from this process. In fact, the
professor in the class described above will be competent to lead it and to
read and grade student papers if, and only if, above all she views herself
as a professional and fellow pilgrim on the personal and professional
myth-way. The notion that law professors (and law schools) are somehow
exempt from the process of inculcating professionalism because they
are engaged in more lofty and arcane pursuits is an attitude the legal
profession can no longer afford (if it ever could). A professional school
should be staffed by people who think of themselves as professionals with
perhaps an even greater obligation than practicing lawyers to pass on the
professional creed.

The Bar

We have discussed in chapter 6 how the current realities of practice
inhibit the development and maintenance of professional community,
particularly through the elimination of time and space for mythmaking.
An obvious solution is for law firms to create more of such time and space,
and the typical response to that suggestion is that for "economic reasons"
it cannot be done. A recent report of the Professionalism Committee of
the ABA Section of Legal Education and Admission to the Bar suggests
that it should be done,[15] and, in fact, it can be. The economic reasons cited
are, in most cases, nothing more that the greed referred to by the retired
judge interviewed in my oral history seminar. Law firms allow reduced

work loads for all sorts of reasons: pregnancy, child care needs, leaves of absence, semi-retirement, political activities, pro bono and charitable activities, to name the more obvious. If law firms wish to make more time and space for mythmaking, they can do it, and some of them are. One outstanding example, uncovered by one of my oral history students, is the firm of Everett, Gaskins, Hancock & Stevens in Raleigh, North Carolina, a mid-sized firm which represents numerous corporate clients, including Raleigh's primary newspaper. According to the oral history of Ed Gaskins, one of the founding partners,[16] the firm sets a 1,400 hour-per-year target in billable hours for partners and associates. If a firm member exceeds more than 120–130 hours in a month, one or more senior partners will meet with that member to counsel with him in order to determine why. In addition, the office closes at noon on Fridays, and it is expected that absent some serious reason (such as a trial the following week), no one will work between noon on Friday and Monday morning. Clients, according to one member of the firm, find the idea of the firm closing at noon on Friday "refreshing."[17] Admittedly, for the present, such firms are rare exceptions, and it may be that larger firms which are wedded to the corporate track with its commensurate salaries and are competing with increasing intensity for clients will never be willing to adopt more open and less demanding work schedules. But these firms do not have to be the only model.* They do not have to be the only model even for large corporate firms. What I am proposing here is a change in the ethical and moral culture of practice and in the way lawyers and firms run their lives. This is a philosophical reorientation and requires a new (or *re*newed) understanding of the meaning of professionalism and of the lawyer's role as a catalyst in profession-building. Part of that role is the lawyer's service as a Gournemand, as a model of the professional ideal. In that role a lawyer can offer a vision of the ideal to which other lawyers can aspire. But Gournemands are also teachers, and in the teaching role they are also

---

*As noted in chapter 11, at least one legal scholar has suggested that, as the demand for a more humane work ethic grows, the profession may begin to divide into different groups which place different degrees of emphasis on billable hours and work quota requirements. See Wilkins, "Who Should Regulate Lawyers," and "How Should We Determine Who Should Regulate Lawyers?" (cf. chap. 11, n. 52). Such a division in the profession might lead to different ethical rules and standards for the separate parts and even different ideals of professionalism. While such a split, or even fragmentation, of the legal profession may eventually come to pass, I hope it will be resisted for as long as there is hope of reconstituting and maintaining a comprehensive legal community. A great profession should not solve its moral quandaries over image and standards by "bowing to the (economically) inevitable" but by persevering through it.

essential to the maintenance of the profession. Just as Gournemand taught Parcival the chivalric code and manners of a knight and drilled him in the skills of arms, Gournemands of the legal profession teach other lawyers fundamentals of professional skills and professional behavior. This is the archetypal role of the professional elder as keeper of the professional heritage. And just as there is a Parcival in each of us who needs to be taught, there must be Gournemand in each of us who has the obligation to teach other members of the community.

Part of the role of being a lawyer, then, should be the desire and obligation to teach other lawyers. That obligation is the intergenerational commitment to being a member of a profession. It implicitly assumes that we have a professional heritage which must be preserved and a professional future to which that heritage is essentially relevant. Without a professional commitment to teaching and serving as mentors to other lawyers, how will professional values be nurtured, critiqued, and passed on? And without professional values—vibrant and relevant professional values—how can we call ourselves a profession?

Once upon a time, professional mentoring of initiates by elders was the primary method by which initiates entered into professional status in the law.[18] Law schools did not exist in the United States prior to the middle of the nineteenth century. Even then, most lawyers followed Abe Lincoln's advice on the "cheapest, quickest and best way" to become a lawyer: "Read Blackstone's Commentaries, Chitty's Pleadings, Greenleaf's Evidence, Story's Equity and Story's Equity Pleading, get a license, and go to the practice and still keep reading."[19] Young men who wished to become lawyers read law in the offices of a member of the bar and were examined for admission to practice by a bar member or committee of two or more lawyers.* Some of this mentoring was excellent instruction. An example of such a mentor was the famous judge John L.

---

*Abraham Lincoln was a notoriously easy examiner for admission to the Illinois Bar. He would ask a few simple questions, tell a few stories, and certify the applicant's admission. One applicant described his examination by Lincoln in Lincoln's hotel room on the court circuit while Lincoln was padding about half-dressed, giving himself a bath: "As he continued his toilet, he entertained me with recollections—many of them characteristically vivid and racy—of his early practice and the various incidents and adventures that attended his start in the profession. The whole proceeding was so unusual and queer, if not grotesque, that I was at a loss to determine whether I was really being examined at all or not. After he had dressed, we went down-stairs and over to the clerk's office in the courthouse, where he wrote a few lines on a sheet of paper, and inclosing it in an envelope, directed me to report with it to Judge Logan, another member of the examining committee, at Springfield. The next day I went to Springfield, where I delivered the letter as directed. On reading it, Judge Logan smiled, and, much to my surprise, gave me the required certificate without asking a

Bailey, who served as teacher to numerous North Carolina lawyers in the days before law schools: "Nothing could equal the graciousness of the Judge's manner, nor the clearness with which the principles of law were enunciated. . . . The highest ideals were inculcated in his students, the utmost courtesy in handling a case, and a thorough study of the principles of law from the time of Coke and Littleton to the modern times."[20] And some of the instruction under this system was poor, as William Livingston of New York testified: "The Imputation of Injustice and Dishonesty [to lawyers] . . . is no more visible and notorious, than in their conduct towards their Apprentices. . . . I averr [sic] that it is a monstrous Absurdity to suppose, that the law is to be learnt by a perpetual copying of Precedents."[21] But what was most important was the assumed duty of bar members to instruct new attorneys and the expectation of young attorneys (occasionally, no doubt, unrealized) that their elders would be sure they learned the necessary skills and tenets of the profession. This active engagement in the intergenerational educational process *is* professionalism. When we talk about professionalism, we tend to engage the subject in terms of a set of values to which lawyers should adhere. These are important. But professionalism is primarily practice—the active practice of the skills, values, and moral standards of the profession and the veneration of them by teaching them and passing them on to others. And one of those values which must be taught and passed on is that of the commitment to teaching itself, an internalizing of the duty owed by each lawyer to the profession and to her fellow-lawyers. That is the essence of professionalism, and that is what is currently missing in the attitude of many members of the bar. As the young Parcival learned, professionalism is more than status; it is an internalized appreciation of the values of one's profession and the willing acceptance of the obligation to teach those values to other professionals.

So the first step for the bar in restoring professional ideals is to resurrect the individual obligation of bar members to educate initiates (and other members of the bar generally) in professional values and aspirations. And this should be a duty assumed by all members of the bar, regardless of age or professional experience, although, certainly age and experience may weigh heavily in the degree of help one member of the bar can give to another. This is a positive step which should appeal to most lawyers and

---

question beyond my age and residence, and the correct way of spelling my name. The note from Lincoln read: 'My dear Judge:—The bearer of this is a young man who thinks he can be a lawyer. Examine him, if you want to. I have done so, and am satisfied. He's a good deal smarter than he looks to be.'" Woldman, *Lincoln Lawyer,* 165.

which law firms should be able to identity and to provide time for if they are committed to being active supporters of professionalism. However, it will take a positive commitment, and bar leaders (and bars themselves) must be willing to devote energy and resources to programs that promote this kind of professional teaching. That may mean hiring state-wide mentoring coordinators to work with local bars, devising structured mentoring models for use by firms and local bars,* offering continuing education credit in ethics for mentoring activities, and encouraging firms to build in time for firm members to serve as both teachers and learners to other members of the bar.[22]

Some law firms have begun to implement mentoring programs for young associates. Arnold and Porter, for example, has begun a mentoring program which matches young associates with partners in their practice area who are *not* partners the associates work with on a daily basis. Mentoring couples are expected to meet for at least two hours a month, with the firm paying expenses for shared lunches, etc. The relationship is confidential and lasts for at least one year. Moore and Van Allen in Charlotte, North Carolina, relies on a team approach with partners assigned to advise both an associate and a paralegal on the culture of the firm and to act as a sounding board for concerns about work loads and employment status. Mentoring programs are increasingly being implemented as a way for firms to curtail the economic loss resulting from attorney work dissatisfaction and high turnover. The turn to mentoring among large firms has reached the proportion that consulting groups are beginning to market advice to law firms on how to implement mentoring programs.[23]

The obligation to mentor other lawyers should not be limited to other members of one's firm or even to particular individuals. Every member of the bar should feel an obligation to help any other member of the bar in need.† That may seem a strong statement to some, and this may seem even more so: In order to have an effective professional community, we need to develop a culture of mutual dependence and mutual obligation. This does not mean that whenever another lawyer in need calls on us, we should drop what we are doing and respond. But it should mean that when we know, for example (as statistics on bar ethical complaints

---

*Appendixes A and B provide comprehensive plans for a statewide mentoring of law students and young lawyers. These plans were developed by committees working under the sponsorship of the North Carolina Bar Association.

†The Inns of Court program, which is in place in numerous local bars throughout the country, is an excellent step toward reviving the mentoring tradition among lawyers. One wishes, however, that it was more widespread and that the mentoring aspect of the program was more structured and intense.

indicate), that solo practitioners have more trouble than most lawyers with issues of ethics and malpractice, we should feel an obligation to address that problem in a meaningful way. This might mean that the firm we belong to would devote a certain number of hours to helping solo practitioners in need of advice. Or, it might mean that our firm would "adopt" several beginning lawyers in solo practice to help them in finding their way in legal work and in the profession. It might mean that older, more experienced solo practitioners should extend a helping hand to younger, less experienced ones. It might mean that we would participate in activities in our local or state bar associations which are designing programs to deal with the problems of solo practitioners.

Assistance to other lawyers and to the profession can occur in ways other than what we now think of as mentoring. A serious problem in many state bars is the disaffection many African-American lawyers feel with the institutions within the bar, the established firms, and the bar itself. This kind of disaffection does not bode well for profession-building. The established firms and bar associations could make significant efforts to understand the sources of this disaffection and to take steps to remedy it. For example, bar associations could hold consciousness-raising seminars on race relations and gender relations within the bar. They could make concerted efforts to see that women and racial minorities are adequately represented among members of their staffs and officers. They could tailor continuing education offerings to be certain that areas of the law are addressed in which women, African-Americans, and other ethnic minorities show particular interest. And established firms could make a conscious effort to hire racial minorities. This might begin with a firm-directed reevaluation of the attitude of firm members toward persons of other races and cultures. If the effort is serious, it will almost inevitably lead to a reevaluation of the hiring criteria many firms use—criteria which could use reevaluation anyway in light of the new types of skills being called for in lawyers' work.

Finally—and this may be the most important step of all—the bar needs to make it a top priority to preserve its professional history and tell its unfolding story. As an institution, the bar of every state, and the organizations within it (bar associations, local bars, subgroup organizations, practice groups, and firms) need to accept the essential storytelling and story-gathering responsibility. Every state bar should have an oral history program where lawyers visit other lawyers and record their life stories so that the bar can make those stories available for its members to see and learn from. Local bars can do the same thing. So can law firms. All of these organizations can maintain some form of archives for important documents, photographs, and memorabilia of professionalism. Histories of bars and bar associations can be commissioned and written, as has recently be done by the North Carolina Bar Association[24] and is now underway in the Mecklenberg County (Charlotte), North Carolina bar. As we have seen, this work of history-gathering, story-gathering and, ultimately, myth-building used to occur naturally within the profession. But it is clear that this is no longer the case. How will we develop a new, positive, profession-building mythology unless we, through our professional institutions, consciously make time and space for doing that and give priority to the effort? This is bedrock work, and the profession will suffer as a profession without it. Beyond that, the history of lawyers and their work is important to everyone. The work of the legal profession is honorable and highly important. The people who do that work are some of the most important people to the welfare of the country and to their local communities. We should be preserving this story, and it should be passed down from generation to generation as part of our professional treasure.

The work of the profession to rebuild itself will have to take place on both the institutional and individual levels. And the work on those two levels must, for those who undertake it, feel interrelated and directed toward the same goal. "One for all, and all for one," was the motto of the Three Musketeers. It signifies a commitment to the group and a devotion to and dependence upon each other which the legal profession would do well to emulate. This sort of unity is the best defense against those outside the profession (and within) who seem so resigned to the profession's demise.

The Cult of the Red Knight

Perhaps the greatest impediment to engendering this type of "other-directedness" among lawyers is the current dominance of the masculine ideal, personified in the Parcival myth by the Red Knight. If the accepted image of the successful lawyer is one who is ruthless, totally self-directed, and independent of moral obligations to anyone other than himself and his client, ambitious lawyers are not apt to devote much time to helping other lawyers and to working to build a professional community. From my observation as a former trial lawyer and judge, many practicing lawyers view courtesy toward other lawyers and opposing parties and activities which are community-directed to be at best useless and at the worst a sign of weakness. As long as this attitude prevails or is even present in a significant number of lawyers, it will be difficult to engender widespread support for community-building and support systems for lawyers. The Red Knight is the kind of warrior who will dominate the scene around him if he is not challenged and defeated. And, as we have noted previously, for most lawyers, challenging the Red Knight in others has involved asserting the Red Knight in oneself.

It is instructive to note where in the Parcival myth the Red Knight appears. Basically he is Parcival's first test, one Parcival must meet and pass before he can even begin the long process of moral development. The mythological implications of this are that where the Red Knight is in control of the individual psyche, personal growth will not occur, and where Red Knights dominate a culture, effective moral community will not be possible. This is not a startling revelation. It should be clear to anyone who is a close observer of the current state of the legal profession or who reads the numerous complaints about attorney behavior. Red Knights scoff at the values of selflessness and other-directedness. And their attitude, exemplified in the legal profession by the tendency of many attorneys to scoff at conciliatory efforts of other attorneys or at attempts by the bar to promote civility and build a professional community, is precisely the attitude that inhibits reconciliation, creates incivility, and destroys community. And it is an attitude that is blind to its own limitations. It is as though the profession has a disease of such a nature that the disease itself prevents the patient from seeing how sick he is or from implementing a cure.

As long as the Red Knight is in the saddle, the legal profession will not recover from its current malaise. In fact, it will not even be able to begin the long quest to heal itself. As was true for Parcival, subduing the Red Knight is the first task we must undertake. And it is important to understand what "subdue" means in this context. Parcival kills the Red Knight, but he takes the Red Knight's armor and weapons for his own use. Henceforth, the power of the Red Knight will continue to exist and be used, but it will be directed toward the achievement of personal consciousness and the welfare of the entire kingdom. Killing the Red Knight does not mean obliterating masculine power. It simply means bringing that power under control and directing its use. This must be done as part of the internal work of individual lawyers as well as the community-building work of the profession itself.

Recent efforts among various bars and bar associations to encourage civility among lawyers are one method of combating Red-knightism. A more effective method might be to confront it head-on. Bars and bar associations might, for example, provide high-prestige annual awards to attorneys who exhibit civility and courtesy toward other lawyers and persons in general. Recognition to lawyers for outstanding efforts at facilitation (as well as recognition for large verdicts) would serve to elevate the more relational aspects of law practice and provide an alternative ideal to which young lawyers may aspire. It also helps when prominent members of the bar speak out in court and publicly against aggressive and abusive tactics and behavior by lawyers. Finally, it would help for more lawyers to complain of such tactics to bar grievance committees and for grievance committees to take more seriously complaints of such tactics. Rule 4.4 of the *ABA Model Rules of Professional Conduct* specifically requires attorneys to respect the rights of other lawyers, parties, jurors (and, perhaps, witnesses). That rule should be expanded to include all persons with whom lawyers come in contact as part of their work as attorneys.

Cooperation Between the Bar and Law Schools

In regard to issues of professionalism, bars and law schools have recently—at least until the last few years—resembled two baseball outfielders who let the ball drop between them because each assumes the other player will catch it. Law schools were not established to teach professionalism. When law curricula began to be designated as separate departments in American universities in the latter part of the nineteenth century, professional behavior was assumed to be part of one's upbringing and code of honor as a gentleman. Bars and professional organizations assumed the same thing. As practice evolved in the twentieth century, it became more apparent that this assumption was no longer true. Yet neither bars nor law schools accepted the essential responsibility of educating law students and young lawyers about the tenets of professionalism and the moral responsibility of professional status. Law schools tardily and grudgingly began to teach courses in the ethical rules but held the attitude that teaching professionalism was the job of the profession and that the profession was "out there" and not really present in law school. The bar looked to law schools to teach the rules of professional ethics and consoled itself that law school courses on legal ethics were what was needed to insure professionalism among law school graduates.

Both of these attitudes are changing, but the change should be much more profound. Law schools and the bar must come to see themselves as part of the same professional community with mutual, interdependent duties to promote and pass on the tenets of professionalism. For law schools, this means understanding their critical role as the threshold of the profession and accepting the responsibility of producing young *professionals* (and not merely persons who are highly educated in the skills of legal reasoning and advocacy). Law students should be viewed as aspirants to professional status, who must be steeped in the traditions of professionalism and confronted with the question of whether they are willing to accept the moral responsibility that entry into the profession entails. This confrontation should begin in the law school admission process. Every applicant to every American law school should be required to read and sign an oath of commitment to professionalism such as the following:

COMMITMENT TO PROFESSIONALISM

I, _____, the undersigned, have read this Commitment, and I understand that I am applying to a professional school dedicated to teaching the knowledge, basic skills, and ethics of the legal profession. I understand that if I am admitted to law school, an essential part of my work during my matriculation will be to learn and practice the tenets of professionalism, including honesty, personal integrity, open-mindedness, and respect for and courtesy toward others, in addition to the formal rules of professional ethics. I further understand that for a professional, the learning process upon which I wish to embark is a life-long process involving continuing education, periodic self-examination, and recommitment. I am willing to assume this life-long responsibility.

Signed: _____

Regardless of LSAT scores and grade point averages, applicants to law school who are not willing to accept the responsibility of such an oath should not be admitted to law school. This is true even for those who ultimately do not plan to practice. Law schools cannot correct their current drift away from inculcating true professionalism if one segment of their student bodies is excused from professional commitment.

Law school curricula and the attitudes of law school teachers must be changed to support that commitment. I have suggested some curriculum changes in the preceding discussion and commended law school programs which I feel are steps in the right direction. But such changes will be of little overall value unless law school teachers and administrators themselves believe in and support commitment to the profession and to passing that commitment on to their students. Law professors must begin to conceive of themselves as members of the legal profession as well as the academic profession. This means a change in attitude for many of them. It will mean establishing through practice a closer relationship to the working bar. Every law dean and law professor should be required to maintain membership in the American Bar Association and, if possible, in the bar association in the state in which his law school is located.* He should be expected to participate, and should receive tenure credit for participating, in the work of local, state, and national bars and bar associations—work such as membership on disciplinary boards and ethics committees, bar admission committees, professionalism committees, and task forces to study particular problems of the profession and practicing lawyers. This sort of work brings legal academicians together with "real" lawyers. It teaches them about the profession which they are presumably teaching students to enter.

As important as the practice of professionalism is in bringing law professors and law schools into the work of preserving the profession, the attitude of legal academia toward the practice of law and practicing lawyers is equally important. Currently many law professors see themselves as above the hurly-burly of practice and somehow superior to those who engage in it. This is an astoundingly *un*professional attitude, and it is not lost upon law students who frequently (once the first-semester grades have "selected them out" from the ranks of the truly brilliant) develop a disdainful attitude toward their profession-disdaining professors. That attitude often follows students into practice, where they tend to look back on some of their law school professors as "eggheads," isolated in academic theory and insulated in academic lifestyles, and useless as guides in the rough-and-tumble life of legal practice. People viewed this way are not good models for professionalism. In fact, they are harmful to the concept.

The practicing bar also should accept a measure of responsibility for the professional education of law students and young lawyers. This will require a degree of cooperation between the bar and legal academy which is often not present. Improving those relations is a job for law school deans and bar leaders. Law professors should be expected to serve on bar committees which deal with legal education and professional issues and should be given career incentives to do so. They should be encouraged to find ways to bring lawyers and judges into the classroom to talk about the duties of professionalism. Bars and bar organizations should inform themselves about current law school offerings in ethics and professionalism and seek ways to assist law schools in promoting professionalism

---

*I intend a distinction here between state bar associations and state bars, the latter of which are licensing and regulatory institutions. In North Carolina at least, one does not have to be a member of the state bar in order to be a member of the North Carolina Bar Association.

among students from the first day students enter law school. The unifying idea here is that building professionalism is a continuing task which begins with the first step toward professional status and continues throughout one's career. And everyone who undertakes to achieve that status has a duty to earn it, promote it, and preserve it, depending upon where one is in the professionalism continuum.

REFLECTIONS

The suggestions for change which I have proposed in the preceding chapter and in various places throughout this book present a daunting task. And while there are encouraging signs that the task is underway, it will be a long time—and perhaps never—before the task is completed and the legal profession completely restored. Unlike the wound of the Fisher King in the Parcival myth, the ailment of the legal profession is real and complex, and it has not occurred from the thrust of one spear but has been brought about by many decades of change and neglect. It will take decades of change and attention to rebuild and restore what has been lost.

But the important thing to remember is that it can be done. We still possess the means to save ourselves as a profession. Through the long night in which we now find ourselves, true knights have persevered in the quest, preserving the ideals of the profession in the face of mounting obstacles such as billable hours, specialization, impersonalizaton, and Red-knightism. New heros and heroines have continued to emerge and are providing new and expanded ideals of professionalism for a renewed profession. The means of creating a new mythology are there. It only remains for us to consciously and collectively assume the task of profession-building. And, above all, this must be done consciously. If we let things take their natural course, we have seen where they will lead.

While the task is daunting and the quest for professional wholeness is a long one, it is worth the effort. How would it feel to work in a profession where we could always expect professional behavior from our fellow lawyers? How would it feel to work in a profession which was justly proud of its professional status, which yielded a mythology of purpose that made the work of lawyering more than a just a job, but a calling, as attorney Robert McMillan sees his work in the quotation from his oral history? How would it feel to be a member of a profession which was so honorable in its ethical standards that others would measure themselves by those standards? How would it feel to see one's life work as something to which others should aspire—not because of the material rewards—but because of the ideals it embodied? How would it feel to know that one's work toward personal wholeness and service to others was supported by a profession of people with similar goals and ideals, people upon whom one could rely for help through the inevitable hard places? How would it feel to be a member of a profession which society looked up to and valued for its ideals and contributions to the public good?

We can be that kind of profession. We have the capacity to become what we would like to become. We have the people. We have the remnants of the ideal. We lack only the effort and desire. And even those are present—coming to life in places, still dormant in others.

What will give us the courage to take on this task and to persist in it? It will not be enough, I suggest, to merely "want" a restoration of the profession. In face of the largely market-driven, technologically enhanced forces mounting against us, a mere longing for professionalism has so far been insufficient to prompt us to take the steps necessary to save ourselves, and there is no reason to believe that it will suffice in the future. It will take something deeper than that. We need to see professionalism and our profession as more than a preferred status and more even than a set of ideals. In order to restore our profession, we must somehow wed our individual journeys to the journey of the profession as a whole. To do this, we need to see professionalism in its narrative entirety. Being a professional must ultimately mean how we tell our life stories. Professionalism is telling one's life story consciously so that it has a narrative purpose, so that we see a reason for telling the story to others and to our society, so that it has mythological significance as a story which teaches others, is worth listening to, and is worthy of a preeminent place among the other narratives about our lives.

Return for a moment to the images of narrative we discussed at the end of chapter 12. Even the traditional hero's myth, often thought of as the archetypal linear story, is circular, or a spiral, proceeding in revolutions toward the conclusion. And with each revolution, the hero grows in consciousness toward himself and awareness of a higher purpose. That is an apt metaphor for the progression of the well-lived professional life and the life of a worthy profession. Both the spiral of the heroic myth and the spiral of a professional life eventually end. Only the memories of their stories continue. But the spiral of the profession does not have to end. It only has to renew itself by revolutions through the heroic lives of its members. Those revolutions can go on indefinitely. The story can go on. And the stories of lawyers, the questing knights who have faded into the mists of Avalon, can live on in the mythology of the profession and through the lives of future generations of lawyers.

So here at the advent of the twenty-first century we stand in a moment of choice. Either we can give up, throw down our lance, dismount from our horse, and take up the less visionary lives of money-makers and power-brokers. Or we can continue the quest for a vision of a new profession. We can look for the divinity in ourselves and the divine purpose in our life's work, always questing, always learning, moving toward the unreachable and yet attainable ideal. And the profession will live on, renewing itself though the lives of devoted lawyers. It is a process of recovering ourselves and the profession at the same time. It is a way to connect our lives to the eternal. As T. S. Eliot tells us in the final lines of his *Four Quartets*:

> Through the unknown remembered gate
> When the last of earth left to discover
> Is that which was the beginning;
> At the source of the longest river
> The voice of children in the apple-tree
> Not known, because not looked for
> But heard, half-heard, in the stillness
> Between two waves of the sea.
> Quick now, here, now, always—
> A condition of complete simplicity
> (Costing not less than everything)
> And all shall be well and
> All manner of thing shall be well
> When the tongues of flame are in-folded
> Into the crowned knot of fire
> And the fire and the rose are one.[1]

APPENDIX A

A Model Mentoring
Program for Young Lawyers

INTRODUCTION

Mentoring is a time-tested and effective method for educating lawyers in the values, skills, and heritage of the profession and is part of the duty lawyers owe to each other, to the profession and to the greater community. The following program is a suggested model for deepening and expanding mentoring within a state bar, but it may also be adapted to a local bar or even at the individual firm level.*

I. GOALS

    A. *Primary Goals*

        1. To provide a basis for enriching the relationships among members of the bar and rebuilding, strengthening, and maintaining the professional community of lawyers.

        2. To pass on to succeeding generations of lawyers the values of the profession.

        3. To create a learning relationship for both mentor and protégé in which both can reflect upon what it means to be a professional and upon the professional's duty to maintain and advance professional responsibility in a changing society.

---

*The model mentoring programs appearing as Appendixes A and B are the work product of two subcommittees of the Legal Education and Professionalism Task Force of the North Carolina Bar Association (1996–97): The Subcommittee on Mentoring of Young Lawyers (membership: Judge Sidney S. Eagles Jr.; attorneys Dorothy C. Bernholz, G. Stevenson Crihfield, Nancy Byerly Jones, Pender R. McElroy, Caryn C. McNeill, Alice Neece Mosley, Gina L. Reyman, Horace E. Stacy Jr., and James D. Wall; law professors Walter H. Bennett Jr. and Lisa Morgan Crutchfield); and the Subcommittee on Mentoring of Law Students (membership: Professor Walter H. Bennett Jr., University of North Carolina Law School, attorney Howard Clement, Associate Dean Johnny Chriscoe, Campbell University Law School, Professor Lisa Morgan Crutchfield, North Carolina Central University Law School, Associate Dean Susan L. Sockwell, Duke University Law School, and Dean Robert Walsh, Wake Forest Law School).

4. To encourage reflection by all members of the bar on the ethics of the profession.

5. To assist lawyers with problems related to establishing and learning the practice of law; managing and succeeding as a lawyer outside of private practice; learning the culture of the legal profession; making career choices; balancing professional duties with personal life; resolving conflicts between personal values and the duties of a professional; managing the stress of professional life; and confronting and dealing with special problems of being a professional including problems related to issues of gender and ethnicity.

6. To provide special assistance in all aspects of lawyering for attorneys who, because of inexperience or physical or professional isolation, are in need of advice and guidance.

B. *Secondary Goals*

1. To assist lawyers in acquiring and developing skills for practicing law.

2. To assist lawyers with specific legal problems.

3. To assist lawyers with specific ethical problems.

II. PARTICIPATION

It is strongly recommended that all lawyers entering the state bar who have practiced law for less than five years and all other members of the bar who, for whatever reason, feel they would benefit from being involved in a mentoring relationship with a more experienced lawyer, be afforded the opportunity to participate as protégés in this program.[*] All lawyers entering the bar of the state on any given year who have practiced less than five years will be contacted in writing and invited to participate and specifically urged and recommended to participate—particularly if they have not participated in a mentoring program of comparable quality in another bar, a law school of this state, or law school located elsewhere.

III. ORGANIZATION

A. *State Mentoring Coordinator:* A state-wide office (with appropriate facilities and staff and called the "State Mentoring Coordinator") will be established and maintained by the state bar/bar association. The duties of the state-wide Mentoring Coordinator will be as set forth in Attachment A hereto.

B. *Oversight Committee:* The State Mentoring Program will be under the direction of an oversight committee composed of . . . [Here it is suggested that membership include representatives from the active, legal

---

[*]The subcommittee considered recommending that participation in the state mentoring program be required of all persons entering the North Carolina bar. While there was general agreement among subcommittee members that mandatory participation might be desirable if it could be implemented, there was concern that because of the substantial funding which would be required, the state bar was unlikely to require universal participation.

professional organizations within the state in order to insure diversity in age, background, locale, areas of practice, race, and gender. In addition, membership should include members of the judiciary and law school faculty within the state as well as lay members and persons from other professions.] The Oversight Committee will have the power to hire and fire the State-wide Mentoring Coordinator, to assist in fund-raising efforts for the establishment and operation of the program, and will serve as the ultimate authority for the operation of the program.

C. *Participation of Local, District Bars:* Local bars will be requested to cooperate with efforts of the State Mentoring Coordinator by designating a local bar Mentoring Coordinator (or by acceptance of that role by the local bar president). That person will assist and advise the State Mentoring Coordinator in designing the local bar program based on this model, informing and educating mentors and protégés, appropriate mentors, matching mentors and protégés, and following up to see that quality mentoring is occurring. Where a local bar, for whatever reason, fails to designate anyone to function as a local mentoring coordinator, the State Mentoring Coordinator will act insofar as possible to fulfill that role.

D. *Use of and Incorporation of and Cooperation with Ongoing Mentoring Efforts:* It is the intention of this program to assist the implementation of quality mentoring throughout the state bar. Where ongoing mentoring efforts exist among organizations within the state bar or on a local level, this program will, where possible, attempt to build upon those efforts. This may involve incorporation of or cooperation with ongoing mentoring programs.

IV. MENTORING PROGRAM(S)

The following are suggested components of a program for effective mentoring of young lawyers. All of the suggested components may not be desirable or feasible in all parts of the state. Some components, described below as "essential components," are necessary for an effective mentoring program. Other components not so described may be very helpful and important to effective mentoring but are not considered absolutely necessary. In designing local programs, local bars should not simply opt for a minimalist approach but should design a program best suited for accomplishing the goals of mentoring in their bars.

A. *Essential Components*

1. A basic mentoring relationship of a least one year's duration between a protégé and at least one older, more experienced lawyer in practice a minimum of five years, and which includes the following:

a. An initial meeting, arranged by the mentor(s) contacting the protégé, in which the partners meet and discuss the purposes for and goals of the relationship and how they will continue to maintain contact throughout the mentoring process.

    b. Additional, periodic, face-to-face meetings no less than three times during the course of the year as follows:

        1. A second meeting within 60 days of the initial meeting.

        2. A third meeting within 120 days of the second meeting.

        3. A fourth meeting before the end of the mentoring year.

    c. An obligation on the part of the mentor(s) to respond promptly and attentively to attempts to inquire or otherwise communicate by the protégé and to listen to, advise, counsel, and teach the protégé in order to effectively achieve the goals of the relationship outlined in Section I above.

  2. Selection of mentors who are committed to the concept of mentoring and who will read carefully and follow through on the "Responsibilities of Mentors" [to be developed by the State Mentoring Coordinator as set forth in Attachment A.]

  3. Enthusiastic support by local bars of mentoring efforts, including, where possible, appointment of a local Mentoring Coordinator to assist the State Mentoring Coordinator in finding mentors, seeing that the local program functions properly, and assuring that mentors and protégés are recognized at bar functions and in newsletters and other appropriate methods of support.

B. *Additional Components*

  1. A training session for mentors in which prospective mentors are taught the benefits of and techniques of effective mentoring from available literature and/or engage in consciousness-raising exercises on professional values, the meaning of being a professional, and how these values can be taught through the mentoring process.

  2. A reception/dinner/luncheon by the local bar for mentors and protégés to "kick off" the mentoring relationship.

  3. A recognition reception/dinner/luncheon by the local bar for mentors and protégés to conclude the formal mentoring program.

  4. A day-long retreat for mentors and protégés in which some of the exercises from Subsection IV-C below are completed (if possible this should be held early in the mentoring process as a "kick off" event).

  5. Organizing mentors and protégés into six- or eight-person groups for periodic meetings/lunches/suppers in which issues of ethics, professional values, or quality of life are presented and discussed. Such groups might be organized under and in conjunction with local Inns of Court. (This approach is a valuable tool to increase contact between mentoring partners, expose protégés to other mentors (and to other protégés), and to bring mentoring partners of the same race or gender into contact with persons of other genders or

ethnicity. It may also be helpful to form groups to include mentors of various ages and time in the profession.)

C. *Examples of Possible Exercises for Mentoring Partners or Groups of Mentoring Partners.* (It is anticipated that the State Mentoring Coordinator will, consistent with his duties outlined in Attachment A, modify and amend this list):

EXERCISE ONE: The mentor and protégé will spend at least an hour sharing with each other recollections of incidents from their own pasts which describe events or people that influenced the formation of their moral value systems and discuss how that has affected (or will/might affect) their values as a professional.

EXERCISE TWO: The mentor will inform the protégé of a "real life" ethical/moral issue that has arisen in the course of the mentor's practice (or of which he/she is otherwise aware), and the mentoring partners will discuss the problem and try to arrive at possible solutions.

EXERCISE THREE: The mentor and protégé will discuss the meaning of professionalism and professional values and try to identify and list, (a) the attributes of a professional and, (b) what constitute professional values.

EXERCISE FOUR: The mentor and protégé will be given a number of hypothetical ethical/legal problems to talk over and propose solutions. These problems might include suggested solutions to which the mentoring partners can refer after their discussion.

EXERCISE FIVE: The mentor and protégé will be given a list of activities to undertake and complete together, such as attending court together, attending an administrative hearing, attending a mediation or arbitration, visiting the clerk's office and register of deeds, attending a local or state bar function, etc.

EXERCISE SIX: The protégé will "take" the oral history (life story) of the mentor by researching the life of the mentor and interviewing (and tape recording) the mentor's telling of his/her life story, how he/she became a lawyer, how he/she has lived a life in the profession, and what it has meant to be a professional.

EXERCISE SEVEN: The mentor and protégé will be given a list of reported cases from which they can select cases to read and discuss in terms of the law of the case and the role of courts and lawyers.

EXERCISE EIGHT: The mentor and protégé will be given a reading list of literary works, studies of lawyers and the profession,

historical accounts of legal cases and legal history, and bi-
ographies of lawyers and judges, from which they can select a work (or works) to read and discuss together (or in
groups of mentors and protégés) in order to further their
understanding of the profession and the place of law and
lawyers in society. (Examples might be, *Billy Budd,* by Herman Melville; *To Kill a Mockingbird,* by Harper Lee; *Native Son,* by Richard Wright; *A Man for All Seasons,* by
Robert Bolt; selections from *Legal Fictions: Short Stories
about Lawyers and the Law,* Jay Wishingrad, editor; a biography of Abraham Lincoln or of his life as a lawyer [*Lincoln,*
by David Donald or *Lincoln Lawyer,* by Albert Woldman];
Simple Justice, by Richard Kluger; *The Lost Lawyer,* by Anthony Kronman; *A Nation under Lawyers,* by Mary Ann
Glendon; *The Soul of the Law,* by Benjamin Sells; *Law vs.
Life,* by Walt Bachman; *Women Lawyers,* by Mona Harring-
ton; *The Alchemy of Race and Rights,* by Patricia Williams; *In
Search of Atticus Finch,* by Mike Panpantino; *Transforming
Practices,* by Steven Keeva; *In the Interests of Justice,* by
Deborah Rhode.)

V. SELECTION OF MENTORS AND MATCHING MENTORING PARTNERS

   A. *Selection of Persons as Appropriate Mentors and Role Models*

   1. The State Mentoring Coordinator will prepare and circulate to
      participating local bars standards for selection of persons to serve
      as mentors. Those standards will include degree of moral integrity,
      appreciation of ethical rules of the bar and ethical standards of
      the community, ethical standing within the local and state bars,
      understanding of and appreciation for the ethical issues faced by
      attorneys, respect by fellow professionals, devotion to their work
      and to the profession and commitment to the concept of mentoring
      and the mentoring program.

   2. Using these standards, the local bar Mentoring Coordinator (or
      the State Mentoring Coordinator where no local Mentoring Coor-
      dinator is available) will recruit and select persons to act as suit-
      able mentors. The State Mentoring Coordinator will establish and
      maintain a list of those persons, together with names, addresses,
      business telephone numbers, type and area of practice (corporate,
      large firm, litigation, domestic, real estate, solo practice, etc.) and,
      where the mentor consents, ethnic designation.

   3. The State Mentoring Coordinator will communicate with local
      bars on an annual basis to ensure that the state-wide list is current,
      expanded, and renewed. Both the local bar Mentoring Coordina-

tors and the State Mentoring Coordinator will work to ensure that persons are not on the list who have been disciplined by the state bar or the bar of any other jurisdiction.

4. Where appropriate, the State Mentoring Coordinator will seek to obtain CLE credit approval for participation of mentors in mentoring training sessions.

B. *Matching Mentors and Protégés*

1. Each year, the State Mentoring Coordinator will, with the assistance of the state bar, write to and otherwise communicate with all persons entering the bar of the state in order to determine which of them wish to participate in the state mentoring program. The State Mentoring Coordinator will also undertake to inform all members of the bar—and particularly those engaged in solo practice—of the existence of the mentoring program and the possibility of participation as a protégé for all who are interested. For all persons who apply to participate as protégé, the State Mentoring Coordinator will inquire of the following:

   a. Geographic location of practice.

   b. Type of practice and area of interest.

   c. Special concerns and need for assistance, if any.

   d. Preference, if any, for being matched with a person of like gender or ethnicity.[*]

   e. Whether the protégé is a sole practitioner.

   f. Any other factors which the State Mentoring Coordinator deems pertinent to match the new lawyer with the most appropriate mentor.[†]

2. Using information gathered on mentors and potential protégés, the State Mentoring Coordinator will match the mentoring partners and so inform each of them and the local bar Mentoring Coordinator (where one exists) so that the mentoring process can begin. Where the protégé is a sole practitioner, the State Mentoring Coordinator will attempt to match the protégé with a mentor who, by virtue of experience and expertise, can advise the protégé on issues of practical skills and practice management as well as issues of professional values.

---

[*]There were different views among subcommittee members on whether race or gender should be a factor in assigning mentors. At least one subcommittee member felt that young lawyers would benefit from being assigned mentors who were specifically not of their race and/or gender.

[†]The subcommittee considered recommending use of the Myers-Briggs Multiple Personality Inventory test for assignment of mentors and proteges, but finally determined that such testing would be too expensive and might be objectionable to some participants.

VI. FOLLOW-UP/EVALUATION The State Mentoring Coordinator will devise and implement yearly evaluations of this mentoring program to ensure that the goals of this program, set forth in Section I, above, are being substantially met. The yearly evaluations will solicit comments on the effectiveness of the program from (at least a representative number of) both mentor and protégé participants.

APPENDIX B

A Model Mentoring
Program for Law Students

INTRODUCTION

Mentoring is a time-tested and effective method of educating students and young professionals in the values, skills, and heritage of a profession. The following program is a model for use by law schools in the state for that purpose and is a guide for persons participating in any such program either as mentors or as student-protégés.* It is anticipated that law schools will use this document as an aspirational model only and should provide mentoring for students according to the judgments of their administrations and faculties and allocation of limited resources.

I. GOALS
    A. *Primary Goals*
        1. To assist law students in making the transition from law school to the profession and practice of law.
        2. To introduce law students to the ideals of professionalism and the life and work of lawyers and to pass on to succeeding generations of lawyers the values of the profession.
        3. To bring each law student participant into close contact and communication with at least one member of the profession who can serve as a role model and advisor to the student.
        4. To provide a basis for enriching the relationships between law students and members of the state bar and among members of the bar themselves and rebuilding, strengthening, and maintaining the professional community of lawyers.

---

*This model mentoring program for law students is the work product of a subcommittee of the Legal Education and Professionalism Task Force of the North Carolina Bar Association (1996–97). See footnote A in Appendix A for details.

5. To create a learning relationship for both mentor and protégé in which both can reflect upon what it means to be a professional and the professional's duty to maintain and advance professional responsibility in a changing society.

6. To encourage reflection by law students and members of the bar on the ethics of the profession.

7. To assist law students with problems related to the study of law in law school; establishing and learning the practice of law; learning the culture of the legal profession in the state; making career choices; balancing professional duties with personal life; resolving conflicts between personal values and the duties of a professional; and confronting and dealing with special problems of being a professional and working in the legal profession in the state, including problems related to issues of gender and ethnicity.

B. *Secondary Goals*

1. To teach law students about specific areas of practice and about the skills necessary for practicing law.

2. To teach law students about how to solve specific legal problems.

3. To assist third-year law students in taking the formal steps necessary for application for admission to the bar and the attitudinal steps necessary to prepare themselves for the bar exam.

II. PARTICIPATION While a high-quality mentoring experience is desirable for all law students, the actual degree of participation by students will depend upon the time and resources each law school is able to devote to mentoring. Where resources do not permit high-quality mentoring for a large number of students, law schools should ensure that where mentoring occurs, it is a deep and meaningful experience for those involved and should strive for quality of the experience over quantity of students served.

III. ORGANIZATION

A. *Law School Mentoring Director/Coordinator/Administrator:* Each law school should designate an administrator or faculty member as Mentoring Director/Coordinator/Administrator (for simplicity, hereinafter referred to as "Mentoring Director") who is responsible for establishing and maintaining the mentoring program in the law school. The duties of this position will be:

1. To administer the law school's mentoring program to best meet the goals and purposes listed in Section I above.

2. To recruit high-quality mentors to participate in the program.

3. To match mentors with students in mentoring relationships which are most likely to accomplish the goals and purposes listed in Section I above.

4. To cooperate with the State Mentoring Coordinator (or some other designee from the bar—see Attachment A) in order to, where

possible, coordinate the law school's mentoring efforts with the mentoring of young lawyers in the state bar.

    5. To cooperate with Mentoring Directors at other law schools in this state and elsewhere to exchange information and ideas in order to constantly improve the mentoring of law students in this state.

B. *Inter-Law-School Advisory Committee:* There should be a committee composed of the deans of the state's law schools and/or Mentoring Directors of the law schools, other designated faculty representatives of the law schools, and at least two representatives from the state bar (who are not law school faculty or staff) to share information about the mentoring of law students and to communicate with the state bar/bar association regarding issues affecting mentoring in law schools.

IV. MENTORING PROGRAM(S) The following are suggested components of a program for effective mentoring of law students. While all of the suggested components will not be desirable or feasible for every law school or every law student, some of them are minimally necessary for an effective mentoring experience. Those components are described below as "essential components," but other components not so described may be very helpful and important to effective mentoring. In designing a mentoring program for students, law schools should not simply opt for a minimalist approach but should design a program best suited for accomplishing the goals of mentoring as set out in this model.

A. *Essential Components*

    1. A basic mentoring relationship of at least one year's duration between a qualified and dedicated lawyer in practice a minimum of five years and a law student (protégé), which includes the following:

        a. An initial "kick off" event, such as a retreat, seminar, reception, or dinner, in which mentors and protégés are brought together in a group and introduced to each other and to the purposes, methods, and expectations of the mentoring process. This should include or be closely followed by a meeting between the mentor and protégé in which the two partners discuss the purposes for and goals of the relationship and how they will continue to maintain contact throughout the mentoring process.

        b. Additional, periodic, face-to-face meetings no less than three times during the course of the year as follows:

            1. A second meeting within 30 days of the initial meeting.
            2. A third meeting within 120 days of the second meeting.
            3. A fourth meeting before the end of the mentoring year.

        c. An obligation on the part of the mentor to respond promptly and attentively to attempts to inquire or otherwise communicate by the protégé and to listen to, advise, counsel, and teach the protégé in order to effectively achieve the goals of the relationship outline in Section I above.

    d. An obligation on the part of the protégé to respect the schedule and time constraints on the part of the mentor in advising and counseling the protégé.

    e. Completion by the mentoring partners of Exercises (One, Two, Three and Four) in the list of exercises in Subsection IV-C below.

2. Selection of mentors who are committed to the concept of mentoring and who will read carefully and follow through on the "Responsibilities of Mentors" (to be developed by the Mentoring Director).

3. Enthusiastic support by law schools of the mentoring program, including emphasis of the mentoring program in the curriculum, and recognition of mentors and protégés at law school functions and in newsletters and other appropriate methods of support.

B. *Additional/Aspirational Components*

1. A training session for mentors of one hour or more in which prospective mentors are taught the benefits of and techniques of effective mentoring from available literature and/or engage in consciousness-raising exercises on professional values, the meaning of being a professional, and how these values can be taught through the mentoring process.

2. A reception/dinner/luncheon for mentors and protégés to conclude the mentoring experience.

3. Organizing mentors and protégés into six- or eight-person groups for periodic meetings/lunches/suppers in which issues of ethics, professional values, or quality of life are presented and discussed. Smaller groups may be organized under and in conjunction with local Inns of Court. (This approach is a valuable tool to increase contact between mentoring partners, expose protégés to other mentors [and to other protégés] and to bring mentoring partners of the same race or gender into contact with persons of other genders or ethnicity. It may also be helpful to form groups to include mentors of various ages and time in the profession.)

4. In order to strengthen and support the mentoring process, where possible it would help to relate the mentoring experience to the law school curriculum in professionalism and legal ethics (or other aspects of the curriculum). This might occur, for example, by making the mentoring experience part of a class on legal ethics for which credit is given. Or, it might occur as a noncredit adjunct to such a class. Or, it might occur by using mentors as speakers in substantive courses (i.e., using district attorneys and criminal

defense attorneys in a class on criminal law) or having mentors and protégés speak to an orientation for first-year students.

C. *Possible Exercises for Mentoring Partners or Groups of Mentoring Partners*

EXERCISE ONE: The mentor and protégé will spend at least an hour sharing with each other stories of incidents from their own pasts which describe events or people that influenced the formation of their moral value systems and discuss how that has effected (or will/might effect) their values as a professional.

EXERCISE TWO: The mentor will inform the protégé of a "real life" ethical/moral issue that has arisen in the course of the mentor's practice (or of which he/she is otherwise aware), and the mentoring partners will discuss the problem and try to arrive at possible solutions.

EXERCISE THREE: The mentor and protégé will discuss the meaning of professionalism and professional values and try to identify and list (a) the attributes of a professional and (b) what constitutes professional values.

EXERCISE FOUR: The protégé will visit the mentor and spend a workday "shadowing" the mentor during a day of work.

EXERCISE FIVE: The mentor and protégé will be given a number of hypothetical ethical/legal problems to talk over and propose solutions to.

EXERCISE SIX: The mentor and protégé will be given a list of activities to undertake and complete together, such as attending court together, attending an administrative hearing, attending a mediation or arbitration, visiting the clerk's office and register of deeds, attending a local bar function, etc.

EXERCISE SEVEN: The mentor will visit the protégé in law school and attend a class or spend the day.

EXERCISE EIGHT: The protégé will "take" the oral history (life story) of the mentor by researching the life of the mentor and interviewing (and tape recording) the mentor's telling of his/her life story, how he/she became a lawyer, how he/she has lived a life in the profession, and what it has meant to be a professional.

EXERCISE NINE: The mentor and protégé will be given a list of reported cases from which they can select cases to read and discuss in terms of the law of the case and the role of courts and lawyers.

EXERCISE TEN: The mentor and protégé will be given a reading list of literary works, studies of lawyers and the profession, historical accounts of legal cases and legal history, and bi-

ographies of lawyers and judges, from which they can select a
work (or works) to read and discuss together (or in groups of
mentors and protégés) in order to further their understanding
of the profession and the place of law and lawyers in society.
(Examples might be, *Billy Budd,* by Herman Melville; *To
Kill a Mockingbird,* by Harper Lee; *Native Son,* by Richard
Wright; *A Man for All Seasons,* by Robert Bolt; selections
from *Legal Fictions: Short Stories about Lawyers and the
Law,* Jay Wishingrad, editor; a biography of Abraham Lincoln or of his life as a lawyer [*Lincoln,* by David Donald
or *Lincoln Lawyer,* by Albert Woldman]; *Simple Justice,* by
Richard Kluger; *The Lost Lawyer,* by Anthony Kronman; *A
Nation under Lawyers,* by Mary Ann Glendon; *The Soul of
the Law,* by Benjamin Sells; *Law vs. Life,* by Walt Bachman;
Women Lawyers, by Mona Harrington; *The Alchemy of Race
and Rights,* by Patricia Williams; *In Search of Atticus Finch,*
by Mike Papantino; *Transforming Practice,* by Steven Keeva;
In the Interests of Justice, by Deborah Rhode.)

EXERCISE ELEVEN: Where the mentoring program is part of or
otherwise connected to a class in the law school, the mentor
could be invited to speak to the student's class on a pertinent
subject or could serve on a panel with other mentors to
address the class of a particular subject.

V. SELECTION OF MENTORS AND MATCHING OF MENTORING PARTNERS

A. Selection of Persons as Appropriate Mentors and Role Models: Each
Mentoring Director should develop guidelines for selection of mentors
which will insure that the persons serving as mentors provide appropriate role models for law students. Standards for qualification as a mentor
for law students should include: moral integrity, ethical standing within
the local and state bars, understanding of and appreciation for the ethical
and life-quality issues faced by attorneys and law students, respect by
fellow professionals, devotion to their work and to the profession, and
commitment to the concept of mentoring and the mentoring program.

B. *Matching Mentors and Protégés:* In matching mentors with protégés,
Mentoring Directors should consider the following factors:

1. Geographic location of the mentor in relation to the law school.
2. Type of practice of the mentor and area of interest of the student.
3. Special concerns of the student and need for assistance.
4. Preference of the student and mentor for being matched with a
person of like gender or ethnicity.[*]

---

[*]Some subcommittee members speculated that young lawyers might benefit more from
being assigned mentors who were specifically not of their race and/or gender.

5. Any other factors which the Mentoring Director deems pertinent to match the law student with the most appropriate mentor.

VI. FOLLOW-UP/EVALUATION

The Mentoring Director will devise and implement yearly evaluations of this mentoring program to ensure that the goals of this program, set forth in Section I above, are being substantially met. The yearly evaluations will solicit comments on the effectiveness of the program from (at least a representative number of) both mentor and protégé participants.

ATTACHMENT A

Duties of Statewide Mentoring Coordinator

The state bar/bar association will establish and maintain a State Mentoring Coordinator whose duties will be:

A. *General Duties*

To actively promote mentoring among members of the state bar and within the law schools and various legal, professional organizations of this state so that mentoring may be recognized as an essential component of professionalism and essential to the character and duties of a professional.

B. *Duties in Regard to Mentoring of Lawyers*

1. To continue to develop and administer the state-wide mentoring program for lawyers in the state.

2. To inform local and district bars of this mentoring program and to solicit participation of all local and district bars in the effort to mentor lawyers.

3. To assist local bars in identifying and soliciting as mentors members of the state bar who have the desire and capacity to act as mentors for other lawyers.

4. To identify all lawyers entering the state bar each year and to notify them of the option of participating in the mentoring program and to inform all members of the state bar—and especially those engaged in solo practice—of the existence and availability of this program.

5. To cooperate with the state bar to ensure that lawyers entering the bar of the state who qualify for participation in this program are properly identified.

6. To match mentors with protégés and to assist local bars and other mentoring programs in the state in the matching of mentors with protégés, including the development of matching criteria and, where feasible, the development of and administering of evaluation tools for matching complementary personality and work types.

7. To create and distribute to all mentors a statement of "The Responsibili-

ties of Mentors" and to all protégés a statement of "The Responsibilities of Proteges."

8. To provide training for mentors and to assist local bars in the training of mentors, the orientation of proteges and in the development of mentoring programs by providing advice and developing materials for use in mentoring, such as guides for mentoring, orientation materials, training materials, and films about the profession.

9. To consult with and coordinate with mentoring projects in other bar-wide organizations to ensure that efforts are not duplicated and that expertise and information about mentoring of young lawyers is shared to the betterment of all such programs.

10. To follow-up on all mentoring relationships, insofar as possible, to ensure that quality mentoring is occurring, including:

    a. Developing checklists, report forms, and guidelines for participants.
    b. Assisting and resolving communication problems between mentors and protégés.
    c. Replacing mentors where the situation warrants.
    d. Assisting mentors in developing program plans for unique situations.
    e. Receiving and processing complaints, concerns, and recommendations from program participants, the public, other attorneys, or legal support staff regarding the program or its participant.
    f. Developing and administering feedback/evaluation tools for biannual/annual updates from participants which are to be completed and signed by all participants.

11. Developing forms and documents necessary to assist the mentoring relationship, including any disclaimer and release forms and forms protecting attorney/client confidentiality.

C. *Duties in Regard to Mentoring of Law Students*

1. To advise and assist the law schools of this state in implementing and administering programs they may establish for the mentoring of young law students.

2. To assist law schools in identifying mentors and matching mentors with protégés.

3. To assist law schools in the training of mentors and orientation of mentors and protégés.

4. To exchange with law schools information on mentoring, including training materials and guidelines and other source materials to ensure a quality mentoring program.

5. To operate as a liaison among the law schools of this state so that information about mentoring programs may be shared and, where feasible, to encourage and assist law schools to cooperate with each other in joint mentoring ventures.

NOTES

Epigraphs

1. Oliver Wendell Holmes, "The Profession of the Law," in *The Essential Holmes: Selections from the Letters, Speeches, Judicial Opinions, and Other Writings of Oliver Wendell Holmes, Jr.,* ed. Richard A. Posner (Chicago: The University of Chicago Press, 1992), 218–19.

2. From one of the Four Maori Cosmologies, "The Creation, First Period *(thought)."* The Maori are Polynesian natives of New Zealand whose theories of creation and spiritual growth are both intricate and vivid. They "envision a gradual evolution of Being-Itself, described as pure thought, first into not-being (the void, chaos, darkness) and then into being (sky and earth, order, light). . . . They argue that gods evolved with the specific forms of being." Barbara Sproul, *Primal Myths: Creation Myths around the World* (San Francisco: HarperSanFrancisco, 1979), 337.

Introduction

1. North Carolina Bar Association, *Report of the Quality of Life Task Force and Recommendations,* June 20, 1991.

2. The oral histories of lawyers and judges upon which I rely from time to time in this book are the product of a seminar I taught at the University of North Carolina Law School. Tapes and transcripts of the oral history interviews are archived in the Southern Historical Collection in the William Round Wilson Library, University of North Carolina at Chapel Hill.

3. Interview with attorney Wade Smith, Raleigh, N.C., March 9, 1992, by UNC law student Kimberly G. Thigpen.

4. Interview with attorney James E. Ferguson, Charlotte, N.C., March 3, 1992, by UNC law student Rudolph Acree Jr.

5. Interview with attorney Malcolm Ray "Tye" Hunter, Durham, N.C., November 8, 1994, by UNC law student Devon Sanders.

Chapter One

1. One commentator has perceptively referred to the current malaise in the profession as "a great sadness." Patrick J. Schiltz, "Legal Ethics in Decline: The Elite Law Firm, the Elite Law School, and the Moral Formation of the Novice Attorney," *Minnesota Law Review* 82 (1998): 705, 787.

2. A 1997 Harris Poll shows that only 19 percent of the public thinks that the law is a

"very prestigious" occupation, a drop from 36 percent in 1977, and a drop unmatched in any other profession. A 1993 American Bar Association poll revealed that 46 percent of persons surveyed had an unfavorable impression of lawyers. Numerous surveys reveal high levels of depression, job dissatisfaction, and alcohol abuse among lawyers. See Robert Kurson, "Who's Killing the Great Lawyers of Harvard," *Esquire*, August 2000, 82; Patrick J. Schiltz, "On Being a Happy, Healthy, and Ethical Member of an Unhappy, Unhealthy, and Unethical Profession," *Vanderbilt Law Review* 52 (May 1999): 871; and Michael P. Schutt, "Oliver Wendell Holmes and the Decline of the American Lawyer: Social Engineering, Religion, and the Search for Professional Identity," *Rutgers Law Journal* 30 (1998): 143, 147–51, for summaries of statistics and commentaries on lawyer unpopularity and low morale.

3. I owe the idea of the Parcival myth as a metaphor for the lawyer's life journey to psychologist Pat Webster of Chapel Hill, North Carolina, who with her husband, attorney William L. Thorp, used that myth very effectively in two excellent retreats they conducted for lawyers and law students. The sources upon which I rely primarily for the Parcival narrative are the version by the twelfth century French writer, Cretien de Troyes, *Le Contes del graal,* and three continuations of that account by Gerbert de Montreuil, Manesier, and an unknown author, and the version by the twelfth century German writer Wolfram von Eschenbach. Accessible translations of these accounts may be found in Cretien de Troyes, *The Story of the Grail,* ed. Rupert T. Pickens, trans. William W. Kibler (New York: Garland Pub., 1990); Cretien de Troyes, *Perceval: The Story of the Grail,* trans. Nigel Bryant (Cambridge, England: D. S. Brewer, 1982); and Wolfram von Eschenbach, *Parzival,* ed. and trans. Andre Lefevre (New York: Continuum, 1991). Other, secondary sources upon which I have relied are: E. Jane Burns, *Arthurian Fictions: Rereading the Vulgate Cycle* (Columbus: University of Ohio Press, 1985); Norma Lorre Goodrich, *The Holy Grail* (New York: Harper Collins, 1992); Arthur Groos, *Romancing the Grail: Genre, Science, and Quest in Wolfram's "Parzival"* (Ithaca: Cornell University Press, 1995); Urban T. Holmes, *Cretien de Troyes* (New York: Twayne Publishers, 1970); Roger Sherman Loomis, *Arthurian Tradition and Cretien de Troyes* (New York: Columbia University Press, 1949); Roger Sherman Loomis, *The Grail: From Celtic Myth to Christian Symbol* (Cardiff: University of Wales Press, 1963); Helaine Newstead, *Bran the Blessed in Arthurian Romance* (New York: Columbia University Press, 1939); Arthur Edward Waite, *The Holy Grail: The Galahad Quest in Arthurian Literature* (New Hyde Park, N.Y.: University Books, 1961); Hermann J. Weigand, *Wolfram's Parzival,* ed. Ursula Hoffman (Ithaca: Cornell University Press, 1969); Jessie L. Weston, *From Ritual to Romance* (New York: Doubleday, 1957).

CHAPTER TWO

1. 12 N.W. 332 (Iowa 1882).

2. Oliver Wendell Holmes, "The Path of the Law," *Harvard Law Review* 10 (1897): 457.

3. Roger C. Cramton, "The Ordinary Religion of the Law School Classroom," *Journal of Legal Education* 29 (1978): 247, 253–55. Cramton refers primarily to a "value skepticism" produced in students by various aspects of legal education. Clearly, however, in its most advanced stages, the "skepticism" qualifies as cynicism toward any sort of higher moral purpose in legal work—"there are no *right* answers, just *winning* arguments" (ibid., 255).

4. See endnote 2.

5. Holmes, "The Path of the Law," 457.

6. Ibid., 459.

7. Ibid.

8. As a leading pragmatist and legal positivist, Holmes distrusted moral terms and the subjectivities of personal conscience as universal guides in human affairs. See Robert W. Gordon, "Introduction," in *The Legacy of Oliver Wendell Holmes,* ed. Robert W. Gordon

(Stanford: Stanford University Press, 1992), 6–7; J. W. Burrow, "Holmes in his Intellectual Milieu," in idem, 23–25; and Morton J. Horwitz, "The Place of Justice Holmes in American Legal Thought," in idem, 38–39, 66–70.

9. Edward G. White, *Justice Oliver Wendell Holmes* (New York: Oxford University Press, 1993), 23.

10. Holmes, "The Path of the Law," 459–60.

11. Ibid., 460.

12. Narrative is a very difficult term to define. The definition I am using here is a composite of those of other commentators. See Hayden White, "The Value of Narrativity in the Representation of Reality," in *On Narrative,* ed. W. J. T. Mitchell (Chicago: University of Chicago Press, 1980); and Stephen Winter, "The Cognitive Dimension of the Agony Between Legal Power and Narrative Meaning," *Michigan Law Review* 87 (1989): 2225.

13. Reynolds Price, *A Palpable God* (San Francisco: North Point Press, 1970), 19.

14. Numerous narrative theorists have noted the primal, a priori importance of the narrative process to the way man thinks and communicates, both with others and with himself. According to Robert Scholes, "Narrative is a place where sequence and language, among other things, intersect to form a discursive code." Robert Scholes, "Language, Narrative and Anti-Narrative," in *On Narrative,* 200–208. Hayden White states: "To raise the question of the nature of narrative is to invite reflection on the very nature of culture and, possibly, even on the nature of humanity itself. So natural is the impulse to narrate, so inevitable is the form of the narrative for any report of the way things really happened, that narrativity could appear problematical only in a culture in which it was absent— absent or, as in some domains of contemporary Western intellectual and artistic culture, programmatically refused." White, "The Value of Narrativity in the Representation of Reality," 1.

Commentators from the legal academy have also recognized the primacy of narrative in the way people think and talk. Steven Winter states: "The attraction of narrative is that it corresponds more closely to the manner in which the human mind makes sense of experience than does the conventional, abstracted rhetoric of law. The basic thrust of the cognitive process is to employ imagination to make meaning out of the embodied experience of the human organism in the world. In its prototypical sense as storytelling, narrative too proceeds from the ground up. In narrative, we take experience and configure it in a conventional and comprehensible form." Winter, "The Cognitive Dimension of the Agony Between Legal Power and Narrative Meaning," 2228. See also Patricia Ewick and Susan S. Silbey, "Subversive Stories and Hegemonic Tales: Toward a Sociology of Narrative," *Law & Society Review* 29 (1995): 197; Jane B. Baron, "Resistance to Stories," *Southern California Law Review* 67 (1994): 255, 261–62; and Robert M. Cover, "The Supreme Court, 1982 Term—Forward: Nomos and Narrative," *Harvard Law Review* 97 (1983): 4; Richard Delgado, "Storytelling for Oppositionists and Others," in *Narrative and Legal Discourse: A Reader in Story Telling and the Law,* ed. David Ray Papke (Liverpool: Deborah Charles, 1991).

15. The phrase "go for the jugular" was apparently originally used by the great appellate advocate John W. Davis, in Davis, "The Argument of an Appeal," *A.B.A. Journal* 26 (1940): 895, 897. The phrase often appears in the law school lexicon in its more innately animalistic form as "instinct for the jugular."

16. In a recent book, attorney and former ABA president Walt Bachman recommends leading this type of dual life in order to be a successful lawyer and to maintain successful personal relationships. Walt Bachman, *Law v. Life* (Rinebeck, N.Y.: Four Directions Press, 1995), 71–85. Bachman's argument is that the practice of law requires behavior (such as lying, manipulation, and secret-keeping) which is harmful to personal relationships, and therefore, professional and personal lives should be lived under different sets of moral

precepts. Other commentators have warned about the moral costs of a morally bifurcated life. See Gerald J. Postema, "Moral Responsibility in Professional Ethics," *N.Y.U. Law Review* 55 (1980): 63, 73–81; Richard Wasserstrom, "Roles and Morality," in *The Good Lawyer,* ed. David Luban (Totowa, N.J.: Rowman & Allanheld, 1984), 34–37.

17. See David Luban, "The Adversary System Excuse," in *The Good Lawyer,* 83–122; Alan Donagan, "Justifying Legal Practice in the Adversary System," in idem, 124–36; Murray L. Schwartz, "The Zeal of the Civil Advocate," in idem, 150; and Thomas L. Shaffer, "The Unique, Novel and Unsound Adversary Ethic," *Vanderbilt Law Review* 41 (1988): 697.

18. This position is, of course, strongly contested. See Luban, "The Adversary System Excuse."

CHAPTER THREE

1. See Maxwell Bloomfield, "Law and Lawyers in American Popular Culture," in *Law and American Literature,* ed. Carl Smith, John P. McWilliams, and Maxwell Bloomfield (New York: Knopf, 1983), 125.

2. Maxwell Bloomfield states that stories of American lawyers (both fictional and historical) were heavily influenced by the social and political cultures of the times in which they were told. Ibid., 131–33. As these cultures changed and the ideals and values which underlay them changed, the stories of lawyers evolved to meet new needs and definitions. This process is very like that of the creation of myths, which are a more specific version of narrative that provide theological and psychological explanation and understanding. See William Bascom, "The Forms of Folklore: Prose Narrative," in *Sacred Narrative,* ed. Alan Dundes (Berkeley: University of California Press, 1984), 9.

3. James Boyd White writes: "Literature works on different terms [from analytic discourse], on a different sense of language and meaning. A literary text is not a string of propositions, but a structured experience of the imagination." James Boyd White, "What a Lawyer Can Learn From Literature," *Harvard Law Review* 102 (1989): 2014, 2016. White goes on to say that literature and "other humanistic" texts are "not propositional but experimental and performative, not language-free, but language bound and language centered; not reducible to other terms—especially not to logical outline or analysis—but expressing their meanings through their form; not bound by the rule of noncontradiction but eager to embrace competing or opposing strains of thought; not purely intellectual, but affective and constitutive, and in this sense integrative, both of the composer and of the audience, indeed in a sense of the culture in which they work" (ibid., 2018).

4. Anthony Kronman, *The Lost Lawyer: Failing Ideal of the Legal Profession* (Cambridge, Mass.: Harvard University Press, 1993), 362–63. An excellent discussion of Kronman's thesis and other aspects of the decline of the professional ideal appears in Michael P. Schutt, "Oliver Wendell Holmes and the Decline of the American Lawyer: Social Engineering, Religion, and the Search for Professional Identity," *Rutgers Law Journal* 30 (1998): 143.

5. Ibid., 363.

6. Kronman's sources generally reference the lives of "great" lawyer-statesmen in American history or treatises on the same. Ibid., 11–17.

7. The role of the ideal of the lawyer-statesman in the early republic has been well established by scholars and commentators from both within and outside the profession and from Tocqueville to modern times: Maxwell Bloomfield, "David Hoffman and the Shaping of a Republican Legal Culture," *Maryland Law Review* 38 (1979): 673; Alexis de Tocqueville, *Democracy in America,* trans. George Lawrence, ed. J. P. Mayer (Garden City, New York: Harper & Row, 1966), 163–270; Robert W. Gordon, "The Independence of Lawyers," *Buffalo University Law Review* 68 (1988): 1, 11–30; Charles R. McManis, "The

History of First Century American Legal Education," *Washington University Law Quarterly* 59 (1981): 597, 601–37; Perry Miller, *The Life of the Mind in America: From the Revolution to the Civil War* (New York: Harcourt, Brace & World, 1965), 109–16; Russell G. Pearce, "Rediscovering the Republican Origins of the Legal Ethics Codes," *Georgetown Journal of Legal Ethics* 6 (1992): 241, 250–58; Michel J. Sandel, "America's Search for a New Public Philosophy," *The Atlantic Monthly,* March 1996; Gordon S. Wood, *The Radicalism of the American Revolution* (New York: Vintage, 1993), 104–109, 194–212.

8. Kronman, *The Lost Lawyer,* 26–52; Gordon, "The Independence of Lawyers," 14–19; Pearce, "Rediscovering the Republican Origins of the Legal Ethics Codes," 250–56.

9. Pearce, "Rediscovering the Republican Origins of the Legal Ethics Codes," 251.

10. McManis, "The History of First Century American Legal Education," 620–26.

11. Kronman, *The Lost Lawyer,* 167.

12. Interview with Judge James H. Pou Bailey, Raleigh, N.C., February 18, 1992, by UNC law student John Scherer.

13. Interview with attorney Doris Bray, in Greensboro, N.C., March 15, 1993, by UNC law student Stacy Miller.

14. Lawrence M. Friedman, *A History of American Law* (New York: Simon and Schuster, 1985), 261–65; Maxwell Bloomfield, "Law vs. Politics: The Self-Image of the American Bar (1830–1860)," *American Journal of Legal History* 12 (1968): 306. See also Bloomfield, "Law and Lawyers in American Popular Culture," 129–43.

15. Barbara A. Curran and Clara N. Carson, *The Lawyer Statistical Report: The U.S. Legal Profession in 1988* (supp. 1991), 21. In North Carolina approximately 70 percent of all lawyers practice solo or in small firms. See *Report of the North Carolina Bar Association Education Task Force, Law Schools Subcommittee Report,* March 15, 1996.

16. Kronman, *The Lost Lawyer,* 357.

17. There were other lawyer stereotypes at work on the frontier as well—some more in the categories of gamblers, shysters, and adventurers than as pillars of the community. Friedman, *A History of American Law,* 267–69; Bloomfield, "Law and Lawyers in American Popular Culture," 138–43.

18. See David Herbert Donald, *Lincoln* (New York: Simon and Schuster, 1995), 66–118.

19. In his extensive study of the contemporary accounts of people who knew Lincoln, Michael Burlingame concludes that between the ages of 40 and 45 Lincoln went through a mid-life crisis during which he withdrew in large part from public life and undertook the reflection and self-examination which enabled him to move from being a primarily local lawyer and politician to one of national stature. Michael Burlingame, *The Inner World of Abraham Lincoln* (Urbana, Ill.: University of Illinois Press, 1994), 1–14. Recent biographer David Herbert Donald attributes this period of withdrawal and self-improvement to Lincoln's experience in Congress from 1847 to 1849, during which time "he could not help observing that he had less education and professional training than most of his fellow congressmen." Donald, *Lincoln,* 142.

20. Albert A. Woldman, *Lawyer Lincoln* (New York: Carroll & Graf Publishers, 1994), 87–98. Donald, *Lincoln,* 105–106.

21. Woldman, *Lawyer Lincoln,* 90–91. Biographer David Donald reports that J. H. Buckingham, reporter for the *Boston Courier,* traveled the circuit with Lincoln in 1847 and observed that Lincoln "knew, or appeared to know, every body we met, the name of the tenant at every farm-house and the owner of every plat of ground. . . . Such a shaking of hands—such a how-d'ye-do—such a greeting of different kinds as we saw, was never seen before, . . . it seemed as if . . . he has a kind word, a smile and a bow, for every body on the road, even to the horses, and the cattle, and the swine." Quoted in Donald, *Lincoln,* 106.

22. Donald, *Lincoln,* 149, 157.

23. Ibid., 156–57.

24. Three examples that come to mind are Gavin Stevens, in novels and short stories by William Faulkner, Atticus Finch in Harper Lee's *To Kill a Mockingbird,* and Paul Begler in Robert Travers's *Anatomy of a Murder.*

25. Wade Smith interview.

26. Interview with Judge Sam J. Ervin III, Morganton, N.C., February 24, 1993, by UNC law student Hillary Arnold.

27. 4 Wheat 518 (1818)

28. In addition to being a seminal case on the issue of sanctity of public charter and contract, the case was also a political battleground between Jeffersonian Republicans who, along with the president of Dartmouth, John Wheelock, sided with the authority of the State, and Federalists, who controlled the College's Board of Trustees. The latter were, in effect, Webster's clients.

29. The Supreme Court was then comprised of seven members: Chief Justice John Marshall and Justices Gabriel Duval, William Johnson, Henry Brockholst Livingston, Joseph Story, Thomas Todd, and Bushrod Washington.

30. Claude Moore Fuess, *Daniel Webster* (Boston: Little, Brown & Co., 1930), 230.

31. Ibid., 231.

32. Ibid., 232.

33. Justice Story's description is from a manuscript in the Library of Congress and is reprinted in Fuess, *Daniel Webster,* 232, n. 1.

34. Webster's faults and character flaws (along with his tremendous intelligence, power, and achievements) are amply chronicled in a recent biography by Robert V. Remini, *Daniel Webster: The Man and His Time* (New York: W. W. Norton & Co., 1997). See also, Sydney Nathans, *Daniel Webster and Jacksonian Democracy* (Baltimore: Johns Hopkins University Press, 1973).

35. While there was substantial political and financial power on both sides of the case, Webster succeeded in portraying his client as a "little institution: put upon by the great powers of the State." Fuess, *Daniel Webster,* 215–32.

36. Harper Lee, *To Kill a Mockingbird* (New York: Warner Books, 1982), 231.

37. Michael D. Davis and Hunter R. Clark, *Thurgood Marshall: Warrior at the Bar, Rebel on the Bench* (New York: Carol Publishing Group, 1992), 69–77; Richard Klugar, *Simple Justice* (New York: Alfred A. Knopf, 1995), 181–94.

38. 347 U.S. 483 (1954).

39. Owen Wister, *The Virginian* (New York: New American Library, Inc., 1979). This legendary novel has gone through numerous editions and printings and was originally copyrighted in 1902 by the Macmillan Company.

40. Cormac McCarthy, *All the Pretty Horses* (New York: Knopf, 1992).

41. G. Edward White, *The Eastern Establishment and the Western Experience: The West of Frederic Remington, Theodore Roosevelt, and Owen Wister* (New Haven: Yale University Press, 1968), 142.

42. Wister's narrative method in his Western fiction was to have a "tenderfoot narrator" recount the story for the reader. White, *The Eastern Establishment and the Western Experience,* 125. An obvious purpose in this approach was to tell the tale to Easterners, who would comprise his primary reading audience, from a perspective they could understand. The tenderfoot reader learns about the rugged ways of the West along with his tenderfoot guide.

43. Wister, *The Virginian,* 273–74.

44. McCarthy, *All the Pretty Horses,* 293–94.

45. Thomas L. Shaffer, "Law as Moral Discourse," *Notre Dame Lawyer* 55 (1979): 232, 235. The lawyer in the story is so named apparently because in response to his client's request, he tells her she should be horsewhipped.

46. Shaffer, "Law as Moral Discourse," 235, 239, 240, and 243.

47. Lincoln's abandonment of his client under such conditions would violate current ethical rules mandating loyalty to client. See *ABA Model Rules of Professional Conduct* 1.1, 1.3, 1.16 and comments thereto. In one case where Lincoln and his partner, Swett, were defending a man charged with murder, Lincoln simply left the courtroom, saying that he was sure the state's witnesses were truthful and his client was lying and that if his client would not enter a plea, he would not represent him further. Woldman, *Lawyer Lincoln,* 193–94.

48. Virginia Foster Durr, *Outside the Magic Circle: the Autobiography of Virginia Foster Durr* (University, Ala.: University of Alabama Press, 1985); David Garrow, *Bearing the Cross* (New York: William Morrow & Company, Inc., 1986), 13–14; John Salmond, *The Conscience of a Lawyer: Clifford J. Durr and American Civil Liberties, 1899–1975* (Tuscaloosa: University of Alabama Press, 1990), 154–196. Concerning Julius Chambers, see Frye Gaillard, *The Dream Long Deferred* (Chapel Hill: The University of North Carolina Press, 1988).

49. See Gaillard, *The Dream Long Deferred;* Jack Bass, *Taming the Storm: the Life and Times of Judge Frank M. Johnson and the South's Fight Over Civil Rights* (New York: Doubleday, 1993); David Garrow, *Bearing the Cross;* Robert Francis Kennedy, *Judge Frank M. Johnson, Jr.: A Biography* (New York: Putnam, 1978); Tinsley E. Yarbrough, *A Passion for Justice: J. Waties Waring and Civil Rights* (New York, Oxford University Press, 1987); Tinsley E. Yarbrough, *Judge Frank Johnson and Human Rights in Alabama* (University, Ala.: University of Alabama Press, 1981).

50. See Stephen Pepper, "The Lawyer's Amoral Ethical Role: A Defense, A Problem, and Some Possibilities," *American Bar Foundation Research Journal* (1986): 613.

51. See David Luban, "Introduction," in Luban, ed., *The Good Lawyer;* Richard Wasserstrom, "Lawyers as Professionals: Some Moral Issues," *Human Rights* 5 (1975): 1.

52. At the time Davis entered Washington and Lee Law School in the Fall of 1904, it was one of eight law schools in the country that allowed students to complete work for their degree in one year. William H. Harbaugh, *Lawyer's Lawyer: The Life of John W. Davis* (New York: Oxford University Press, 1973), 23. The school had two professors and approximately fifty to sixty students, only a small portion of whom had bachelor's degrees. Davis held a bachelor's degree—also from Washington and Lee. Ibid., 19.

53. The observer was Chief District Judge David Pine of the United States District Court for the District of Columbia. Harbaugh, *Lawyer's Lawyer,* 406 (interview with Judge Pine by the author).

54. By the time of his death in 1955, only two other lawyers in history had argued more cases before the Court: Walter Jones argued three hundred and seventeen, and Daniel Webster argued between one hundred eighty-five and two hundred cases. Harbaugh, *Lawyer's Lawyer,* 531.

55. Harbaugh, *Lawyer's Lawyer,* 128. The statement attributed to Holmes was relayed to the author, William Harbaugh, in his interview with Robert Szold, who served in the Solicitor General's Office with John W. Davis. Of the 67 cases Davis argued before the Supreme Court as Solicitor General, he won 48 of them. Sydnor Thompson, "John W. Davis and His Role in the Public School Segregation Cases—Personal Memoir," *Washington and Lee Law Review* 52 (1996): 1679, 1681.

56. Harbaugh, *Lawyer's Lawyer,* 101, 104, 127–28.

57. Ibid., 404–406.

58. Ibid., 404 (quoting Joseph M. Proskauer, "Letters from Readers," *Commentary,* January 1970, 4).

59. Harbaugh, *Lawyer's Lawyer,* 404 (interview by the author with Learned Hand).

60. Ibid., 410 (quoting Lloyd Paul Stryker, "John W. Davis—A Tribute," *New York Law Forum* 1 [1955]: 206, 207).

61. Ibid., 458 (quoting Phillip M. Stern, with the collaboration of Harold P. Green, *The Oppenheimer Case: Security on Trial* [1970], 507–508).

62. 347 U.S. 483 (1954).

63. Harbaugh, *Lawyer's Lawyer,* 503 (quoting "The Segregation Issue," *Time,* December 22, 1952, 12–13).

64. Ibid., 284, 286–87.

65. Ibid., 310.

66. Davis Polk Wardell Gardiner & Reed. After 1942, Davis Polk Wardell Sunderland & Kiendl.

CHAPTER FOUR

1. Rollo May, *The Cry for Myth* (New York: Delta Publishing, 1991), 15.

2. Ibid., 26.

3. Joseph Campbell with Bill Moyers, *The Power of Myth* (New York: Doubleday, 1988), 38–39.

4. C. G. Jung, "The Psychology of the Child Archetype," *The Collected Works of C. G. Jung,* vol. 9, pt. 1, *The Archetypes of the Collective Unconscious,* trans. R. F. C. Hull, Bollingen Series 20 (Princeton: Princeton University Press, 1959), 154.

5. Kronman, *The Lost Lawyer,* 354.

6. Campbell, *The Power of Myth,* 38–39.

7. In his book tracing various mythological themes through various world cultures, J. F. Bierlein says: (1) "Myth is a unique use of language that describes the realities beyond our five senses. It fills gaps between the images of the unconscious and the language of conscious logic." (2) "Myth is the 'glue' that holds societies together; it is the basis of identity for communities, tribes, and nations." (3) Myth is the essential ingredient in all codes of moral conduct; the rules for living have always derived their legitimacy from their origins in myth and religion." (4) "Myth is a pattern of beliefs that give meaning to life. Myth enables individuals and societies to adapt to their respective environments with dignity and value." J. F. Bierlein, *Parallel Myths* (New York: Ballentine Books, 1994), 6.

8. See Michael Grossberg, "Institutionalizing Masculinity: The Law as a Masculine Profession," in *Meanings for Manhood: Constructions of Masculinity in Victorian America,* ed. Mark C. Carnes and Clyde Griffin (Chicago: University of Chicago Press, 1990).

9. This is the attitude Stephen Pepper condemns as creating an "oligarchy of lawyers." Pepper, "The Lawyer's Amoral Ethical Role: A Defense, A Problem, and Some Possibilities," *American Bar Foundation Research Journal* (1986): 617.

10. In a very perceptive analysis of the current credibility of the ethic of the gentleman-lawyer, Tom and Mary Shaffer posit that its chief failing as a formula for setting professional standards is that it is based upon a moral order of internalized, moral rules which one simply learns "as he learns his language" and then applies without scrutiny or reflection. As a result, say the Shaffers, gentleman-lawyers abused power (failed to see their commonality with their clients and communities and treated them as disconnected "others" subject to control and manipulation according to the gentleman's code of what is good and just); were blind to a true understanding of tragedy (in the sense that, while they accepted the inevitability and "tragedy"—in the classical sense—of moral choice, they failed to see that the tragedy was not in the fact that such choices are a necessity of life but in the equally necessary and painful learning and growing process that follows the making of choices and, therefore, of "being" in a moral life); and were, as a result of the above two, unable to account for the suffering of others (which results from making the moral choice under the gentleman's ethical code). Thomas L. Shaffer with Mary Shaffer, *American Lawyers and Their Communities* (Notre Dame: University of Notre Dame Press, 1991), 127–28.

11. Interview with attorney James K. Dorset, Jr., in Raleigh, North Carolina, March 3, 1993, by UNC law student H. George Kurani.

12. See Judith Welch Wegner, "Lawyers, Learning and Professionalism: Meditations on a Theme," *Cleveland State Law Review* 43 (1995): 191, 211, who notes that over 70 percent of North Carolina lawyers surveyed believed that unprofessional conduct and incivility were more prevalent in today's practice than when they began practicing law. See also *Interim Report of the Committee on Civility of the 7th Federal Judicial Circuit,* 143 F.R.D. 371 (1992); John Marks, "The American Uncivil Wars," *U.S. News and World Report,* April 22, 1996, 66–72; American Bar Foundation, "Uncivil Litigation: Problematic Behavior in Large Law Firms," *Researching Law* 7 (Fall 1996).

13. See American Bar Association, *The State of the Legal Profession* (1991); Andrew Benjamin, Elaine Darling, and Bruce Sales, "The Prevalence of Depression, Alcohol Abuse, and Cocaine Abuse Among United States Lawyers," *International Journal of Law and Psychiatry* 13 (1990): 241.

14. Oliver Wendell Holmes, "The Profession of the Law," in *The Essential Holmes,* 219.

15. C. G. Jung, "Aion: Phenomenology of the Self," *Collected Works,* vol. 9, pt. 2, *Aion: Research into the Phenomenology of the Self,* trans. R. F. C. Hull, Bollingen Series 20 (Princeton: Princeton University Press, 1959), 8–10.

CHAPTER FIVE

1. The villainous lawyer in literature is identified in Maxwell Bloomfield, "Law and Lawyers in American Popular Culture" (see chap. 3, n. 1 above), and in E. F. J. Tucker, *Intruder into Eden: Representations of the Common Lawyer in English Literature 1350–1750* (Columbia, S.C.: Camden House, 1984), 31–50.

2. Elizabeth Ammons and Annette White-Parks, eds., *Tricksterism in Turn-of-the-Century American Literature: A Multicultural Perspective* (Hanover: University Press of New England, 1994); C. G. Jung, "On the Psychology of the Trickster Figure," *Collected Works,* vol. 9, pt. 1: 255–72; Suzanne E. Lundquist, *The Trickster: A Transformative Archetype* (San Francisco: Mellen Research University Press, 1991); Paul Radin, *The Trickster: A Study in American Indian Mythology* (New York: Schocken, 1956); John W. Roberts, *From Trickster to Badman: The Black Folk Hero in Slavery and Freedom* (Philadelphia: University of Pennsylvania Press, 1989); Jeanne Rosier Smith, *Writing Tricksters: Mythic Gambols in American Ethnic Literature* (Berkeley: University of California Press, 1997);

3. While the trickster is not always male, he is most often depicted as male. See Tiffany A. Lopez, "Maria Cristina Mena: Turn-of-the-Century La Malinche and Other Tales of Cultural (Re)Construction," in Ammons and Annette White-Parks, *Tricksterism in Turn-of-the-Century American Literature,* 34–35.

4. Jung identifies aspects of the trickster in stories from the Bible (including attributes of Yahweh in the Old Testament and in some of the characteristics of Christ related in the New Testament), Greek mythology, medieval European pageantry, and shamanism throughout the world. He says: "There is something of the trickster in the character of the shaman and medicine-man, for he, too, often plays malicious jokes on people, only to fall victim in his turn to the vengeance of those whom he has injured. For this reason, his profession sometimes puts him in peril of his life." Jung, *Collected Works,* vol. 9, pt. 1: 256. The trickster also appears in African and African-American culture; see Henry Louis Gates, Jr., *The Signifying Monkey* (New York: Oxford University Press, 1988); Julia B. Farwell, "Goophering Around: Authority and the Trick of Storytelling in Charles W. Chestnut's 'The Conjure Woman,'" in Ammons and White-Parks, *Tricksterism in Turn-of-the-Century American Literature,* 79–92; and John W. Roberts, *From Trickster to Badman;* in Asian-American culture, see Annette White-Parks, "We Wear the Mask: Sui Fin Far as One Example of Trickster Authorship," in Ammons and White Parks, 1–20; in Hispanic-American culture,

see Tiffany A. Lopez, "Maria Cristina Mena: Turn-of-the-Century La Malinche and Other
Tales of Cultural (Re)Construction," in Ammons and White-Parks, 21–45. Perhaps one of
the most famous examples of the trickster in African-American folk tales is Brer Rabbit,
adopted (some might say stolen) from the folklore of African-American slaves and made
famous by Joel Chandler Harris. See Arna Bontemps and Langston Hughes, *The Book of
Negro Folklore* (New York: Dodd, Mead, 1958), 1–30.

5. Jung, *Collected Works,* vol. 9, pt. 1: 260.

6. The trickster's abuse of ordinary people sometimes takes a sexual form, and he is
depicted in both African and Native American stories as possessed of an enormous penis.
In this guise the trickster literally takes the form of "fucker" (of others) or "he who fucks."
This characterization, without the over-sized penis, is also applied to female tricksters. See
Lopez, "Maria Cristina Mena," 35.

7. Lundquist, *The Trickster: A Transformative Archetype,* 23–28; Radin, *The Trickster:
A Study in American Indian Mythology.*

8. See Bloomfield, "Law and Lawyers in American Popular Culture," 32–35; Friedman,
A History of American Law, 94–95.

9. Friedman, *A History of American Law,* 96 (quoting from H. T. Lefler, ed., *North
Carolina History as Told by Contemporaries* [1956]).

10. Bloomfield, "Law and Lawyers in American Popular Culture," 39–50. Maxwell
Bloomfield attributes some of the distrust of lawyers after the revolution to the identification
of American lawyers with the common law—a British legacy, and one perceived to value
individual rights above morality. Ibid., 34.

11. Alexis de Tocqueville, *Democracy in America,* 263–70.

12. Bloomfield, "Law and Lawyers in American Popular Culture," 42–43.

13. "The Republic of Beasts," *Columbian Magazine* 2 (September 1788): 538; quoted
in Bloomfield, "Law and Lawyers in American Popular Culture," 41.

14. Interview with Justice Henry Ell Frye, North Carolina Supreme Court, February 18,
1992, by UNC law student Amy E. Boening.

15. P. W. Grayson [pseud.], *Vice Unmasked, an Essay: Being a Consideration of the
Influence of Law upon the Moral Essence of Man* (1830), quoted in Perry Miller, *The Legal
Mind in America: From Independence to the Civil War* (Garden City, N.Y.: Doubleday,
1962), 192–99.

16. June Singer, *Boundaries of the Soul: The Practice of Jung's Psychology* (New York:
Doubleday, 1994), 164–65.

17. Jung, *Collected Works,* vol. 9, pt. 1: 262–63.

18. Lundquist, 31.

19. Jung even refers to the trickster as the "forerunner of the savior, and like him,
God, man and animal at once. He is both subhuman and superhuman, a bestial and divine
being, whose chief and most alarming characteristic is his unconsciousness." Jung, *Collected
Works,* vol. 9, pt. 1: 263.

CHAPTER SIX

1. Joseph Campbell, *Myths to Live By* (New York: Penguin Books, 1993), 10–11.
Campbell's thesis is supported by the work of Carl Jung: Myths . . . have a vital meaning. Not merely do they represent, they *are* the psychic life of the primitive tribe, which
immediately falls to pieces and decays when it loses its mythological heritage, like a man
who has lost his soul. A tribe's mythology is its living religion, whose loss is always and
everywhere, even among the civilized, a moral catastrophe." C. G. Jung, "The Psychology
of the Child Archetype," *Collected Works,* vol. 9, pt. 1: 248. For a critique of Campbell's
thesis, see Robert A. Segal, "Joseph Campbell's Theory of Myth," in *Sacred Narrative,*
256–69.

2. Sydnor Thompson, "John W. Davis and His Role in the Public School Desegregation Cases—A Personal Memoir," 1692 (cf. chap. 3, n. 55 above).

3. My evidence for this is largely anecdotal and comes from numerous conversations with older members of the profession and from the oral histories of lawyers and judges taken by UNC students in the seminar I taught on the oral histories of lawyers and judges.

4. Lawrence J. Landwehr, "Lawyers as Social Progressives or Reactionaries: The Law and Order Cognitive Orientation of Lawyers," *Law and Psychology Review* 7 (1982): 39. Landwehr finds that the majority of lawyers are at Lawrence Kohlberg's fourth stage of ethical thinking: "The law and order orientation . . . an orientation toward authority, fixed rules, and the maintenance of social order. Right behavior consists of doing one's duty, showing respect for authority, and maintaining the given social order for its own sake" (ibid., 40, quoting Kohlberg, "The Cognitive-Developmental Approach to Moral Education," in *Reading in Moral Education,* ed. P. Scharf [1978]).

5. Campbell, *Myths to Live By,* 11.

6. Interview with Judge Frank W. Snepp, Mecklenburg County Superior Court, Charlotte, N.C., February 25, 1993, by UNC law student Kevin B. Bunn.

7. James Hollis, *Tracking the Gods: The Place of Myth in Modern Life* (Toronto: Inner City Books, 1995), 22.

8. Campbell, *The Power of Myth,* 16.

9. Cynthia Ozick, *Metaphor & Memory* (New York: Random House, 1991), 282–83.

10. Interview with attorney James K. Dorset, Raleigh, N.C., March 11, 1993, by UNC law student H. George Kurani.

11. Interview with Judge James B. McMillan, Charlotte, N.C., November 1, 1991, by Walter H. Bennett Jr.

12. Interview with attorney Emil F. Kratt, Charlotte, N.C., October 4, 1996, by UNC law student David F. Shives.

13. See Deborah K. Holmes, "Learning from Corporate America: Addressing Dysfunction in the Large Law Firm, *Gonzaga Law Review* 31 (1995–96): 373, 381–84; Renee M. Landers et al., "Rat Race Redux: Adverse Selection in the Determination of Work Hours in Law Firms," *American Economic Review* 86 (1996): 329; Note, "Why Law Firms Cannot Afford to Maintain the Mommy Track," *Harvard Law Review* 109 (1996): 1375, 1378–80.

14. Harry T. Edwards, "The Growing Disjunction Between Legal Education and the Legal Profession," *Michigan Law Review* 91 (1992): 34, 72–73. See F. Leary Davis, "Back to the Future: The Buyer's Market and the Need for Law Firm Leadership, Creativity and Innovation," *Campbell Law Review* 16 (1994): 147.

15. An insightful examination of the effect of billing practices upon lawyers' working conditions appears in Michael Trotter's study of large firms in Atlanta, *Profit and the Practice of Law: What's Happened to the Legal Profession* (Athens, Ga.: University of Georgia Press, 1997), 81–89, 112–13; See also Landers et al, "Rat Race Redux."

16. Trotter, *Profit and the Practice of Law,* 27–32, 97; Landers et al., "Rat Race Redux."

17. Interview with Judge George F. Bason, Raleigh, N.C., February 15, 1993, by UNC law student Jeannette S. Graviss.

18. See Edwards, "The Growing Disjunction between Legal Education and the Legal Profession." See also Luban, "The Adversary System Excuse"; Schwartz, "The Zeal of the Civil Advocate"; Shaffer, "The Unique, Novel and Unsound Adversary Ethic" (cf. chap. 2, n. 17 above).

19. Interview with attorney Howard Twiggs, Raleigh, N.C., March 9, 1993, by UNC law student Kimberly W. Rabren.

20. Interview with attorney H. James Thomas, Princeton, N.J., in Richard A. Moll, *The Lure of the Law* (New York: Viking, 1990), 134.

21. This term was first used in regard to lawyers by Richard Wasserstrom in "Lawyers as Professionals: Some Moral Issues" (cf. chap. 3, n. 51 above).

22. See Monroe H. Freedman, *Understanding Lawyer's Ethics* (New York: Matthew Bender & Company, Inc., 1990), 14–65; Charles J. Fried, "The Lawyer as Friend: The Moral Foundations of the Lawyer-Client Relation," *Yale Law Journal* 85 (1976): 1060; Pepper, "The Lawyer's Amoral Ethical Role" (cf. chap. 3, n. 50 above); Simon Rifkind, "The Lawyer's Role and Responsibility in Modern Society," *The Record* 30 (1975): 534.

23. See Alan H. Goldman, *The Moral Foundations of Professional Ethics* (Totowa, N.J.: Rowman and Littlefield, 1980); essays in Luban, *The Good Lawyer;* Luban, "The Adversary System Excuse"; Shaffer, "The Unique, Novel and Unsound Adversary Ethic"; Postema, "Moral Responsibility in Professional Ethics"; Simon, "The Ideology of Advocacy."

24. Quoted in Fried, "The Lawyer as Friend: The Moral Foundations of the Lawyer-Client Relation," 1060, n. 1.

25. Perhaps the most famous example of such zealousness was the performance of attorneys for both sides in the O. J. Simpson case. Numerous critics have castigated the ethics and professionalism of those involved. See Jeffry Toobin, *The Run of His Life: The People v. O. J. Simpson* (New York: Random House, 1996); Jeffrey Rosen, "The Bloods and the Crits: O. J. Simpson, Critical Race Theory, the Law and the Triumph of Color in America," *The New Republic* 215, n. 24 (December 9, 1996).

26. Sharon Smith Leaman, "Long Distance Law Firms: Intranets that Help Lawyers Keep in Touch Are Opening New Possibilities for Branch Offices," *The Legal Times,* January 26, 1998.

27. John V. Pavlik, *New Media Technology: Cultural and Commercial Perspectives* (Boston: Allyn and Bacon, 1998), 290–91, 320–21; Stephen L. Talbott, *The Future Does Not Compute* (Sebastopol, Calif.: O'Reilly & Associates, Inc., 1995), 232–33.

28. Talbott, 233.

CHAPTER SEVEN

1. Roscoe Pound, *The Lawyer from Antiquity to Modern Times* (St. Paul: West, 1953), 5.

2. *Shapero v. Kentucky Bar Association,* 486 U.S. 466 (1988), Justice O'Connor, joined by Chief Justice Rhenquist and Justice Scalia, dissenting.

3. Interview with Justice Henry Ell Frye, North Carolina Supreme Court, February 18, 1992, by UNC law student Amy E. Boening.

4. Interview with attorney Ellen Gerber, High Point, N.C., February 18, 1992, by UNC Law Student Kristen Gislason.

5. Carl Bogus, "The Death of an Honorable Profession," *Indiana Law Journal* 71 (1996): 911; Russell G. Pearce, "The Professional Paradigm Shift: Why Discarding Professional Ideology Will Improve the Conduct and Reputation of the Bar," *New York University Law Review* 70 (1995): 1229. See also James M. Dolliver, "Law as a Profession: Will It Survive?" *Gonzaga Law Review* 26 (1990–91): 267; and Trotter, *Profit and the Practice of Law* (cf. chap. 6, n. 15 above).

6. Pearce, "The Professional Paradigm Shift"; Ronald Gilson and Robert Mnookin's work has also been interpreted in this vein. See William H. Simon, "Babbitt v. Brandeis: The Decline of the Professional Ideal," *Stanford Law Review* 37 (1985): 565, 576–84, discussing Gilson and Mnookin, "Sharing among the Human Capitalists: An Economic Inquiry into the Corporate Law Firm and How Partners Split Profits," *Stanford Law Review* 37 (1985): 313.

7. I take it as no longer open to question that a lawyer's work inevitably ranges far beyond pure, Holmesian, legal analysis into questions of economics, politics, social issues, and other moral concerns. Anybody who has practiced law—particularly where clients are individuals—knows this. It is also recognized in the professional codes. See *ABA Model Rule of Professional Conduct* 2.1 and comments thereto.

Chapter Eight

1. Approximately 44 percent of people entering law school in 1993 were women. American Bar Association Commission of Women in the Profession, *Elusive Equality: The Experiences of Women in Legal Education* (1996). See also American Bar Association Commission on Women in the Profession, *Women in the Law: A Look at the Numbers* (1995), which shows that in 1990 women comprised close to a third of those admitted to the bar in the United States. Despite these gains, women account for less than 15 percent of partners in major firms. See Jennifer L. Rosato, "The Socratic Method and Women Law Students: Humanize, Don't Feminize," *Southern California Review of Law and Women's Studies* 7 (1997): 37 and studies cited therein at 56.

2. See James Rogers, "The Journey Continues," *A.B.A. Journal* 102 (April 1997); Rick L. Morgan and Kurt Snyder, eds., *Official American Bar Association Guide to Approved Law Schools* (New York: Macmillan, 1998).

3. This was my observation of students at the University of North Carolina Law School over the twelve years I taught there. I have heard this from a fair number of colleagues from UNC and other law schools as well.

4. Nancy J. Crimm, "A Study: Law Students' Moral Perspectives In the Context of Advocacy and Decision-Making Roles," *New England Law Review* 29 (1994): 1.

5. See Gisila LaBouvie-Vief, *Psyche & Eros: Mind and Gender in the Life Course* (Cambridge: Cambridge University Press, 1994), 39–61.

6. Ibid., 33–43.

7. Michael Grossberg, "Institutionalizing Masculinity," 135–36 (cf. chap. 4, n. 8 above). If Professor Grossberg is correct in this assertion, it is notable that the masculinization of the bar occurred in tandem with (and perhaps as a necessary corollary to) the rise of the lawyer-statesman. See Janet Rifkin, "Toward a Theory of Law and Patriarchy," *Harvard Women's Law Journal* 3 (1980): 83, also contending that the patriarchal nature of the legal profession is culturally based and was conceived and enforced purposefully by men to keep men in power. See also Jennifer L. Rosato, "The Socratic Method and Women Law Students: Humanize, Don't Feminize," for a discussion of studies (particularly the "Guinier Study" at the University of Pennsylvania Law School) showing the negative effects of traditional law school teaching methods on women students.

8. Emma Jung and Marie-Louise Von Franz, *The Grail Legend,* trans. Andrea Dykes (Boston: Sigo Press, 1986), 56–58; Robert Johnston, *He: Understanding Masculine Psychology* (New York: Harper and Row Publishers, Inc., 1989), 21–24.

9. Numerous other commentators have recognized this aspect of lawyer-think. See James R. Elkins, "Moral Discourse and Legalism in Legal Education," *Journal of Legal Education* 32 (1982): 11; and others who have noted its masculine cast: Katherine T. Bartlett, "Feminist Perspectives on the Ideological Impact of Legal Education upon the Profession," *North Carolina Law Review* 72 (1994): 1259; Lucinda M. Finley, "Breaking Women's Silence in Law: The Dilemma of the Gendered Nature of Legal Reasoning," *Notre Dame Law Review* 64 (1989): 886; Lani Guinier et al., *Becoming Gentlemen: Women, Law School and Institutional Change* (Boston: Beacon Press, 1997); Janet Rifkin, "Toward a Theory of Law and Patriarchy"; Deborah L. Rhode, "Missing Questions: Feminist Perspective on Legal Education," *Stanford Law Review* 45 (1993): 1547.

10. For a more complete discussion of the masculine nature of legal discourse (and its effect on women lawyers and law students), see Taunya L. Banks, "Gender Bias in the Classroom," *Journal of Legal Education* 38 (1988): 137, 141–42; Lucinda M. Finley, "Breaking Women's Silence in Law"; Lani Gunier et al., *Becoming Gentlemen;* Carolyn Jin-Myung, "Questioning the Culture-Biased Assumptions of the Adversary System: Voices of Asian-American Law Students," *Berkeley Women's Law Journal* 7 (1992): 125; Carrie Menkel-Meadow, "Portia in a Different Voice: Speculations on Women's Lawyering Process,"

Berkeley Women's Law Journal 1 (1985): 39, and "Portia Redux: Another Look at Gender, Feminism, and Legal Ethics, *Virginia Journal of Social Policy and Law* 2 (1994): 75; Judith Resnik, "Gender Bias: From Classes to Courts," *Stanford Law Review* 45 (1993): 2195; Robin West, "Jurisprudence and Gender," *University of Chicago Law Review* 55 (1988): 1. Studies of women students at specific law schools are: Robert Cranfield, "Contextualizing the Different Voice: Women, Occupational Goals, and Legal Education, *Law and Policy* 16 (1994): 1 (Harvard Law School); Suzanne Homer and Lois Schwartz, "Admitted but Not Accepted: Outsiders Take an Inside Look at Law School," *Berkeley Women's Law Journal* 5 (1989–90): 1; Janet Tabor et al., "Gender, Legal Education, and the Legal Profession: An Empirical Study of Stanford Law Students and Graduates," *Stanford Law Review* 40 (1988): 1209; and Catherine Weiss and Louise Melling, "The Legal Education of Twenty Women," *Stanford Law Review* 40 (1988): 1299. For a more general discussion of the differences between men's and women's moral reasoning, see Carol Gilligan, *In a Different Voice: Psychological Theory and Women's Development* (Cambridge: Harvard University Press, 1982) and Carol Gilligan, Janie Victoria Ward, and Jill McLean Taylor, eds., *Mapping the Moral Domain: A Contribution of Women's Thinking to Psychological Theory and Education* (Cambridge: Harvard University Press, 1998).

11. Cramton, "The Ordinary Religion of the Law School Classroom" (cf. chap. 2, n. 3 above); Griswold, "Intellect and Spirit" (cf. chap. 2, footnote C).

12. Cramton, "The Ordinary Religion of the Law School Classroom," 260–62. A recent study of graduating law students attributes the legal profession's (including both men and women members) preference for "masculine," "rights based" thinking as opposed to a "feminine" ethic of care largely to the training they received in law school. Crimm, "A Study: Law Students' Moral Perspectives In the Context of Advocacy and Decision-Making Roles," 29–30.

13. See Stanley Fish, *There's No Such Thing as Free Speech and It's a Good Thing, Too* (New York: Oxford University Press, 1994), 3–28, 200–230; Jerome Frank, *Law and the Modern Mind* (New York: Brentano's, 1930); Duncan Kennedy, "Freedom and Constraint in Adjudication: A Critical Phenomenology," *Journal of Legal Education* 36 (1986): 518.

14. Lawrence J. Landwehr, "Lawyers as Social Progressives or Reactionaries: The Law and Order Cognitive Orientation of Lawyers," *Law and Psychology Review* 7 (1982): 39, 44. For more in-depth discussions of the application of Kohlberg's methods to legal education, see Elliott M. Abramson, "Puncturing the Myth of the Moral Intractability of Law Students: The Suggestiveness of the Work of Psychologist Lawrence Kohlberg for Ethical Training in Legal Education," *Notre Dame Journal of Law, Ethics and Public Policy* 7 (1993): 223; and Kurt M. Saunders and Linda Levine, "Learning to Think Like a Lawyer," *University of San Francisco Law Review* 28 (1994): 121, arguing that law students can be influenced morally and are not, therefore, immutably bound to Kohlberg's fourth level.

15. See LaBouvie-Vief, *Psyche & Eros*, 253–61; Hilary M. Lips and Nina Lee Colwill, *The Psychology of Sex Differences* (Englewood Cliffs, N.J.: Prentice-Hall, 1978), 41–43; Edward C. Whitmont, *Return of the Goddess* (New York: Crossroad, 1992), 180–204.

16. White, *Justice Oliver Wendell Holmes,* 91 (cf. chap. 2, n. 9 above).

17. Oliver Wendell Holmes, "Harvard Law School," *American Law Review* 5 (1870): 177.

18. Holmes, "The Path of the Law," 459 (cf. chap. 2, n. 2 above).

CHAPTER NINE

1. Reported as "Feminist Discourse, Moral Values, and the Law—A Conversation," *Buffalo Law Review* 34 (1985): 11. The other panelists were Ellen C. DuBois, Mary C. Dunlap, and Carrie J. Menkel-Meadow. Moderators were Isabel Marcus and Paul J. Spiegelman.

2. See Gilligan, *In a Different Voice*, 22–63 (cf. chap. 8, n. 10 above).

3. "Feminist Discourse, Moral Values, and the Law," 62–63.

4. Ibid., 63.

5. Ibid., 73–75.

6. Jungian psychologist Edward C. Whitmont writes: "The political and social goals of the women's movement deserve fullest endorsement. They are vital in establishing equal human rights and dignity on the social level. However, an egalitarianism that disregards human differences, and deals with sociological problems as though there were no difference between archetypal masculinity and femininity, is a remnant of the repressive, monotheistic, and monolithic patriarchal outlook. It prevents the liberation of the devalued and repressed Yin nature." Whitmont, *Return of the Goddess* (New York: Crossroad, 1992), 151.

7. See Linda Brannon, *Gender: Psychological Perspectives* (Boston: Allyn and Bacon, 1995), 208–17. A psychologist with whom I have discussed the relation between judgment and anger (Dr. Pat Webster, Chapel Hill, North Carolina) states that judgment is frequently a manifestation of anger that is not otherwise honestly expressed and occurs in two scenarios: We tend to judge others as inferior when we feel threatened or bested by them and need to practice one-upmanship; and, we tend to judge others when we see in them some aspect of ourselves we do not like or of which we are ashamed.

8. MacKinnon seems to believe that, if women were free to express themselves, we would see a new kind of power emerge, which, to my knowledge, she has never defined or envisioned. She simply says that if men will take their feet off the throats of women, we will see women's power. MacKinnon, "Feminist Discourse, Moral Values, and the Law: A Conversation," 75. How that would differ from what Gilligan describes as feminine values and methodology is not clear.

9. Psychologist Edward Whitmont pays glowing tribute to feminine power: "Femininity can no longer be limited to responsiveness, passivity, and mothering. It will discover and express its active, initiating creative, and transformative capacity." And:

"The archetypal role of the new femininity is to stand as a priestess of the fullness of life as it is, with its unpredictable pitfalls and unfathomable depths, richness and deprivation, risks and errors, joys and pains. She insists on personal experiencing and personal response to the needs of the human condition." Whitmont, *Return of the Goddess,* 189 and 197.

10. See Lips and Colwill, *The Psychology of Sex Differences* (cf. chap. 8, n. 15 above); C. G. Jung, "Syzygy: Anima and Animus," *Collected Works,* vol 9, pt. 2: 11–22; June Singer, *Boundaries of the Soul: The Practice of Jung's Psychology,* 178–208 (cf. chap. 5, n. 16 above); Edward C. Whitmont, *The Symbolic Quest: Basic Concepts of Analytical Psychology* (Princeton: Princeton University Press, 1991), 185–215.

11. Jung, *Collected Works,* vo. 9, pt. 2: 11–22. Jung's use of these definitions has come under criticism by feminist critics who fault his limited male perspective—in particular his tendency to equate the anima (his understanding of it from his own experience) with feminine traits in women, and his equation of the animus in women with his own understanding of masculinity. See Mary Daly, *Gyn/Ecology: The Metaethics of Radical Feminism;* Naomi Goldenberg, *Changing of the Gods: Feminism and the End of Traditional Religions* (Boston: Beacon Press, 1979); Demaris S. Wehr, *Jung and Feminism* (Boston: Beacon Press, 1987); Carol Christ, "Some Comments on Jung, Jungians and the Study of Women, *Anima* 3, no. 2 (Spring Equinox 1977); Naomi Goldenberg, "A Feminist Critique of Jung," *Signs: Journal of Women in Culture* 2, no. 2 (1976): 443–49. For defenders of Jung in this debate, see Ann Ulanov, *Receiving Women: Studies in the Psychology and Theology of the Feminine* (Philadelphia: Westminister Press, 1981); June Singer, *Boundaries of the Soul,* 178–208; June Singer and Stephanie Halpern, "Two Responses to Naomi Goldenberg," *Anima* 4, no. 1 (Fall Equinox 1977).

12. See West, "Jurisprudence and Gender," 15–28 (cf. chap. 8, n. 10 above); Shaffer, "The Unique, Novel and Unsound Adversary Ethic," 707–709 (cf. chap. 2, n. 17 above).

13. Interview with attorney Mary Ann Talley, Fayetteville, N.C., March 4, 1993, by UNC law student Maureen O'Neill.

14. I owe my knowledge of the Psyche myth as an example of feminine power to psychologist Pat Webster, who practices in Chapel Hill, N.C.

15. Professor Gisela Labouvie-Vief traces the rise of *logos* in civilization—and the corresponding decline of *mythos*—to the beginning of literacy, which enabled "vertical" (as opposed to "horizontal") thinking. Plato showed us what was possible in terms of vertical thinking, and the age of reason followed in which mythological explanations and sensory intuition were denigrated as inferior forms of knowing. As a result, according to Labouvie-Vief, the human mind was "demythified": Nature became "disenchanted" and instead the subject of theoretical and scientific study. Labouve-Vief, *Psyche & Eros: Mind and Gender in the Life Course,* 53–54. The concept of human nature also changed: "More and more, the belief emerged that the mature mind could be described without reference to an intersubjective, collective reality. Instead thinking was to be described exclusively by propositional forms, universal ideas, and stable principles that transcended the dynamics of social order and interpersonal exchanges. These new laws of thinking were to replace the forms of decision making of the past, forms that had relied primarily on the authority of myth, tradition, and social power. Instead, the Greeks envisioned a new form of decision making that was located purely in the realm of the abstract and the universal. In that realm, everybody could examine statements and be lead to the same conclusion. The individuality of the thinker, then, no longer entered into the process of thinking, except in the sense that one might make an error of logic" (ibid., 57).

Chapter Ten

1. All quotations from students used in this book are taken from year-end course evaluations administered by the UNC Law School.

2. Interview with attorney Roger W. Smith, Raleigh, N.C., October 8, 1996, by UNC law student Steven Wall.

3. Interview with attorney Katherine Holliday, Charlotte, N.C., March 16, 1994, by UNC law student Charlotte Gaskins.

4. Interview with attorney William L. Thorp, Chapel Hill, N.C., November 14, 1994, by UNC law student Debra Lloyd.

5. See Carrie Menkel-Meadow, "The Trouble with the Adversary System in a Postmodern, Multicultural World," *William and Mary Law Review* 38 (1996): 5.

6. William L. Thorp interview.

7. Interview with attorney Ben Bridgers, Silva, N.C., November 11, 1995, by UNC law student Amber Corbin.

8. Wade Smith interview.

Chapter Eleven

1. Fried, "The Lawyer as Friend: The Moral Foundations of the Lawyer-Client Relation," 1060 (cf. chap. 6, n. 22 above).

2. See Shaffer, "The Unique, Novel and Unsound Adversary Ethic," 707–709 (cf. chap. 2, n. 17 above). Professor Richard Abel states that because of the differences between types of lawyers, differences and lack of contact between lawyers from a myriad of jurisdictions, and the lack of any cohesive factor such as commonality of ethnicity or race, community is "an attractive but elusive goal" for the legal profession. Richard Abel, *American Lawyers* (New York: Oxford University Press, 1989), 36–37. These problems are serious, but there is another side to the equation, as many lawyers know when they walk into a room

of strange people and find there is another lawyer present. There is—at least for some members of the profession—a strong feeling of commonality through shared outlook and experience. In addition, there have been eloquent calls from the legal academy for a return to professional community. See Colin Croft, "Reconceptualizing American Legal Professionalism: A Proposal for Deliberative Moral Community," *New York University Law Review* 67 (1992): 1256; Thomas L. Shaffer, "The Legal Ethics of Belonging," *Ohio State Law Journal* 49 (1988): 703.

3. See Robert Bellah et al., eds., *Habits of the Heart: Individualism and Commitment in American Life,* updated ed. (Berkeley: University of California Press, 1996), vii–xxvii; Richard Neuhaus, *The Naked Public Square: Religion and Democracy in America* (Grand Rapids, Mich.: Eerdmans, 1984); Robert D. Putnam, *Bowling Alone: The Collapse and Revival of American Community* (New York: Simon and Schuster, 2000); Putnam, "The Strange Disappearance of Civic America," *The American Prospect* no. 24 (Winter 1996); Putnam, "Bowling Alone: America's Declining Social Capital," *Journal of Democracy* 6, no. 1 (1995). This has been a historical struggle in the United States. See Peter Berkowitz, "The Art of Association," *The New Republic,* June 24, 1996, 44, reviewing Joshua Mitchell, *The Fragility of Freedom: Tocqueville on Religion, Democracy, and the American Future* (Chicago, University of Chicago Press, 1995).

4. See Alasdair MacIntyre, *After Virtue* (Notre Dame: University of Notre Dame Press, 1984), 6, 252; Jeffrey Stout, *The Flight from Authority* (Notre Dame: University of Notre Dame Press, 1981); David Hollenbach, "Justice as Participation: Public Moral Discourse and the U.S. Economy," in *Community in America: The Challenge of "Habits of the Heart,"* ed. Charles Reynolds and Ralph Norman (Berkeley: University of California Press, 1988).

5. See Michael J. Sandel, *Democracy's Discontent: America in Search of a Public Philosophy* (Cambridge, Mass.: Belknap Press, 1996), 123–67; Sandel, "America's Search for a New Public Philosophy" (cf. chap. 3, n. 7 above); Wood, *The Radicalism of the American Revolution,* 216–18.

6. Sandel, "America's Search for a New Public Philosophy," 58.

7. Tocqueville, *Democracy in America,* 263–70.

8. William A. Galston, *Liberal Purposes: Goods, Virtues, and Diversity in the Liberal State* (New York: Cambridge University Press, 1991), 140.

9. See Joseph Raz, *Ethics in the Public Domain: Essays in the Morality of Law and Politics* (New York: Oxford University Press, 1994), 64.

10. Numerous social philosophers have discussed the implications of value pluralism in constituting the modern state. See Nancy Fraser, "Rethinking the Public Sphere: A Contribution to the Critique of Actually Existing Democracy," in *Habermas and the Public Sphere,* ed. Craig Calhoun (Cambridge, Mass.: MIT Press, 1992); Galston, *Liberal Purposes;* Jürgen Habermas, *The Structural Transformation of the Public Sphere,* trans. T. Burger and F. Lawrence (Cambridge, Mass.: MIT Press, 1989); Thomas E. Hill, Jr., *Respect, Pluralism, and Justice: Kantian Perspectives* (Oxford: Oxford University Press, 2000); Louis Marcil-Lacoste, "The Paradoxes of Pluralism," in *Dimensions of Radical Democracy: Pluralism, Citizenship, Community,* ed. Chantal Mouffe (New York: Verso, 1992); Kirstie McClure, "On the Subject of Rights: Pluralism, Plurality and Political Identity," in *Dimensions of Radical Democracy;* John Rawls, *Political Liberalism* (New York: Columbia University Press, 1993); Raz, *Ethics in the Public Domain.*

11. Fraser, "Rethinking the Public Sphere," 129.

12. Ibid., 130, quoting Jane Mansbridge, "Feminism and Democracy," *The American Prospect* 1 (1990): 131. Fraser goes on to say: "In general, there is no way to know in advance whether the outcome of a deliberative process will be the discovery of a common good in which conflicts of interest evaporate as merely apparent or rather the discovery that conflicts of interests are real and the common good is chimerical. But if the existence of a

common good cannot be presumed in advance, then there is no warrant for putting any strictures on what sorts of topics, interests, and views are admissible in deliberation."

13. See Stout, *The Flight from Authority;* Hollenbach, "Justice as Participation."

14. MacIntyre, *After Virtue,* 6.

15. Thomas L. Shaffer, "Towering Figures, Enigmas, and Responsive Communities in American Legal Ethics," *Maine Law Review* 51 (1999): 229.

16. MacIntyre, *After Virtue,* 253.

17. Rawls, *Political Liberalism,* xvii–xx, 3–4; Raz, *Ethics in the Public Domain,* 178–82.

18. Rawls, 144.

19. Rawls, 42.

20. Hollenbach, "Justice as Participation," 226–27. One of the most noted calls for a broader view of justice to include economic and social justice appears in Amy Gutman and Dennis Thompson, *Democracy and Disagreement* (Cambridge, Mass.: Harvard University Press, 1996).

21. Christopher Lasch, "The Communitarian Critique of Liberalism," in *Community in America,* ed. Reynolds and Norman.

22. Michael Sandel, *Liberalism and the Limits of Justice* (Cambridge: Cambridge University Press, 1982), 150.

23. MacIntyre, *After Virtue,* 254.

24. Sandel, "America's Search for a New Public Philosophy," 70–72.

25. Ibid., 58.

26. See Jeffrey Stout's discussion of this aspect of communitarian critique in Jeffrey Stout, "Liberal Society and the Languages of Morals," in *Community in America,* ed. Reynolds and Norman, 137.

27. Alasdair MacIntyre, "Politics, Philosophy and the Common Good," in *The MacIntyre Reader,* ed. Kelvin Knight (Notre Dame: University of Notre Dame Press, 1998), 235–52; Stanley Hauerwas, *The Peaceable Kingdom: A Primer in Christian Ethics* (Notre Dame: University of Notre Dame Press, 1983), 99–113.

28. Milner S. Ball, *Called by Stories: Biblical Sagas and Their Challenge for Law* (Durham, N.C.: Duke University Press, 2000), 141.

29. MacIntyre, "Politics, Philosophy and the Common Good," 240–41.

30. See Hollenbach, "Justice as Participation"; Michael Walzer, *Spheres of Justice: A Defense of Pluralism and Equality* (New York: Basic Books, 1983).

31. Hollenbach, "Justice as Participation."

32. Ibid., 74.

33. Holmes, "Path of the Law," 457 (cf. chap. 2, n. 2 above).

34. Janet Reno, "Address Delivered at the Celebration of the Seventy-Fifth Anniversary of Women at Fordham Law School," *Fordham Law Review* 63 (1994): 5, 8; Institute for Survey Research at Temple University, for the American Bar Association's Consortium on Legal Services and the Public, *Report on the Legal Needs of the Low-Income Public: Findings of the Comprehensive Legal Needs Study* (January 1999); United States Census Bureau, *Poverty in the United States: 1998;* Talbot D'Alemberte, "Racial Injustice and American Justice," *American Bar Association Journal* 78 (August 1992): 58–59; See Statement of Doreen D. Dodson, Chair of ABA Standing Committee on Legal Aid and Indigent Defendants, before the Senate Subcommittee on Commerce, Justice, State, the Judiciary and Related Agencies of the Committee on Appropriations (March 24, 2000).

35. Barbara Curran, "Report of the 1989 Survey of the Public's Use of Legal Services," *American Bar Foundation* (1989); Deborah Rhode, "The Rhetoric of Professional Reform," *Maryland Law Review* 45 (1986): 274.

36. Russell Engler, "And Justice for All—Including the Unrepresented Poor: Revisiting the Roles of Judges, Mediators and Clerks," *Fordham Law Review* 67 (April 1999): 1987.

37. Deborah Rhode, "Cultures of Commitment: Pro Bono for Lawyers and Law Students," *Fordham Law Review* 67 (April 1999): 2415, 2419.

38. While estimates of the number and percentage of lawyers doing pro bono work for poor people are relatively low nationwide (between and 10 and 20 percent), there are some who faithfully do it. Deborah Rhode, "Cultures of Commitment," 2415.

39. Thomas L. Shaffer, *On Being a Christian and a Lawyer* (Provo, Utah: Brigham Young University Press, 1981), 21. See also Stephen Ellman, "The Ethic of Care as an Ethic for Lawyers," *The Georgetown Law Journal* 81 (1993): 2665, and, more generally, Nel Noddings, *Caring: A Feminine Approach to Ethics and Moral Education* (Berkeley and Los Angeles: The University of California Press, 1984).

40. See David Luban, *Lawyers and Justice: An Ethical Study* (Princeton, N.J.: Princeton University Press, 1988); Robert W. Gordon, "Corporate Law Practice as a Public Calling," *Maryland Law Review* 49 (1990): 255; William Simon, "Ethical Discretion in Lawyering," *Harvard Law Review* 101 (1988): 1083.

41. Pepper, "The Lawyer's Amoral Ethical Role," 617 (cf. chap. 3, n. 50 above).

42. Quoted in David Luban, "Partisanship, Betrayal and Autonomy in the Lawyer-Client Relationship: A Reply to Stephen Ellman," *Columbia Law Review* 90 (1990): 1004.

43. Richard Wasserstrom, "Lawyers as Professionals: Some Moral Issues" (cf. chap. 3, n. 51 above). Wasserstrom cites the "role differentiated amorality" (13) of lawyers which allows them to pursue their clients goals, regardless of what they might be, as long as those goals are not illegal. See also Monroe H. Freedman, *Understanding Legal Ethics;* Stephen J. Ellman, "Lawyering for Justice in a Flawed Democracy" (Book Review) *Columbia Law Review* 90 (1990): 16; Stephen L. Pepper, "The Lawyer's Amoral Ethical Role."

44. See Bachman, *Law v. Life,* 74–76; Postema, "Moral Responsibility in Professional Ethics" (cf. chap. 2, n. 16 above for both).

45. Virginia Woolf, *Three Guineas* (New York: Harcourt, Brace and Company, 1938), 109–110.

46. Lawyers are specifically permitted by Rule 2.1 of the *ABA Model Rules of Professional Conduct* to advise clients on "moral, economic, social and political factors, that may be relevant to the client's situation."

47. Wade Smith interview.

48. Interview with attorney Robert L. McMillan Jr., Raleigh, N.C., February 2, 1992, by UNC law student Grady Ballentine.

49. Malcom Ray "Tye" Hunter interview.

50. Robert L. McMillan interview.

51. Thomas L. Shaffer, "The Christian Jurisprudence of Robert E. Rhodes, Jr.," *Notre Dame Law Review* 73 (March 1998): 737, 746–47.

52. David B. Wilkins, "Who Should Regulate Lawyers?" *Harvard Law Review* 105 (1992): 755; David B. Wilkins, "How Should We Determine Who Should Regulate Lawyers? Managing Conflict and Context in Professional Regulation," *Fordham Law Review* 65 (1996): 465.

53. Ball, *Called by Stories,* 137.

54. Gordon, "The Independence of Lawyers," 17.

CHAPTER TWELVE

1. Emma Jung and Marie-Louise von Von Franz, *The Grail Legend,* 61 (cf. chap. 8, n. 8 above).

2. MacIntyre, "Politics, Philosophy and the Common Good," 248 (cf. chap. 11, n. 27 above).

3. Shaffer, "Towering Figures, Enigmas, and Responsive Communities in American Legal Ethics," 230 (cf. chap. 11, n. 15 above).

4. Interview with attorney Daniel Joseph Walker, Burlington, N.C., February 11 and 25, 1992, by UNC law student Laurie Stegall; Judge Sam J. Ervin III interview.

5. Interview with attorney Elreta Alexander Ralston, Greensboro, N.C., February 18, 1993, by UNC law student Anna Barbara Perez.

6. Oliver Wendell Holmes, "The Profession of the Law," 219 (cf. Epigraphs, n. 1 above).

7. Interview with Lee Smith, novelist, in Chapel Hill, N.C., July 19, 1996, by Linda Byrd, *Shenandoah* 47 (Summer 1997): 105.

8. Kathryn Allen Rabuzzi, *Motherself: A Mythic Analysis of Motherhood* (Bloomington: Indiana University Press, 1988), 13. See Demaris S. Wehr, *Jung and Feminism,* 114–17 (cf. chap. 9, n. 11 above), criticizing generally the use of myths created in a patriarchal culture to explain feminine psychology.

9. Compare Edward C. Whitmont, *Return of the Goddess,* 149–78 (cf. chap. 9, n. 6 above), which attempts to interpret the more traditional, linear quest in a form meaningful to both men and women to Maureen Murdock, *The Heroine's Journey* (Boston: Shambhala, 1990), which frames woman's quest as a circular journey through obstacles which work peculiarly to women to lead to an integrated personality. See also Jean Shinoda Bolen, *Crossing to Avalon: A Woman's Midlife Pilgrimage* (San Francisco: HarperSanFrancisco, 1994), 49–81, a personal interpretation of a woman's quest; and James Hollis, *Tracking the Gods: The Place of Myth in Modern Life,* 53–78 (cf. chap. 6, n. 7 above), the "eternal return" and the hero's journey—masculine and feminine archetypes of the quest as applied to the realities of modern life.

10. See Jean Shinoda Bolen, *Goddesses in Everywoman* (New York: Harper and Row, 1985); Christine Downing, *The Goddess: Mythological Images of the Feminine* (New York: Crossroad, 1992). Other commentators in this field have suggested that society as a whole is on the threshold of developing a new mythology and psychic orientation altogether, which is no longer patriarchally oriented. See Riane Eisler, *The Chalice and the Blade: Our History, Our Future* (Cambridge, Mass.: Harper and Row, 1987); Jean Houston, *The Search for the Beloved* (New York: G. P. Putnam's Sons, 1987).

11. T. S. Eliot, *The Four Quartets,* lines 239–42.

CHAPTER THIRTEEN

1. Mary Rose O'Reilly, *The Peaceable Classroom* (Portsmouth, N.H.: Boynton/Cook Publishers, 1993), 136.

2. The Association of American Law Schools conducts yearly workshops for new law teachers and in the year 2001 will conduct a workshop entitled *New Ideas for Experienced Teachers: We Teach, But Do We Learn?* See the AALS Website: http://www.aals.org/profdev/newideas/index.html. Perhaps the most innovative work in new methods of law school teaching occurs at the annual conferences hosted by Gonzaga Law School's Institute for Law School Teaching. Subjects of previous conferences and information on the conference scheduled for 2001 can be found at http://www.law.gonzaga.edu/ilst/ILST.htm.

3. Other commentators have called for similar changes in (and enhancement of) law school curricula, though in different terms. Roger C. Cramton and Susan P. Koniak, "Rule, Story, and Commitment in the Teaching of Legal Ethics," *William and Mary Law Review* 38 (1996): 145; Colin Croft, "Reconceptualizing American Legal Professionalism: A Proposal for Deliberative Moral Community, *New York University Law Review* 67 (1992): 1256; E. Michelle Rabouin, "Transforming Law Students into Ethical Transactional Lawyers," *Depaul Business Law Journal* 9 (1996): 1.

4. Numerous law school teachers are calling for more effective use of narrative in law school classrooms. Examples in the area of legal ethics are: Cramton and Koniak, "Rule, Story, and Commitment in the Teaching of Legal Ethics"; James R. Elkins, "The Stories We Tell Ourselves in Law," *Journal of Legal Education* 40 (1988): 577; Thomas L. Shaffer,

American Legal Ethics: Text, Readings, and Discussion Topics (New York: Matthew Bender, 1985); and Mark Weisberg and Jacalyn Duffin, "Evoking the Moral Imagination: Using Stories to Teach Ethics and Professionalism to Nursing, Medical, and Law Students," *Change* (January-February 1995). In more general contexts, see Kathryn Abrams, "Hearing the Call of Stories," *California Law Review* 79 (1991): 971; Jane B. Baron, "The Many Promises of Storytelling in Law," *Rutgers Law Journal* 23 (1991): 79 (reviewing *Narrative and Legal Discourse: A Reader in Storytelling and the Law,* ed. David R. Papke [Liverpool: Deborah Charles, 1991]); William N. Eskridge Jr., "Gaylegal Narratives," *Stanford Law Review* 46 (1994): 607; Marc A. Fajer, "Authority, Credibility, and Pre-Understanding: A Defense of Outsider Narratives in Legal Scholarship," *The Georgetown Law Journal* 82 (1994): 1845; Judith G. Greenberg and Robert V. Ward, "Teaching Race and the Law Through Narrative, *Wake Forest Law Review* 30 (1995): 323; Toni M. Massaro, "Empathy, Legal Storytelling, and the Rule of Law: New Words, Old Wounds?" *Michigan Law Review* 87 (1989): 2099; Kin Lane Schepple, "Forward: Telling Stories," *Michigan Law Review* 87 (1989): 2073; Stephen L. Winter, "The Cognitive Dimension of the Agony Between Legal Power and Narrative Meaning," *Michigan Law Review* 87 (1989): 2225; James Boyd White, "What a Lawyer Can Learn From Literature," *Harvard Law Review* 102 (1989): 102 (reviewing Richard A. Posner's *Law and Literature: A Misunderstood Relation* [Cambridge: Harvard University Press, 1988]).

5. See James R. Elkins, "Writing Out Lives: Making Introspective Writing a Part of Legal Education," *Willamette Law Review* 29 (1995): 45; Cathaleen A. Roach, "A River Runs Through It: Tapping into the Informational Stream to Move Students from Isolation to Autonomy," *Arizona Law Review* 36 (1994): 667; Auturo L. Torres and Karen E. Harwood, "Moving Beyond Langdell: An Annotated Bibliography of Current Methods for Law Teaching," Special Edition, *Gonzaga Law Review* 1 (1994); Margaret M. Russell, "Beginner's Resolve: An Essay on Collaboration, Clinical Innovation, and the First Year Core Curriculum," *Clinical Law Review* 1 (1994): 135; Dennis Turner, "Infusing Ethical, Moral, and Religious Values into a Law School Curriculum: A Modest Proposal," *University of Dayton Law Review* 24 (1999): 285; James Boyd White, "Doctrine in a Vacuum: Reflections on What a Law School Ought (and Ought Not) to Be," *University of Michigan Journal of Law Reform* 18 (1985): 251.

6. Robert McCrate, "Educating a Changing Profession: From Clinic to Continuum," *Tennessee Law Review* 64 (1997): 1099.

7. Ibid., 1130–31. Jane Harris Aiken, "Striving to Teach 'Justice, Fairness, and Morality,' " *Clinical Law Review* 4 (1997): 1; Nancy Cook, "Legal Fictions: Clinical Experiences, Lace Collars and Boundless Stories, *Clinical Law Review* 1 (1994): 41; Carolyn Grose, "A Field Trip to Benetton . . . and Beyond: Some Thoughts on 'Outsider Narrative' in a Law School Clinic," *Clinical Law Review* 4 (1977): 109; James E. Moliterno, "Professional Preparedness: A Comparative Study of Law Graduates' Perceived Readiness for Professional Ethics Issues," *Law and Contemporary Problems* 58 (1995): 259; Christine Mary Ventner, "Encouraging Lawyer's Responsibility: An Alternative Approach to Teaching Legal Ethics," *Law and Contemporary Problems* 58 (1995): 287.

8. Moliterno, "Professional Preparedness"; Russell, "Beginner's Resolve."

9. A detailed description of these programs at UNC Law School appears in Walter H. Bennett Jr. "The University of North Carolina Intergenerational Legal Ethics Project: Expanding the Contexts for Teaching Professional Ethics and Values," *Law and Contemporary Problems* 58 (1995): 173. See also Walter H. Bennett Jr. and Judith W. Wegner, "Lawyers Talking: UNC Law Graduates and Their Service to the State," *University of North Carolina Law Review* 73 (1995): 846.

10. Fran Quigley, "Seizing the Disorienting Moment," *Clinical Law Review* 2 (1995): 37, 51; Aiken, "Striving to Teach 'Justice, Fairness, and Morality," 23–50.

11. The resurgence of law and literature courses in law schools owes a great debt to Professor James Boyd White, whose pioneering book *The Legal Imagination* (Boston: Little, Brown and Company, 1973) has served as inspiration and text for law and literature teachers and others attempting to introduce narrative and narrative techniques into law school classrooms. See Richard Weisberg, "Coming of Age Some More: 'Law and Literature' Beyond the Cradle," *Nova Law Review* 13 (1988): 107, for a historical review of the pedagogical practice and theory of law and literature in American law schools.

12. An excellent survey of and bibliography for law and literature courses in American law schools appears in Elizabeth Villiers Gemmette, "Law and Literature: Joining the Class Action," *Valparaiso Law Review* 29 (1995): 665.

13. Weisberg and Duffin, "Evoking the Moral Imagination."

14. Flannery O'Connor, *Mystery and Manners,* ed. Sally and Robert Fitzgerald (New York: The Noonday Press, Farrar, Straus & Giroux, 1957), 67–68.

15. American Bar Association, "Teaching and Learning Professionalism."

16. Interview with attorney E. D. Gaskins Jr., Raleigh, N.C., November 6, 1996, by UNC law student Anderson Caperton.

17. Ibid.

18. For a discussion of the decline of mentoring in the profession, see Patrick J. Schiltz, "Legal Ethics in Decline: The Elite Law Firm, the Elite Law School, and the Moral Formation of the Novice Attorney," *Minnesota Law Review* 82 (1998): 705.

19. Quoted in Jack Northrup, "The Education of a Western Lawyer," *American Journal of Legal History* 12 (1968): 29.

20. Quoted in Albert Coates, "The Story of the Law School at the University of North Carolina," *North Carolina Law Review* 47 (1968): 1, 8.

21. Anton-Hermann Chroust, *The Rise of the Legal Profession in America* (Norman: University of Oklahoma Press, 1965), 31–32, quoting *New-York Weekly Post-Boy,* August 19, 1745. Other legal apprentices in early America also complained of their treatment by their masters, but John Jay and John Quincy Adams found their apprenticeships to be of the highest quality (ibid., 33).

22. Significant mentoring programs are underway in numerous locations around the country. Two notable bar programs are the Bill Kitts Mentor Program in the New Mexico Bar and the Colleagues Program in the Nashville, Tennessee, Bar. See programs described in Bennett, "The University of North Carolina Intergenerational Legal Ethics Project"; Patrick R. Hugg, "Comparative Models for Legal Education in the United States: Improved Admissions Standards and Professional Training Centers," *Valpariso University Law Review* 30 (1995): 51; and *Mentor Program Resource Guide,* ABA Senior Lawyers Division (1996).

23. One such organization is Eastpoint Consulting Group, Inc. in Newton, Massachusetts (E-mail: Info@eastpt.com).

24. J. Edwin Hendricks, *Seeking Liberty and Justice: A History of the North Carolina Bar Association 1899–1999,* ed. Lynn P. Roundtree (Charlottesville, Va.: Lexis Publishing, 1999).

REFLECTIONS

1. T. S. Eliot, *The Four Quartets,* lines 243–59.

Index